Norwich, an Expanding City 1801-1900

by Rosemary O'Donoghue

To Gerald,

Memories of a lovely summer day.
in Norfolk.

Rosemary

Larks Press

Published by the Larks Press

Ordnance Farmhouse, Guist Bottom, Dereham,
Norfolk NR20 5PF
01328 829207
Larks.press@xlnmail.com
Website: www.booksatlarkspress.co.uk

Printed by Short Run Press, Exeter
March 2014

About the author:

Rosemary O'Donoghue has a degree in English from London University and a Cambridge University Board of Extra-Mural Studies certificate in English Local History. In 1988 her article 'A Victorian Suburb: Some aspects of Town Planning in 19th-century Norwich' was published in Norfolk Archaeology and she continues researching the history of Norwich in the 19th century. She was for many years in charge of the Office and Library at the Castle Museum. Since her retirement, she has done voluntary work in the library of Norwich Castle Museum and latterly at the library of the Norfolk & Norwich Archaeological Society.

Front cover: *London Street c. 1885, from*
Industries of Norfolk & Suffolk Business Review

Back cover: *Tombland c. 1900, an old postcard*

British Library Cataloguing-in-Publication Data
A catalogue record for this book is available
from the British Library

ISBN 978 1 904006 71 8

CONTENTS

ILLUSTRATIONS

Chapter 1. The Condition of English Towns in the 19th century

The population of Britain doubled between 1801 and 1851 and the increased number of people living in towns and cities was responsible in large part for a deterioration in living conditions. Local government before 1835 did not have adequate powers to address the problems associated with the growing population; there was no central control and each local authority acted independently. Parliament had made attempts to correct the worst abuses but with only limited success. The challenges which the factory system posed - population growth and expanding towns - demanded a national, not a local, solution. Parliament no longer served the interests of the majority of the people especially as the growing manufacturing interest was not represented. The Electoral Reform Act, passed in 1832, led to many manufacturing towns being represented for the first time and although it did not greatly increase the franchise, its effects were far-reaching. Prior to 1832, the party in power governed in the country interest; now, for the first time, the interest of the manufacturers was to be taken into account.

A good example of how government had been unable to change was Manchester. Despite its importance and growing population, it was considered a village and not a Municipal Borough. It would have been unaffected by the Municipal Corporations Act, which only applied to the old boroughs, had it not also made provision for the creation of new boroughs by Royal Charter.[1]

An enquiry into municipal corporations in 1833 had found no single system of local government throughout the country; some corporations were effective, some were not, and many were corrupt and incompetent. This lack of system had not caused any great problems in the past, but it was not equipped to deal with the industrial age. The unreformed corporations varied in their zeal for improvement, but there was no system of control to ensure success.

Even the most effective found it difficult to make improvements because changes could only be brought about by a local Act of Parliament and each Act related not only to a specific town but to a specific area and could not be adapted to take into account future town expansion. This made it impossible for later changes to take effect without a further Act and this was one of the reasons for the deterioration of town life during a period of rapid growth.

There are many examples of improvements that failed to improve: the Norwich water bill in 1794 which improved the existing system but was not able to bring water to the entire city within the walls,[2] the provision of water to Exeter in 1811[3] which was not successful because the system installed was inadequate and not available to every house. There are many instances of water being laid on, but not being universally available: in Newcastle, because of complaints about shortages of water, supplies had been improved by 1805 but the supply was restricted and consequently only a small number of better-quality houses had water laid on, the remainder of the population obtaining water from stand-pipes, private wells and the river.[4] Even when a satisfactory system was in operation in Southampton, where a reservoir was made in 1803 and two more added in 1830 and 1831, the improved water supply was not available to newly-built parts of the city.[5]

Before 1835 Parliament had approved a large number of local Acts for paving and cleaning streets and to bring lighting, but here again the results were patchy. One reason for the lack of success (and many commentators spoke about the terrible state of the streets and pavements) was the often half-hearted approach to improvement. There were some early successes: it was noted that in Portsmouth health improved after the town was paved in 1769;[6] in Exeter improvements commenced in 1819 with the demolition of the south gate and the widening of roads nearby.[7]

Because of the desire to keep the local rates as low as possible there was always strong opposition to any proposed changes, but the single most important factor militating against improvement was population increase. For instance, the census returns show that the population of Manchester grew from 75,000 in 1801 to 303,000 in 1851. In such cases, it is not surprising that the traditional system of local government was inadequate. Even smaller increases could bring problems. Norwich, where the population grew from 36,000 in 1801 to 68,000 by 1851 was similarly affected, which suggests that the system itself was incapable of coping with even relatively small expansion.

The difficulty with many of the Improvement Acts both before and after 1835 was that the towns grew so fast that the Acts were soon obsolete as they did not cover areas not yet developed. In Norwich, despite considerable opposition, acts for the better paving, lighting, cleaning, watching and otherwise improving the city were passed in 1806 and 1825 but only related to the city within the walls and did not include the hamlets.[8] A paving, lighting and watching Act was passed in Southampton in 1770 which did not include the eastern and north-eastern suburbs.[9]

The problems arising because of the lack of over-all planning were not solved by the Municipal Corporations Act of 1835. This Act brought consistency to the organisation of town councils, a slight measure of democracy with triennial elections by all rate-payers, but otherwise made little difference. The changes were largely cosmetic in effect as they did not give the Corporations power to act independently: as before, each new measure required a special local Act of Parliament and Treasury permission to raise loans.

The attitude of the reformed corporations varied. Some enlightened councils were anxious to make improvements, some were unwilling to do anything which might lead to increased rates, but the greatest bar to improvement was the continuing population growth which resulted in more and more overcrowding with uncontrolled building in the expanding towns. This made any alteration to the *status quo* virtually impossible. In Newcastle there had been legislation to provide for the maintenance of sewers and pavements in the principal streets since 1835 but, as in so many other towns, this related only to areas within the medieval borough and did not cover new streets, which were built without drainage.[10] There were some cosmetic changes: Liverpool opened a public bath and wash-house in 1842; there were private swimming baths in Leeds and Westminster where the working-class could swim,[11] but in general corporations often seemed not to have the will to bring about change and there was much opposition to any would-be reformers. In 1839 a small group of individuals failed to obtain an Act of Parliament to include the hamlets of Norwich within the provisions of the 1825 Act for Paving Lighting and Watching the City due to the Corporation's extreme opposition.[12] There seems no reason to suppose that this situation was unique. A further disincentive was the expense of obtaining a bill and presenting it to Parliament because, until 1877, all Acts submitted had to be funded by individuals and could not be charged to the rates.

Even though flawed in conception, the Municipal Reform Act was important because it was compulsory. Before 1835 it was widely felt that the proper unit of local government was the parish, and Parliament should not interfere in purely local matters. There was considerable opposition to the Act which seems to have been received with most hostility in ancient towns which were jealous of their privileges. In Norwich a resolution was passed inviting other corporations 'to make common cause with them in endeavouring to defeat any design that might be in contemplation for wresting from them their ancient charters, franchises and liberties' and at a special assembly the Corporation declared that the Municipal Commission was illegal and unconstitutional.[13] In August 1835 evidence was given before the House of Lords in opposition to the Bill. This loss of ancient privileges was long mourned: the plea to the House of Commons reported in the Exeter Council Minutes on 12th May 1859 'to take the earliest opportunity of repealing all laws which, by centralising power in London, have deprived the Provincial Corporation and other Public Bodies of that independence which they have hitherto enjoyed'[14] shows the continued strength of feeling.

Although the 1835 Act brought consistency to local government, it did nothing to address the problems associated with population growth and the expansion of towns. The lack of a safe water supply and the inadequate and often non-existent sewers were responsible for outbreaks of typhus and other diseases. Things were particularly bad in London and there were outbreaks of cholera in 1836 and 1837. The reports that were submitted in 1838 detailing the causes of the spread of fever in London led the government to call for an investigation into the rest of the country. The Report of the Health of Towns Committee was published in 1840, and in 1842 Edwin Chadwick published *Report on the Sanitary Condition of the Labouring Population of Gt. Britain* and, as a result, a Royal Commission was appointed and the Health of Towns Commission published reports in 1844 and 1845.

The scope of Chadwick's report was far-reaching and few towns escaped criticism. Inspectors spoke of the deficient sewerage system in Leeds, with offensive drains and overflowing sewers; in Stockport[15] there were insanitary privies and refuse was thrown into the gutters; in the courts of Liverpool there were filthy, inadequate privies.[16] Bradford was described as 'the dirtiest, filthiest and worst regulated town in the Kingdom'[17] and in Nottingham 8,000 of a total of 11,000 houses were back-to-back.[18] The old county towns were not exempt from criticism: in York the well water was contaminated by graveyards and the York Water Company drew its water unfiltered from the River Ouse, the supply was inadequate and midden privies were common.[19] In 1832 the water in Exeter was still mostly being obtained from private wells and a few public pumps.[20] In Newcastle, despite attempts to bring a sufficient supply during the 18th and early 19th centuries, there was a chronic water shortage and in 1845 the supply was still inadequate and was polluted by the discharge from the common sewers and thirty-three streets were found to be without drains and sewers.[21] Even smaller towns such as Canterbury[22] had problems with drainage and Tiverton in Devon had open drains and sewers.[23]

As a result of these reports, the Health of Towns Act received royal assent in 1848. It is perhaps the most significant piece of

legislation to be passed in the 19th century as it was the first time that the government had intervened so directly in the lives of the people. The Act created a central Board of Health which delegated authority to local boards and could be created on the petition of 10% of the ratepayers, but it was only compulsory if the death-rate of the population in a locality exceeded 23 per thousand. Consequently, and despite the overwhelming necessity for improvement, the Act was timid, being permissive when it should have been mandatory. It was also limited to only five years and, given its general unpopularity, the Board of Health's limited powers and the dilatory nature of local government, had only limited success. Its weakness was that even towns that adopted the plan could prevaricate. The evidence shows that in the worst areas the opposition of owners of slum properties was sufficient to delay implementation. However, even though the Act had many weaknesses, this was an important piece of legislation. Its significance lies in its universal application. In theory it affected everybody in every town and city and was applicable to all and, if implemented, would give everybody clean water and proper drainage.

Nevertheless, and despite the lack of compulsion, the proposals met with much hostility and indignation. The possibility of compulsion, however tenuous, was seen as a threat to liberty. Another complaint was that the cost of implementing the reforms would be borne by landlords of substandard property who, in turn, would have to increase the rent charged and thus be unpopular with tenants. Whether or not Norwich Councillor Osborn Springfield's remark that 'persons living next the river ought not to be taxed for water which they could take from the river'[24] displays a particular East Anglian foible, it is likely that his reason for objection was not unique. Other objectors felt it unnecessary for a constant supply of water to be available at all and in many cases there was indignation that ratepayers would have to pay for improvements which they did not need, as they themselves already had sewers and an adequate water supply. In Southampton, despite the Medical Officer of Health's damning report on conditions, there was much opposition to the adoption of the Act

because of widespread suspicion of a Central Board of Health.[25] In Exeter the bill was described as 'involving provisions of a most unconstitutional and arbitrary character'[26] and *The Times*, although in favour of reform, seems not to have liked the element of compulsion, declaring 'it would rather take its chance of cholera and the rest than be bullied into health by the Public Health Board'.[27]

There was much talk about people being *forced* to take the water, whether they liked it or not. This seems to have been the view of the editor of the *Norfolk Chronicle* who said the measures proposed by the Board of Health would be 'enforced',[28] an allegation denied more than once by the Inspector appointed to enquire into the sanitary conditions of Norwich. And although over 200 authorities adopted the Act, the results were patchy and had little effect. For instance, in Southampton, which passed the Act in 1848, the sewerage system started in 1849 was left unfinished; improvements were not continued and although there was an outbreak of cholera in 1868, the threat by the Local Government Board in 1871 to force the Borough Council to improve drainage was considered 'unwarrantable interference'.[29] In Newcastle, the Health of Towns Act had little effect except for the erection of some public baths and washrooms for the use of the poor and the closure of church grounds for burials.[30] In Norwich sewage was allowed to flow untreated into the river Wensum and it was only the threat of legal action that brought improvement.[31] In general the lack of improvement was disappointing and in 1869 the Royal Sanitary Commission reported that although there had been some improvement, drinking-water was still being polluted by local authorities allowing sewage to flow into the rivers.

The strength of opposition to the Act had been such that only compulsion would have brought real improvement. The response had varied, but that of Leeds: 'there is a strong feeling in Leeds that the local authority can manage their own affairs...better and more economically than if they were placed under government inspection'[32] seems to have been pretty general as even those who professed to be sympathetic to the reforms, interpreted them in their own way. How

else to explain the continued lack of sewage disposal and inadequacies of water supply in the slums? In 1900 the Medical Officer of Health in York noted the prevalence of typhoid fever, the continued use of midden privies and the lack of a proper water supply: in one area there were only thirty taps for 442 houses.[33] The general ambivalence about the importance of the Act can best be exemplified by Norwich which adopted the Public Health Act in 1851. As late as 1899, a Building Control Plan submitted for a terrace of eighteen houses in Waddington Street was approved with earth closets.[34]

Although the report on sanitary conditions was mainly concerned with the lack of pure water and the disposal of sewage, the Inspectors drew attention to the unsatisfactory state of the houses in the courts and yards of the large English cities and towns. In Leeds, Manchester and Liverpool large numbers of people were living in cellars in the 1840s and in Leeds 71% of houses were back to back - 49,000 by 1886. Large numbers of back-to-back houses had been built in Manchester, Liverpool and Bradford by the 1840s although many towns passed bye-laws forbidding their erection later in the decade.[35] Things were little better in Exeter, York and Norwich where old mercantile houses had become overcrowded tenements in multiple occupation - once grand houses were now slum dwellings,[36] and in Southampton former fashionable areas behind the High Street had become slums by 1850.[37] In Newcastle, grand houses, some still retaining vestiges of past glory, had been turned into slums.[38] In Manchester by the 1830s the private houses in the centre of the town were being converted into warehouses and factories whilst the middle-classes went to live in the suburbs.[39]

Expansion outside the town centres proceeded apace during the 19th century, fuelled by the population increase, and the type of houses built varied according to area. In many instances, the nearby hamlets and villages were incorporated into the town. In Southampton the borough was extended to include the hamlet of Freemantle and the village of Shirley in 1895 although both had become residential areas before then.[40] In 1852 Freemantle House had been purchased by an

industrialist and nearly 20 roads were built on its grounds which were soon covered by small buildings and in Shirley high-class villas and country mansions had been built for wealthy Southampton merchants and professional men from about 1830.[41] In York the population expanded outside the walls and the city was extended by the Extension & Improvement Acts of 1884 and 1893,[42] and in Norwich, although many professional men continued to live in the City itself, large numbers moved to the prosperous suburbs as the city expanded outside the walls during the century. The better-off lived in houses built north of the River Wensum in Thorpe Hamlet and south along the Newmarket Road or by other thoroughfares leading out of the City.

Although there were areas of deprivation both within the manufacturing towns and in the nearby villages, there were also better-quality houses in both. The expansion of large cities such as Manchester, Birmingham and Leeds had extended to many villages: in Birmingham middle-class houses were built in the village of Edgbaston.[43] In 1835 Newcastle was enlarged by the incorporation of the townships of Westgate, Elswick, Jesmond, Heaton and Byker and there were superior houses in Jesmond and artisan buildings in Elswick and Byker near the shipyards and engineering shops by the river.[44] In Bradford the contrast between the better-off areas and the slums was immense: Silsbridge Lane was said to be unhealthy and 'dingy, dilapidated and depressing' whilst in Manningham Lane there were prosperous villas;[45] in Leeds there were quality villas in the village of Headingley whilst near the centre of the town, in Kirkgate, a typhus epidemic started in 1851 in an area of 222 lodging houses with 2,500 people living in them.[46]

There was some attempt to improve the worst of the slums. In 1865 the Newcastle-on-Tyne Improvement Act was secured, but although some slum property was demolished and some was reconditioned, only one small area was improved and there was no attempt to extend the scheme.[47] In 1868 the Artisans & Labourers' Dwellings Act, which gave corporations authority to force improvements to properties considered dangerous to health, allowed the compulsory purchase and re-building of slum property. It achieved real, if limited, results in Norwich where slums in the parish of St Paul's were acquired and demolished in 1878-9; the land was then sold and new houses built on the vacant site. The difficulty faced by corporations is illustrated by the history of this acquisition: it was expensive and there was opposition from the owners, who placed fanciful values on their property;[48] only a very small part of the extensive slums was improved and it was the only part of the city to be redeveloped until the passing of the Housing of the Working Classes Act in 1890. Judging by the state of slum housing at the end of the century, there seems to have been very little popular enthusiasm for improvement. It is arguable that, given the continued population increase, this was an intractable problem, especially in view of the lack of compulsory legislation.

Despite the many reports which made clear the terrible housing conditions, there was no legislation to deal with slum dwellings and, in general, housing conditions remained unchanged for more than half a century. The corporations did little, the slums remained, growing throughout the century. And, outside the centre, within and beyond the city boundaries, working-class suburbs were built – slums in the making. The cycle was repeated: because of inadequate sanitary facilities and building control, a new slum population lived in these expanded towns and hundreds of badly-built dwellings were erected. In Norwich, south of the city walls, what was called the 'New City', built between 1815 and 1835, was condemned in the Health of Towns report;[49] in Southampton, a new working-class suburb had grown up in Kingsland Place in the parish of St Mary's. This had been described in 1831 as 'almost a little town',[50] but because of deficiencies in sanitation this was one of the areas affected by an outbreak of cholera in 1848-9. In York, apart from the tenement housing within the walls, Rowntree's 1899 survey found substandard working class houses built outside the walls, the buildings being described as small, some situated in narrow alleys or confined courts.[51]

Slums like these were reported both within the cities and surrounding the cities. The writer Robert Blatchford replied, when in 1899 he was asked where the slums were in Manchester, 'They are everywhere. Manchester is a city of slums.'[52]

Regulations affecting new building came after the passing of the Local Government Act of 1858. This gave local authorities the power to draw up bye-laws to deal with the quality of housing and sanitation. Although the 1858 Act was not compulsory and many substandard houses were built by local authorities who did not pass suitable bye-laws, the 1875 Public Health Act which followed was compulsory. This important piece of legislation gave the local authority control over the sanitary conditions of the district, the width of new streets and the construction of new buildings. The Public Health Amendment Act of 1890, which gave the local authority further control over the height of rooms, the placing of privies, etc., the prohibition of infilling of yards and garden ground and control of street width, made the creation of areas that would deteriorate into slums impossible. This deterioration had occurred not only in the centres of the towns, but in the new artisan suburbs where badly constructed houses were extended and added to without any regard to drainage.

Norwich is a good example of the beneficial effects of the passing of bye-laws and Acts on the quality of buildings. The houses built in the second half of the 19th century are well-built, not overcrowded, and the streets are well ordered. Rowntree described property in York built after the Public Health Act and the bye-laws: he divided the dwellings into three classes - the first two with six rooms and outside water-closet or privy, the only difference being size and a third class of house much smaller, with only two or three rooms, but still acceptable. These were all houses built according to the bye-laws.[53] The condition of houses such as this were replicated in similar bye-law houses in other towns and cities throughout the country including Birmingham, Bristol, Sheffield and Coventry. Apart from the very small houses in parts of England, many if not most of them are still standing and have become desirable properties. In Norwich, for example, Thorpe Hamlet and New Catton, just outside the city centre, are virtually unchanged.

The housing acts only related to new property and although it was possible for the first time to control the quality of new houses and the density of housing and to ensure that the water supply and sanitary facilities were adequate, it was nearly impossible to deal with existing property without new legislation. The inner city slums and sub-standard properties built before the various acts were a much more difficult proposition. Although slum property and poverty seem to have been accepted as inevitable, the full extent of poverty only became widely known when John Hollingshead[54] was commissioned by the London newspaper, the *Morning Post,* to report on how the poor of London survived in the winter of 1860/61 when the temperature dropped below freezing for a month. The result, published in newspaper articles in 1861 and in the book *Ragged London,* was a wide-ranging critique of the desperate condition of the poor. Hollingshead was not the only writer to draw attention to the plight of the poor and attempts were made to improve housing by philanthropic societies. Mayhew's report in 1861[55] described widespread slums and chronic overcrowding and Charles Booth's survey of life and labour in London, which started in 1886 and continued until 1902,[56] shows how little changed during the intervening period. Gareth Stedman Jones has described how efforts to improve the housing of the poor before 1875 made the situation worse as unhealthy buildings were demolished but no attempt was made to provide affordable alternative accommodation, leaving those who were displaced with nowhere to go but into other overcrowded buildings. The problem just shifted from one area to another.[57] In addition railway building led to much displacement and the poor in the areas affected had to move from one overcrowded area to another.

Various manufacturers and individuals had attempted to deal with problems of housing the poor. The first model dwellings had been built in the 1840s in an effort to improve the housing stock. The Metropolitan Association for the Improvement of the Dwellings of the

Industrious Classes was founded in 1842 and was followed by other companies in the 1850s and 1860s. However, although initially successful, the rent could not be kept low enough, given that a dividend of 4% was expected. The rents were too high for the poorest and the tenants were drawn from the lower middle classes and upper artisans. More successful, but limited in scope, were the model villages that were built by successful businessmen: Saltaire, begun in 1853 by Sir Titus Salt for the workers in his mohair alpaca mill, and Port Sunlight, begun in 1888 for workers in W.H. Lever's soapworks.[58]

The Public Health Act of 1875 had marked a fundamental change in the attitude of government to town development in that it was intended to be compulsory and universal in its application. As it dealt with water, sewage and the disposal of waste, it was very relevant to slum property which had previously not been affected by any regulations. Like the Public Health Act of 1848, it created local government boards and gave each one powers and responsibilities. Only in 1890 did Parliament address the problem of slum dwellings when the Housing of the Working Classes Act was passed. It extended the power of the corporations to clear insanitary areas and encouraged them to provide new houses by giving them further power to raise loans for this purpose. By 1900 this was already leading to slum clearance but there was still much that needed improvement. In the past, a number of local authorities including Liverpool and Manchester, had taken advantage of previous Acts. In 1869 Liverpool had been the first provincial city to build council houses and by 1912 it had built over 2,000 dwellings, demolished 550 and improved 11,000. Manchester started building its first flats in 1896[59] and in 1898 Norwich started the lengthy process whereby the courts and yards were cleared and the first council houses were planned.[60]

Improvement was patchy. Rowntree's survey of York in 1899, which found a scale of poverty in certain parts of the city that was largely unnoticed, showed the extent of the problem that still remained. Because York was a comparatively small city, Rowntree had been able to make a very detailed and close examination of every slum property and he believed his survey, which covered the slums in their entirety in a way that was impossible in larger cities, was 'fairly representative of the conditions existing in many, if not most... provincial towns'.[61] But despite the surveys and the various acts of Parliament, the degree of improvement in the housing of the very poorest, can be seen in the Medical Officer of Health's 1935 report on unfit conditions in a number of towns and cities including London, Birmingham, Bradford and Sheffield, to name but a few.[62]

By 1900, although to all intents and purposes England was a recognisably modern country with many of the checks and balances that are in place today as far as legislation is concerned, it was still unable to deal successfully with its unregulated past by clearing all the slums. The powers given by the 1890 Act to local authorities were extended in 1900 to allow them to acquire land and build outside their districts. Further powers were given in 1918 and 1919 to accelerate slum clearance, but with a world war intervening and the extent of the problem, it is perhaps not so surprising that the slums persisted until the 1960s.

Notes

1. Manchester is a good example of the difficulties experienced in modernising the country as, despite its importance and growing population, it was not a Municipal borough and therefore unaffected by the 1835 Municipal Reform Act. This Act only applied to the old borough but also made provision for the creation of new boroughs by Royal Charter as a consequence of which Manchester achieved incorporation in 1837
2. See Chapter 9.
3. Newton, Robert *Victorian Exeter 1837-1914*, p. 10
4. Middlebrook, S. *Newcastle upon Tyne Its Growth and Achievement*, p. 113
5. Patterson, A. Temple *Southampton A Biography*, pp. 201-2
6. Chadwick, Edwin *Report on the Sanitary Condition of the Labouring Population of Gt Britain*, p.110
7. Newton, p. 11
8. See Chapter 9
9. Patterson, p. 76
10. Middelbrook, p. 203-4
11. Gregg, Pauline *A Social and Economic History of Britain 1760-1965*, p. 200

12. See Chapter 9 in which is recounted the fate of a proposed new Paving & Lighting Act in 1839

13. Reported in the *Norfolk Chronicle* 9th January 1834

14. Newton, p. 23. This plea seems to have been Exeter's response to its lost status.

15. Chadwick, pp. 91-2

16. Chadwick, pp. 104-5

17. Briggs, Asa. *Victorian Cities*, p. 147

18. Chadwick, p. 6

19 Digby, A. 'The Relief of Poverty in Victorian York.....' in Feinstein, C.N. (Ed.) in *York 1831-1981. 150 Years of Scientific Endeavour and Social Change*, p. 161

20. Newton, p. 136

21 Middelbrook, p. 202

22 Briggs, p. 376

23. Chadwick, pp. 80-81

24. See Chapter 9

25. Patterson, p.134

26. Cited in Newton, p. 83 where the response by Edward Divett, M.P. for Exeter to the adverse report on sanitation by Edwin Chadwick is described.

27. *The Times*, August 1 1854 quoted by Gregg p. 204. Although in favour of reform, the element of compulsion was disliked.

28. Quoted in Mr Lee's report on the sanitary condition of Norwich: Health of Towns Act. *Report of an inquiry held before William Lee of the Sanitary Condition of the City and County of Norwich.*

29. See Patterson, p. 157. This refers to the objections made by the inhabitants of Portswood, one of the new suburbs of Southampton, to paying for improved sanitation which they feared would lead to an increase in rates.

30. Middelbrook p. 206

31. The inhabitants of Thorpe St Andrew, down-river from Norwich, in 1866 threatened to bring proceedings against the City because of the contamination of the river Wensum.

32. Briggs, p. 376. This remark summarises the adverse responses of the majority of corporations.

33. Rowntree, B. Seebohm *Poverty. A Study of Town Life*, pp. 222-6

34. NRO, N/EN/1/12/3772 Waddington Street and Armes Street. See Chapter 9

35. Burnett, John *A Social History of Housing 1815-1985*, p. 58 and 74

36. In Exeter, by 1833 the old houses had been converted into tenements and were occupied by five to fifteen families (Patterson p. ll); in Norwich, Hibgame mourned for the loss of what he called 'quaint' houses which were demolished in accordance with the Artizans & Labourers Dwellings Act of 1868 (cited in Chapter 8 - Substandard Houses and Slum Clearance'); in York the former good-quality houses turned into slum property is mentioned by Digby p. 163.

37. Patterson, p. 139

38. Middelbrook, p. 260 ff.
39. Briggs, pp. 106-7
40. Patterson, pp. 172-3
41. Patterson, pp. 147-8
42. Rowntree, pp. 188 ff.
43. Burnett, p. 115
44. Middelbrook, p. 107
45. Briggs, p. 144
46. Burnett, pp. 62-3
47. Middlebrook 272-3
48. See chapter 8
49. Lee's report on the sanitary conditions of Norwich, p. 56
50. See Patterson, p. 109. This area was so described in the *Hampshire Advertiser* on 2nd July 1831and said to be 'inhabited by many disreputable elements'.
51. Rowntree, p. 29. Feinstein, p. 110 gives a plan of the city with the boundary changes.
52. Quoted by Burnett, p 175. This article by Robert Blatchford 'Nunquam Modern Athens. A City of Slums' was printed in the *Sunday Chronicle* (Manchester, 5 May 1889).
53. Rowntree pp. 183 ff.
54. Hollingshead, John. *Ragged London in 1861.* Everyman Classic, 1986
55. Mayhew, Henry. *The Life and Labour of the People of London,* London 1861-62
56. Booth, Charles. *Life and Labour of the People in London,* 17 volumes 1886-1902.
57. Jones, Gareth Stedman. *Outcast London,* pp. 162-3. OUP 1984
58. Darley, Gillian. *Villages of Vision. A Study of Strange Utopias* (revised and updated edition), Nottingham, 2007
59. Burnett, *A Social History of Housing* pp. 184-85
60. See chapter 8
61. Rowntree, Introduction, p. xvii
62. Burnett, p. 243

Chapter 2. The 18th Century Background

In 1701 Norwich, with 30,000 inhabitants, was the second most populous city in the country, only exceeded in size and wealth by London. In 1723 Daniel Defoe described it as 'an ancient, large, rich and populous city' where everyone was employed, each working in his own garret and where 'the very children after four or five years of age could every one earn their own bread'.[1]

Before the Municipal Corporations Act of 1835, the civil government was composed of a mayor, twenty-four aldermen elected for life, two sheriffs, a recorder, a steward, a town clerk and 60 common councilmen elected annually by the freemen. Only freemen were entitled to take office; they were also entitled to vote in parliamentary elections. In addition, only they were able to engage in trade. Percy Millican in *The Register of the Freemen of Norwich 1548-1713*[2] has listed the requirements for entitlement to the freedom of Norwich as follows:

1. Patrimony: the legitimate son of a freeman was entitled to admission at the minimum age of sixteen years and, if not already apprenticed in some other craft was enrolled in that of his father.

2. Service: an apprentice who had served a Norwich freeman for a term of at least seven years, who had proved himself to be a competent workman and who had become a householder, in whole or in part, was expected to take up his freedom.

3. Purchase: by the 'Ordinances for Crafts,' 1449, 'foreigners,' either dwelling in or without the city, could purchase their freedom on condition that they were exercising and enrolled in their respective crafts and that the Masters of those crafts assented to their enfranchisement. The fees paid for this varied in proportion to their financial ability.

4. Order of the Assembly: The Assembly had power to grant admission to the Freedom to any person who, by virtue of his rank,

learning or great technical skill, would be likely to benefit the community.

The wealth of Norwich was based on textiles. In this it was not unique, but it benefited by having available a large workforce consisting of the wives and children of agricultural workers living in nearby villages. Norwich had the advantage of being near to London. It also had easy access to European markets and, most importantly, the quality of its goods was much better than those of its competitors, being the beneficiary of the skills and innovations of the 'strangers' - refugee textile workers who had come from the Low Countries to escape religious persecution. Because of this, the stuffs of Norwich were much in demand and the industry was little affected initially by the growth of the factory system and competition from the north of England.

To make the pre-eminence of Norwich absolutely sure, attempts were made to stifle competition and to this end, even before mechanization had presented any threat, in 1701 an Act of Parliament was passed prohibiting the importation of calicoes from the far east (11 & 12 W.III c.10) and in 1720 a further Act (7 G.I. c.7) was passed prohibiting the wearing of any calicoes after the 25th December 1722. The ostensible reason for this was to protect the country's woollen and silk manufacture and to assure employment of the poor. However, as its implementation was harmful to the Manchester cotton industry, the Manchester Act was passed in 1736 (9 G.11 c.4). This stipulated that the 1721 Act did not apply to Manchester. The order that court mourning should consist of Norwich crape remained.

In his history of Norwich, Bayne[3] gives a summary of trading conditions in Norwich during the 18th century. He quotes various authorities, including Arthur Young's description in *Tour of England* in 1771 on the state of the industry and the value of exports to Europe and the West Indies. The importance of trade to France, Spain, Portugal, Germany, Poland and Russia is described. Bayne stated that a sign of a flourishing trade was evident when on 2nd February 1759 and again on 24th March 1783, the pageant of the Golden Fleece (also called Bishop Blaize)[4] was held in Norwich. The 1783 pageant was said to be far finer in style than any previous one and in a summary of the social state of the city in the 18th century Bayne said that Norwich was 'in a more flourishing state as regards trade than it has ever since been known.'[5]

Bayne also described the reasons for the decline of the textile industry towards the end of the century: the popularity of cotton goods made in the new mills of Lancashire and Yorkshire affected the sale of worsteds and, as a consequence, Norwich became increasingly dependent on its export trade, markets which were lost because of the American War of Independence, the French Revolution and the war with France.[6] There also seems to have been a degree of complacency and an inability to adapt to change. The physical geography of the north favoured the growth of the factory system where use was made of water power from fast-flowing rivers, easily accessible coal and the newly developed steam locomotion. Norwich had no coal, no fast rivers nor easy access to coal and, at the beginning of the industrial revolution, there had seemed no necessity for mechanisation. It had a prosperous home industry and the danger posed by the new system was not fully understood or accepted. Consequently manufacturers were slow to adapt to modern requirements: in 1773 a letter to a local newspaper refers to 'the great decay of trade in the manufactory of this city' and urges 'the female part of the creation to encourage our Manufactory by giving up Silks and Linens and wearing specimens of the ability of our own ingenious artists in the manufactory.....'[7] This was not the first time that fashion had impacted on the traditional manufacture of stuffs and in 1724 the popularity of calico had led to a disturbance[8] when the clothes were ripped off people wearing them.

The protection of local industry exemplified by the acts of 1701 and 1720 was only a part (although an important part) of the efforts made by the City to protect local industry and the citizens of Norwich from competition. The *Weekly Mercury* reported on 24th November 1722 a complaint that itinerant salesmen were selling spice, earthenware and other goods and the immediate response was that if they continued to do so they would be punished 'as the Law directs'. In 1741 it was decreed that no person be allowed to trade in the city for more than six months without taking out his freedom.[9] This was again decreed in 1755 and again in 1762[10] which suggests that it was a difficult ordinance to enforce. In 1762 it was decided to prosecute Robert Hannington a 'Scotch pedlar' for trading in the city.

Although by the end of the century Norwich's prosperity had declined, the textile industry was still able to compete with the north in the production of high-quality products such as the fine shawls introduced by John Harvey in 1791.[11] Nevertheless although this industry continued during the 19th century, it never regained its pre-eminence and although the opening of two factories by the Norwich Yarn Company was felt to be a new beginning,[12] there were very few manufactories at the start of the 20th century. There seems to have been a gradual decline: spinners were the first to go, unable to compete with the speed of automation, then hand-loom weavers; the market in Norwich shawls, which for a time was very strong, shows that the industry was focussing on an elite market that was very much at the mercy of the vagaries of fashion. At the end of the 19th century the census returns show that the few remaining hand-loom weavers were mostly aged over 65 and lived in the slums. And now, at the beginning of the 21st century, it is as if this important industry had never been. Apart from the Yarn Mill built in 1836, the only evidence is in the Bridewell Museum in Norwich.[13]

Even before the industry went into decline there were riots. In 1720 there were riots because of the growing popularity of calico, in 1752 wool combers encamped at Rackheath, whilst in 1757 there were fears that Wymondham weavers would ride to Norwich 'to make a riot' and Norwich weavers barricaded the Golden Ball Lane entrance to Castle Meadow with a waggon.[14] There were also riots in 1740, in 1754 and in 1796 but these were caused by the high cost of food and subscriptions raised for relieving the poor which rose from £12,000 in 1756 to £29,500 in 1799. Perhaps the most significant signs of the downturn of trade are the population figures, especially towards the end of the century. During a period that saw high population growth (in Manchester, from about 17,000 in 1758, to 76,788 in 1801) that of Norwich fell. In 1752 it was 36,169, having increased from 28,881 in 1693, in 1786 it was 40,051, but in 1801, the year of the first census, the figure was only 36,375. It is possible to quarrel with the accuracy of the figures before the first census, but the trend seems to be down.

The industrial revolution did not affect the prosperity of the City during most of the century. Much of the city was newly paved: the Fish Market in 1727, the Market in 1731, Tombland in 1733 and Gentleman's Walk in 1792. Other improvements included Rochester Lane (Orford Street) being widened and a good carriage-way made across the castle ditches from Griffin Passage into King Street in 1792 (these last two were done by public subscription). Finally, to improve access, most of the city gates were taken down in the 1790s.[15] Further improvements included the building of the Norfolk & Norwich Hospital, erected by public subscription and first opened for in-patients and out-patients in 1772, and the plan to bring water from the New Mills into a reservoir in Chapel-field in 1798.

Norfolk and Norwich Hospital – it was extended in 1883

Housing in Norwich seems also to have improved. In 1662 Dr Fuller's book *Worthies of England* described a visit he had made in 1622 when he hoped the large number of houses with thatched roofs would soon all be replaced. Beatniffe,[16] writing in 1808 (admittedly rather a long time after) said that this had now happened. In a 1795 edition of his book he stated that since 1752, 'a great many of the smaller houses within the gates have been pulled down' and larger ones erected upon their site; also many houses had been built outside the walls to house the displaced people. In the absence of documentation it is difficult to verify this assertion; the population of the Norwich hamlets grew slightly between 1752 and 1801, but there was no widespread growth until after about 1820. However, a number of quality houses were built on Bracondale outside the walls in the late 18th century as well as on the other main roads leading out of the city, most of which remain. Heigham Street, just outside the walls, and the land between the street and the river Wensum, had long been inhabited by tanners and the like. There was some growth of slum property within the city walls as there is mention as early as 1762 that the large house of Sir Nicholas Bacon on Ber Street had been turned into tenements.[17]

The wealth of Norwich at the beginning of the 18th century is illustrated by the houses drawn in the margin of Corbridge's map of the city dated 1727. Most of them have disappeared, but they were identified by Ernest Kent in his manuscript copy of the 1811 Norwich Directory. They were the homes of worsted weavers, drapers, brewers and grocers, some of whom were also sheriffs and mayors. They were large, probably brick-built houses (although this may only be the facing covering a timber dwelling).[18] These houses were situated in all parts of the city; no particular part apparently considered unsuitable for a quality dwelling. The only house that remains is that of Thomas Churchman, situated on St Giles Street. Churchman was a worsted weaver who was sheriff in 1757 and mayor in 1759. Mr Thomas Beevor's house in Magdalen Street (illustrated on Corbridge's map) was demolished and the site divided into a number of lots in 1824 (see chapter 4).

These massive houses made a statement about the wealth and power of their owners and seem very different in size and style from the houses built later in the century when, as mentioned by Beatniffe, substantial town houses, some of them designed by the architect Thomas Ivory, were built in various parts of the city - in All Saints Green, Surrey Street, St Giles Street and Tombland - many of which still remain. The quality of these houses can still be seen in St Giles Street and Tombland. Many of the residents were professional and business men who were engaged in banking and insurance, businesses which were expanding. Large modern houses, within the city itself were still desirable as can still be seen by John Patteson's house in Surrey Street, Surrey House, which was built in 1765. Patteson was in the wool stapling trade and was mayor in 1766. Another large house, St Catherine's Close in All Saints Green, was built in 1780. It was the home of the brewer, John Morse, and was designed by the architect Thomas Ivory. It remained in domestic occupation until the second World War. Ivory also built a row of large terrace town houses in Surrey Street in about 1770.

To complement the new genteel brick-built town houses, the Assembly Rooms had been built 1754-6 on the site of the medieval College of St Mary in the Fields (part of which was incorporated into the building). It had been designed by Ivory and Sir James Burrough. This was a grand building, only exceeded in size by the one in Bath, and it replaced Chapel Field House which had hosted assemblies since about 1692. An anonymous diarist praised the Assembly House then being erected in 1754 as a 'very large, tall, grand affair, by far the tallest in the city.'[19] It was built on land known as the Chapple Field Estate purchased from the Earl of Buckingham by a group of Norwich gentlemen and wealthy businessmen for the purpose of erecting public places of entertainment. There was no lack of backers including physicians, bankers, merchants as well as worsted weavers and grocers.

The New Theatre, built in 1757, was also designed by Thomas Ivory. In order to fund the Theatre, the ground was leased to Thomas Ivory for 400 years and a building fund established, the proprietors buying one share each of £30 to fund the building work. The new theatre was opened on 28th January 1758 to much acclaim. Among those with a financial interest in the theatre was the brewer Charles Weston, and bankers, manufacturers and gentlemen such as Robert Harvey, Jeremiah Ives Harvey, James Beevor, William Fell, Thomas Gostling and William Wilkins (plasterer). It was renamed the Theatre Royal in 1768 after being granted a Royal Patent. The White Swan Playhouse, which it replaced, had been the home of the Norwich Company of Comedians from 1731 to 1757.[20]

The 18th century saw many changes: in the streets, in the houses, in the places of amusement and in the building of Nonconformist chapels after the passing of the Act of Toleration in 1689. Prior to this, worshippers had met in private houses, but the Act allowed dissenters to legalise their meeting houses and a number of chapels were built. The most noteworthy of the new buildings erected were the Quaker meeting houses in Goat Lane in 1698, the Gildencroft in 1699, and the Independent (Congregational) Old Meeting in Colegate in 1693. The Presbyterian Chapel which was founded in 1672 was later replaced by a grander building in 1756, the Octagon Chapel designed by Thomas Ivory. It cost £5,000 of which £4,000 was raised by public subscription.[21] The high quality of these buildings (which still remain) is testament to the wealth of the manufacturers and merchants of Norwich in the 18th century, many of whom were Nonconformists.

In addition there were gardens: Norwich, like London, had its pleasure gardens. Norwich gardens had been long admired and when Thomas Fuller visited the city in 1662[21] he had said 'Norwich is ...either a *City* in an *Orchard*, or an *Orchard* in a *City*, so equally are Houses and Trees blended in it; so that the *Pleasure of the Country* and *populousness* of the City meet here together'. Henry Howard, the Duke of Norfolk's brother, laid out a garden as a place of recreation in 1663-4 and the New Spring Gardens (named after the more famous ones in

London) was opened in 1739. Other gardens followed including Smith's Rural Gardens in 1766 and the Wilderness in 1773. Their clientele varied; the New Spring Gardens sought to appeal to a more exclusive clientele by staging concerts and raising the cost of admission to one shilling.[22]

However, despite improvements and the new building carried out and despite the extensive pleasure gardens, the layout of the city remained largely medieval). At the end of the 18th century Norwich was still a walled city; the city gates were in the process of demolition but the 'polite' traveller, used to impressive townscapes, would probably have expected something grander from a city renowned for its wealth. There were comparatively few modern new buildings and the city was virtually unchanged; the grand houses illustrated in Cunningham's plan were isolated, symbols of past power and wealth. The 19th century would see the disappearance of most. They bore very little relationship to the new houses in Surrey Street and St Giles.

William Chase, who published *The Norwich Directory; or Gentlemen and Tradesmen's Assistant* in 1783 complained 'This city, though bounding in opulence and fashion, has long laboured under great inconvenience on account of the difficulty of ascertaining, precisely, the address of its inhabitants, whether in trade or independent'. According to him, the layout of Norwich did not reflect its importance: the buildings lately erected were a start, but their grandeur was diminished by the medieval plan of the city which made it difficult for the visitor to find his way. There were no street signs, only parish boundary plaques, and the difficulty of finding a particular street was compounded by the fact that one side of a street might very well be in a different parish from the other. In addition to the lack of street signs, houses were not numbered.[23]

By 1800 Norwich had lost its pre-eminence: its industry was declining (although it is likely that the extent of the contraction of the industry was masked by the decline in population) and it seemed unable to compete with the factories in the north. However, by the late 18th century, it was still benefiting from the wealth accrued during the period of prosperity which had been instrumental in the growth of banking and insurance.

Notes

1. Defoe, Daniel *Tour through the Eastern Counties*, East Anglian Magazine 1949, pp. 86-87
2. Millican, Percy *Freemen of Norwich 1549-1713*. Norwich 1934, xiv.
3. Bayne, pp. 569-578 gives a summary of trade in the 18th century.
4. St. Blaise [Blaize], or Bishop Blaise was the patron saint of woolcombers. His feast day was 3rd February and in *Memorials of Old Norfolk* p. 268 (ed. H.J. Dakenfield Astley), it is recorded that there was a special pageant in Norwich with a grand procession in his honour. The pageant which took place in 1783 seems to have been a particularly fine one as it is mentioned in a number of guides to Norwich (i.e. *A Historical Account of Norwich* published by Stacy in 1819) and is recorded in *The Diary of a Country Parson* by James Woodforde who, with his niece Nancy and others, made a special trip to Norwich to see it. Bishop Blaize's pageant was also celebrated on 2nd February 1759 (Blyth, G.K. *The Norwich Guide* p. 68). With the decline of the wool industry, the custom fell into disuse but was revived again in 1836 on laying the foundation-stone of the Norwich Yarn Company (Bayne, A.D. *A comprehensive history of Norwich*, p. 403).
5. Bayne, p. 570
6. Bayne, p. 578
7. Goodwyn, E.A. *Selections from Norwich Newspapers 1760-1790*, p. 13
8. Rudd, Walter R. 'The Norfolk and Norwich Silk Industry' in *Norfolk Archaeology* XXI, 260-2
9. [Crouse, John]. *The History of the City and County of Norwich from the Earliest Accounts to the Present Time*, 1768.
10. Browne, P. *The History of Norwich from the Earliest Records to the Present Time*, Norwich 1814
11. White's 1836 Directory, p. 96
12. See Chapter 4.
13. The Bridewell Museum, which had an excellent display about the woollen trade has been closed for over two years.
14. Rudd, p. 259ff. gives a very detailed picture of the industry. The title of the article is misleading as he writes of the textile industry in general.
15. Browne, P. describes the work carried out.
16. Beatniffe, *The Norfolk Tour or Gentleman's Companion.....* p. 163. Norwich, 1808
17. See Chapter 3
18. Manuscript copy of Berry's 1811 Norwich Directory includes a copy of Corbridge's map which has been annotated by E.A. Kent with the names of some of the

residents of the houses illustrated (found in the Norfolk & Norwich Archaeological Society Library).

19. Stephen, Andrew, *A History of the Assembly House, Norwich.* 2004, p. 17
20. Blackwell, Michael & Carole. *Norwich Theatre Royal. The First 150 Years,* 2007
21. Virgoe, Norma & Williamson, Tom (Eds.) *Religious Dissent In East Anglia,* 1993 describes the funding and building of Nonconformist chapels in Norwich and Norfolk, the preachers and some of the patrons.
22. Quoted in Fawcett, Trevor, *The Norwich Pleasure Gardens,* Norfolk Archaeology 35, 1972
23. Chase,W. *Norwich Directory, or Gentleman and Tradesmen's Assistant, containing An alphabetical list of the principal Inhabitants....,* 1783, p. iii-

Norwich Market Place c. 1890

Chapter 3. The City South of the River - Quality Residential and Commercial Buildings

Norwich Guildhall

Introduction

The most important buildings in Norwich - the Castle, the Cathedral, the Guildhall which housed the Council Chamber, and the Market Place, are south of the river Wensum. The best houses, the wealthiest parishes and the best shops were (and are) also south of the river. Many of the better-quality houses still remain, now no longer residential, but the pockets of poverty in the courts and yards leading from the main streets, which were the subject of slum clearance orders in the late 19th and early 20th centuries, have long since disappeared.

The courts and yards have gone. So too have the factories: Grout & Co. had established a silk mill on the river Wensum on Lower Westwick Street (Westwick Street) in 1814, John Wright & Son had a worsted manufactory on Elm Hill by 1836, Towler, Campin, Shickle and Matthews, also in Elm Hill, was in business by 1845 and P. Haldenstein's boot and shoe manufactory was in Queen Street by 1864. These are just a few of many manufactories which have gone, some large, some small. Also gone are large numbers of small workshops which manufactured a wide range of goods. Gone too are the brewers with premises in King Street and in Upper Westwick Street (St Benedict Street). Most of these businesses had started in a small way, and those that were successful grew in size during the 19th century. The clothing manufactory of F.W. Harmer was established in Bethel Street in 1825 and moved to large new premises in St Andrew's Street in the 1890s. At that time it employed about 1,500 people[1] and it remained there until it was destroyed by enemy action during the Second World War.

If the 18th century was a period of small industrial activity with large manufacturers having small premises only to store and distribute the work to outworkers, the 19th century saw the growth of the factory system with large premises built near or beside the river. The river had been essential to the production of textiles early in the century and continued to be so for the breweries and for other industrial processes. Because of the inadequate road system, the iron trade established their manufactories near the river, upon which they depended for delivery of supplies.

However, factory building was sufficiently far away not to impinge upon those parts of Norwich with good quality houses. Unlike other large cities where a majority of prosperous residents moved to the suburbs, streets such as St Giles, Surrey Street, Tombland and All Saints Green continued to be popular with professional and middle-class residents. And although in Norwich in the 19th century, as in other cities, the tendency was for the more prosperous inhabitants to leave the city centres for the spacious and salubrious suburbs; this happened less in the better residential areas within the city walls.

One reason for the move to the suburbs may have been the lack of quality houses for an increasing number of professional, business and white-collar workers working in banking and insurance. There was little or no building of quality houses within the walls during the 19th century, due to a decline in the popularity of large houses, many of which were converted into boarding houses, hotels, schools and business premises. Many businesses later in the century occupied the good-quality residential houses and others were demolished to be replaced by offices. To put it into context, the Norfolk & Norwich Savings Bank expanded from one room in St Andrew's Hall, to a large house in St Giles Street and then to a large new building in the Haymarket during the 19th century.[2] And, if the type of house built in the suburbs is anything to go by, what the newly educated class wanted were detached houses with garden ground and terrace houses, their type and size depending on income.

Norwich Savings Bank in the Haymarket, erected in 1843 and later demolished to make way for the tram lines

Although the City expanded outside the walls during the 19th century and many houses were built for the so-called 'genteel' classes, the number of professional and business people living within the walls remained constant until late in the century. Examination of the census returns for St Giles, Surrey Street, All Saints Green and Tombland/

Upper King Street – the areas with quality houses – shows that only in Upper King Street was there a sharp decline in residential use, with the 1901 return listing a large number of unoccupied business premises. The number of physicians, surgeons and solicitors living in All Saints Green gradually declined, but despite this, houses here were still desirable for professional persons. As late as 1901, one of the houses there – listed as a 'Servant Girls' House' in 1891 – was taken by the surgeon, Harrington Darrell, and although the number of solicitors living in Surrey Street and St Giles declined, this may have been due to the increase in the number of business partnerships. There was little or no decrease in the number of physicians and surgeons living in these streets.

At the beginning of the 19th century, before the growth of the suburbs it was customary for the family business to be at ground level with living quarters above and one or two employees living with the family. Although their numbers gradually declined, in 1900 a number of skilled self-employed craftsmen still continued this custom. One such was the harness maker who lived on All Saints Green from at least 1851 to 1891. However, this became less common as successful tradesmen moved to the suburbs.

Factories and shops remained within the City. The *Industries of Norfolk and Suffolk*, a trade journal published about 1890 by the British Industrial Publishing Company in Birmingham, lists industries of all sizes in Norwich, none of them in the suburbs. Apart from the benefits of locating a business in the industrial centre, the new suburbs were not inviting places as nearly all the original freeholders had imposed covenants forbidding any sort of industrial activity.

As the suburbs expanded with houses suitable for prosperous businessmen and the growing number of white-collar and skilled manual workers, large numbers of poor and unskilled labourers remained in the increasingly overcrowded courts and yards (the census returns show very few paupers or hand-loom weavers living in the suburbs).

St Giles, Upper St Giles and Bethel Streets

When F.T. Hibgame published *Recollections of Norwich Fifty Years Ago* in 1913, he described the City as he remembered it at that time. He was born 1856/7, so was in a good position to compare St Giles Street as it then was to what it had become early in the 20th century. The main difference he noted was the increase in the number of shops and businesses on the street. It is interesting to make a further comparison with Browne's description of St Giles in 1814. Browne said 'Broad-Street (St Giles) is esteemed the best street in the city'. This accords with Hibgame's praise of the buildings and the street, which were favoured by doctors, dentists and other professional people.[3]

One reason why St Giles Street changed so little was its situation. It was close to the Guildhall, and was fortunate in not having a river location to attract undesirable manufacturing processes. In 1783 it housed the gentry or near gentry. It was the town residence of the Member of Parliament, Sir Harbord Harbord Bart. and Chase's Directory shows a large number of people styled gentleman or esquire. There were also a number of attorneys, merchants and clerics. Residents included Dr Edward Rigby, obstetric surgeon, the founder of the Norfolk Benevolent Medical Society in 1785 and Mayor of Norwich in 1805, and John Hammond Cole, founder of the Norfolk & Norwich Savings Bank, Stamp Distributor in the service of George III and Receiver and Collector for the City and County, who was Mayor in 1811, as well as the manufacturer William Herring, Mayor in 1796.[4]

However, it was not immune from the gradual encroachment of the commercial sector, even though the professions retained a foothold. There are a number of reasons for the continued popularity of St Giles with physicians and surgeons. First of all the houses, to which a surgery was often attached, were large, of as good quality as anything available in the suburbs; they were situated in a convenient position for patients coming in from the county for a consultation. In addition, a large number of the doctors and surgeons resident not only had a private practice, but were on the medical staff of the Norfolk &

Norwich Hospital nearby or were Medical Officers of the Eye Infirmary in Pottergate, the Jenny Lind Infirmary for Sick Children in Pottergate, the Lying-in Charity and the Norwich Dispensary which were also nearby.

Upper St Giles Street in 1886

Sir Peter Eade, one of the physicians at the Norfolk & Norwich Hospital, lived in Churchman House in St Giles Street and wrote *Some Account of the Parish of St Giles, Norwich* in 1886.[5] Today Churchman House is the Norfolk Register Office and the finest building remaining in the street, but in the 1880s it was just one of a number of fine buildings that included, in Upper St Giles, Mann's Mansion House built early in the 18th century which had been the home of the banker Starling Day in 1810. In 1890 it became St Giles College, a boarding and day school for boys.

One important house in St Giles not mentioned by Eade (because it is not in the parish) was that occupied by John Harvey in the late 18th century, a man highly esteemed for having introduced the manufacture of shawls into Norwich in 1791. He was Mayor in 1792 and a partner in Harvey and Hudson's Bank. In later years he lived in

Thorpe Grove, Thorpe St Andrew (the progression of successful manufacturer or businessman to member of the 'gentry' with a grand country estate was not unusual). It became the premises of the Liberal Gladstone Club in 1889.[6]

The quality of the houses can be gauged by their description in extant sale particulars. The house of John Hammond Cole, was sold in 1829, after his death. The sale particulars[7] describe the property: the house was large with three storeys and eight bedrooms. There was an extensive garden with stable, brew-house with pump and large store chambers. Another house in St Giles, sold in 1848,[8] was said to be 'well-adapted for the residence of a professional gentleman'. It had eleven bedrooms and a rear garden containing ample room for a coach-house, stables and carriage. Another house,[9] also sold in 1848, had ten bedrooms and was described as the possible residence of a professional man having been 'for many years a Lodging-House of the first class'

Before the advent of the railway, St Giles Street was a coaching and posting centre and the Norfolk Hotel had been an important coaching inn in the 18th century when it was known as the Woolpack. The Norfolk Hotel is listed in the 1836 Directory and was the headquarters of the Tory party before the 1832 Reform Bill.[10] It did not survive into the 20th century as the freehold of the site was purchased in 1898, the building was demolished and the 'Grand Opera House' opened on the site in 1903. Mortimer's Hotel, situated nearly opposite the Norfolk Hotel, had been built on the site of another coaching inn called the New Inn.[11] It is possible that the large house mentioned above and described as a 'Lodging-House of the first class' later became Mortimer's Hotel.

The large houses in and near St Giles were often used by widows and unmarried women teachers as small private boarding schools. Hannah Larke had a school in a large house in Pottergate and was listed in the 1845 Directory, and Anna [sic] Larke is listed in the 1836 Directory in St Giles Broad Street. (Possibly there was some confusion about the name and even the location as the 1851 census describes

Hannah Larke's school as being on Cow Hill near the junction with Upper St Giles.) Another large house which had once been a school was demolished: Miss Firth's ladies' school, listed in the 1854 Directory. The entry in the 1851 census states that in addition to Miss Firth and an English teacher, there was a French teacher and eleven girls, aged between 9 and 16, eight of them the daughters of gentlemen, the others a clergyman's daughter, a solicitor's daughter and a surgeon's daughter. Miss Firth, the daughter of William Firth esq., Steward of Norwich, who was appointed Attorney-General of Upper Canada in 1807, was born in Toronto, Canada. Clearly this was a school for the gentry or near gentry; the occupation of the fathers of the pupils is often stated in census returns, information that would have been included in any prospectus for would-be parents to show that their child would be mixing with the 'right' sort of people. As it also took day-girls, it is likely that the daughters of the many physicians, surgeons and other professional people who lived nearby went to the school.

Miss Firth's school is listed in the 1854 Directory, but not any later. There are a number of schools listed in the directories and the census returns, but they are often listed only once and only a very few remained into the twentieth century. This building was demolished before 1876. It was one of a number that were replaced by non-domestic buildings in the 19th century. St Giles Hall was erected on the site and opened in 1876 as an ice-skating rink.[12] In 1877 a theatrical licence was obtained and the building became 'The Vaudeville Theatre of Varieties' and in 1879 a circus. In 1882 part of the building was purchased by the Salvation Army and converted into their Citadel and in 1898 the remainder (the skating rink) was sold to Lincoln & Lacey, builder's merchants. (Today a part of the premises is the Loch Fyne Restaurant).

Another large building which, according to Eade[13] was probably re-built in 1792, and was once used as a judge's lodging, was the home of the surgeon G.W.W. Firth by 1854, the brother of Miss Firth, the schoolmistress. It was purchased by the YMCA in 1886. Eade mentions other large buildings which were either demolished or converted to offices. These include the offices of the Norwich & London Accident Insurance Association and the General Hail Storm Insurance Society which occupied two large houses. The Norwich & London was established in 1856 and incorporated the General Hailstorm Insurance in 1898. (Both houses were demolished and a new building was erected on the site in 1906 and the insurance company was absorbed by the Norwich Union in 1908).[14]

Bethel Street, also described by Sir Peter Eade,[15] had (and has) a number of quality houses. Three of them were sold at auction in 1837.[16] Lot 1 of this sale is described as a 'mansion'. It was a large house with seven bedrooms and a walled garden. Lot 2 was another grand house with eleven bedrooms and a large garden. According to the 1881 census, this house and the one beside it (Lot 1) was the residence and the surgery of Mr Robinson, Surgeon at the Norfolk & Norwich Hospital.[17] Haynes S. Robinson occupied the house with his wife, three children, four female servants and one lad described as a 'page'. His surgery was situated in the adjacent house.[18] Lot 3 seems to have been smaller, being called only a 'neat and eligible dwelling house' although it was large enough to contain three sitting-rooms and five bedrooms. At the time of the Ordnance Survey in 1883, only that portion of Bethel Street nearest its junction with St Giles Street had quality buildings. Nearer the Market Place were a boot and shoe manufactory, Harmer's clothing manufactory and a number of tenements in yards.

Sir Peter Eade, speaking about St Giles Street and the parish in general, said that it appeared 'for a long time to have been the favourite residence of Medical Men in Norwich'.[19] This was certainly true in 1886; he listed fifteen physicians and surgeons in addition to surgeon-dentists, nine in St Giles Street alone in 1883. In 1900 a large number of doctors and dentists continued to live in St Giles and Bethel Streets and seven out of a total of fifteen dentists listed lived in St Giles and more than half of the total number of physicians and surgeons.

Surrey Street

Surrey Street was judged by Browne, writing in 1814,[20] to be one of the best in the City with some of the best private buildings. Between 1761 and 1773 the eminent architect Thomas Ivory erected a 'range of elegant buildings' on this street[21] and a number of prominent people lived there in 1810. In 1819 Sir Samuel Bignold, the son of the founder of the Norwich Union Fire Society and the Life Society, moved from Catton Old Hall to Surrey House in Surrey Street. This house, which had extensive garden ground, also housed the offices of the Norwich Fire and the Life Insurance Societies and had formerly been the home of John Patteson Esq. of the wealthy brewing family.[22] Patteson was the President of the Life Society from 1815 to 1833 and Member of Parliament from 1806 until 1817. Sir Samuel Bignold, who became Secretary of both the Fire Office and Life Society in 1818, occupied the building from 1820 until his death in 1875. After his death, because of the increase in business, the building was no longer residential.

Norwich Union Fire Office, Surrey Street

Probably the most important building in Surrey Street was Surrey Court, built before 1546, which had once been the house of the Earl of Surrey. In the 18th century this was partly owned by Alderman William Crowe of Tuckswood House in Old Lakenham and after his death it passed to his son, the surgeon James Crowe, who let it to his son-in-law, Sigismund Trafford.[23] In 1821 Surrey Court was sold by the widow of James Crowe to Miss Unity Mace who let part of the building for a ladies' school; in 1901 the whole building, together with the west side, owned by the proprietor of the *Norfolk Chronicle*, was sold to the Norwich Union who demolished it. A splendid new headquarters for the Norwich Union Life Society was erected on the site and opened in 1905.[24]

As in St Giles Street, other large houses that had once been family residences became private schools and business premises. One large house became a boarding-house - the 'Messrs. Bunting Boarding House for Young Lady Assistants'. According to the 1891 census, thirty girls and women aged 16-21 lived there. They are described as assistant milliners and drapers and nearly all were born in either Norfolk or Suffolk. The Boarding House is listed in Jarrolds Directories from 1885 until at least 1905. Arthur Bunting & Co. (in 1875 Curl & Bunting) were wholesale and retail linen and woollen drapers etc. with a shop on the corner of St Stephen's Street and Rampant Horse Street. (Bunting's Store was destroyed during the Second World War and the business later moved to London Street.)

Although Surrey Street continued to be a desirable place to live throughout most of the 19th century and was popular with physicians and surgeons, it seems likely that increased commercialisation led to a drop in other prosperous professional residents. However, the street remained popular with the medical profession and there were also a significant number of private residents although a comparison with entries in the 1883 and 1890 directories shows how the residential sector contracted, whilst business premises expanded.

All Saints Green (and Upper Surrey Street)

All Saints Green was another street with fine houses, many of which still remain; the largest and best is St Catherine's Close, built in 1778. This large house with extensive garden ground was the residence of Alderman John Morse, Sheriff of Norwich in 1779 and twice Mayor, in 1781 and 1803. The house remained in private occupation until the Second World War (until 2000 it was the headquarters of B.B.C. East). Ivory House, also in All Saints Green was designed by Thomas Ivory and built 1771-72.[25] Edward Temple Booth Chairman of the Norwich Union Fire Office, who was associated with Samuel Bignold in the establishment of the Norfolk & Norwich Joint Stock Bank, lived there in 1827, but by 1867 Ivory House had become the headquarters of the West Norfolk Militia, continuing in use by the military well into the 20th century.

The 1851 census returns show a mixture of professional and prosperous commercial men living in All Saints Green. In 1890 the general draper, milliner, hosier and mantle warehouseman R.A.H. Bond had large premises in Ber Street and lived in a house in All Saints Green near to his business. But by 1900 the business had expanded and incorporated three buildings in Ber Street and a warehouse in All Saints Green, and in 1905 he moved to a house in Christchurch Road. However, the 1901 census shows that All Saints Green was still very largely residential with a number of widows with private means, many self-employed tradesmen and a small number of professional men.

Tombland and Upper King Street

Tombland and Upper King Street has the advantage of being very near to Norwich Cathedral and still has some fine 18th century houses. The 1841 census return shows Tombland was very popular with physicians and surgeons and, to a lesser extent, with solicitors, but gradually declined in popularity throughout the century. Upper King Street (King Street until 1859) was also popular with doctors and solicitors during the first half of the century but was nearly completely commercial by 1891.

Samson and Hercules and Augustine Steward's House in 1900

High-status houses south of the river

The growth of banking and insurance and the expansion of retail premises brought about the growth of quality housing in the suburbs as this type of accommodation was limited within the walls. Population also increased: between 1811 and 1851 the population of Norwich rose from 37,313 to 68,713. The shortage of houses was in itself sufficient to bring about a market for building in the suburbs where new houses ranged in size and quality, from those suitable for artisans to grander ones built for a wealthy solicitors and industrialists. As the status of each house was determined by deeds of covenant, not only were their size and quality secured, but the whole neighbourhood was guaranteed free from industry and commerce and unsuitable housing development. This would have been a great incentive to move out of a city where substandard houses and slum development was growing due to the increase in population.

Exchange Street, London Street - the commercial hub

London Street, Exchange Street and the streets close to the market were the commercial heart of the City throughout the 19th century. However, the street plan was virtually unchanged since the Middle Ages and the growth in the number and size of manufactories and the development of the railway system made an efficient road system essential. During the first half of the century two major streets were built and a number of lanes were widened and improved. Exchange Street was opened in its entirety in 1832, Prince of Wales Road in the early 1860s and London Street was widened between 1848 and 1877.

Exchange Street was built after the Corn Market was removed from St Andrew's Hall in 1824. At that time it was proposed that a Norwich Corn Exchange be erected somewhere near the Market Place but the Corporation opposed the plan and agreed in 1825 that a Corn Exchange be erected on land on a new street that was planned to join the Market Place to St Andrew's Street. This new street, variously called Exchange Street and Post Office Street was opened in 1828. At that time it ran only as far as Lobster Lane but was extended to St Andrew's Street by 1832 (the name Post Office Street was still used as late as 1864). The Corn Exchange was opened in 1828, a post office was opened for business in June 1832 and in 1834 the Norfolk & Norwich Museum moved into a purpose-built museum building on Exchange Street near the Post Office.[27]

The history of Exchange Street in the 19th century is, in the main, the history of retail premises. The proximity to the Market and London Street, as well as the buildings which had already been erected, dictated the development of the street so that, unlike many other streets in the centre of Norwich, Exchange Street has always been mainly commercial in character. In 1836 businesses included a wine and spirit merchant and a jeweller's shop. In 1841 John Betts of Betts Hinde & Co., boarded his shop assistants in two houses in Exchange Street. There were also a number of small shops, including that of a wool draper, a druggist and a haberdasher. Another linen draper is listed in the 1841 and 1854 census returns. However, most of these businesses had disappeared by 1864 and London Street became the premier shopping street for woollens and linens.

By 1881 there were few private residents, most buildings being non-residential and listed as 'offices' (census shorthand for shops and offices). Even a long-resident dentist, George Neep, who had lived and worked in Exchange Street since at least 1841 had moved to Mount Pleasant by 1864, and the cabinet-maker Henry Trevor who lived and had a business in Exchange Street by 1845 (the 1851 census records him living there and employing 30 men) had moved to 'The Plantation' on St Giles Road (Earlham Road) by 1854. His business remained in Exchange Street and was listed as Trevor Page in 1883; it was still in business there in 1900 with another shop in the Royal Arcade, by which time the factory had moved to St Andrew's Street.

The directory entries for 1881 and 1890 show no linen or woollen drapers, but in 1890 J. E. Barnes of the Great Eastern Seed Store had a large four-storeyed building. There had been seedsmen and/or nurserymen with premises on Exchange Street since at least 1836: the seedsman Frederick Mackie (by 1845 Mackie's & Ewing) listed in 1836, had a shop and a nursery on the Ipswich Road. It remained in business and is listed as Daniels Brothers by 1875 with a shop in Exchange Street, moving to the Royal Arcade by 1890. It retained the nurseries on land between Newmarket and Ipswich roads (on Daniels Road) until well into the 20th century (today Notcutts Garden Centre occupies the site). In 1889-90 Chamberlin & Smith, Wine & Spirit Merchants and Poultry Game & Dog Food Manufacturers had a retail and wholesale business and a manufactory in modern two-storey and three-storey premises on Exchange Street. It had premises on both sides of the road and was established about 1850 and combined a wholesale and retail business manufacturing poultry, game and dog food with one of retail wine and spirit merchants. This firm was still in business in the 1890s.[28] Another long-established business was that of Frank Thorns, an ironmonger who had a three-storey building and employed 'a good number of hands'.[29] It is listed in the 1845 directory as Cubitt & Thorns (Thorns is still in business in Exchange Street).

47

London Street (Cockey Lane and London Lane)

During the 19th century London Street was probably the most important shopping street in Norwich despite problems of access. As early as 1783 Chase had complained about the difficulties faced by those travelling either on foot or by carriage in what was then Cockey Lane and London Lane. He spoke of pedestrians having to duck into shops to avoid being run over by carts and carriages and made suggestions for improvement.[30] Although Peck, writing in 1803, praised the alterations recently made in Norwich and the 'superior appearance which the Shops in...London Lane now assume',[31] subsequent developments suggest that Peck's comments must have reflected an optimistic hope rather than genuine improvement. Later in the century Hibgame described London Street as he had known it (about 1870), saying that it consisted only of 'small low shops similar

Shop in London Street c.1836, originally called 'John of All Sorts'
(Litho by H. Ninham)

to the three or four still left'.[32] The widening and subsequent re-building of many of the shops which had started in 1848, was still

48

continuing in 1877. A number of smaller shops disappeared, but, judging by the number of prosperous businesses that continued to be listed in the directories, the protracted nature of the improvement did not injure trade.

The necessity to widen London Street was recognised as early as 1830[33] when the then Paving, Cleansing and Finance Committee of Norwich Corporation asked the Surveyor to draw up a plan of property occupied by the residents who would be affected. The Minutes make no further reference to London Street although other improvements took place and other streets were being widened at that time, including land on each side of Briggs Street which was purchased in 1839. Many schemes were floated for road improvements during this period although not all of them came to fruition.

When the widening of London Street finally started in 1848, it was a rather half-hearted affair and only a short section of the street was affected. On 8th September 1848 Spelman sold by auction the several freehold estates which had been purchased by the Norwich Paving Commissioners. On sale was the site and the whole of the materials of several dwelling houses, shops and other buildings and included that of a Tea and Coffee dealer, a Music Dealer and Preceptor and a Warehouseman.[34] The City was to retain a portion of each site for road widening and release the remainder of the property for sale in lots. The negotiations for the purchase of land were extremely slow and continued for many years, involving a large number of shops and small workshops.

Despite numerous complaints, the widening of London Street was still not complete in 1877. The negotiations, in particular the sale of the affected properties, were protracted. An editorial in the *Norfolk Chronicle* in 1855[35] made the following observation, a not unfair assessment of the state of London Street at that time:

Of late years some improvements have been made in various parts of Norwich by widening the streets, but by far the most important and expensive has been that in London Street. The improvement was badly designed and has cost almost as much already as the cost would have been of pulling down one side of the street entirely. From first to last at least £20,000 has been expended, and the whole street is a bungle after all. The lower part of the street remains as bad as ever, and in the upper part years have been required to make a fourteen feet passage.

Residents of London Street during the first half of the 19th century included men with small workshops, boot and shoe makers, grocers and very many drapers, haberdashers, hatters and other allied trades. The 1841 census returns show the majority of shopkeepers, both large and small, lived in their shops often with their staff. Typical entries include the linen draper Lydia Fairweather, silk mercer Richard Moore, Mary Clark and her sister also silk mercers, and grocer Henry Steel who provided lodging for a male assistant as did the chemist and druggist Richard B. Smith. All these small shopkeepers employed staff who lived with the family on the premises. The second half of the 19th century saw the disappearance of more and more small shops, including those mentioned above, as the growth of large stores employing hundreds of women and girls made these small businesses uneconomic

In 1851 proprietors of large businesses were just as likely to have staff living on the premises as those of smaller ones. According to the census, the tailor and draper John Tipple lived in his shop (he was a manufacturer employing five people) as did the tailor William Banks who employed 16 people. However, as the century progressed, the more successful businessmen whose stores were increasing in size and staffing, moved away and the 1881 census records a large number of premises in London Street termed 'offices'. Typical is W. B. English of English & Son, drapers, who died in the suburbs in 1875 although his predecessor, J. B. English lived in the shop premises in 1854. In 1836 the firm of John B. English is listed in the directory as a linen draper and, according to the *Industries of Norfolk and Suffolk Review* published c.1890 the firm, then known as English & Son, employed a large number of people in their shop and workrooms; the firm had gone out of business by 1911.

Although a great variety of businesses was represented, probably about half were involved in the clothing trade - tailors, hatters, glovers, hosiers, haberdashers, etc. The relative importance of the shops in London Street can be appreciated by the fact that in 1867 the draper and silk mercer I.W. Caley & Co. was able to provide some rich poplins for the Queen and royal family from its own stock supplied by the manufacturer, Willett & Nephew of Pottergate.[36] Caley was established in 1852 and is described in the 1854 directory as Nath.

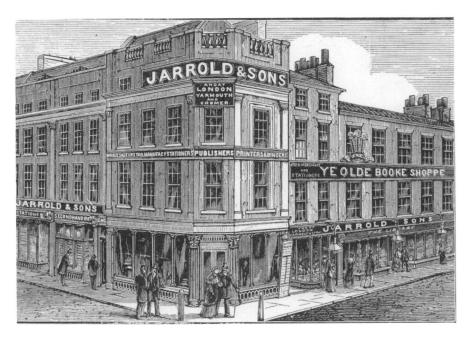

Jarrolds, at the corner of Exchange Street and London Street c. 1890

Hy. Caley, silk mercer. It is listed in Harrods 1877 directory as I.W. Caley & Co. and in 1890 is described as having a large shop with workrooms, employing over 100 girls and women.[37] It was still in business in 1929 as I.W. Caley & Co. Ltd., closing shortly after. All these large stores have disappeared; the only one remaining in business is Jarrold & Sons. Started up in a small way as printers and booksellers in 1823 by John Jarrold and his son, John James Jarrold,[38] it is today transformed into a successful large department store.

London Street had been an important retail shopping street in 1783 and so it remained during the 19th century despite the upheaval caused by the over-extended street widening. Its situation, near to the Cattle Market, the Guildhall, the provision market and the quality houses in the nearby suburbs gave it a commercial advantage.

Prince of Wales Road

Before the building of Prince of Wales Road, the only approach to Thorpe (Norwich) railway station from the centre of Norwich was along Rose Lane. The narrowness and inconvenience of this approach to the station led a group of Norwich businessmen in 1859 to form a company with the purpose of constructing a new road. This involved buying land to a depth of about 108 feet to front a road which was to run from King Street to Foundry Bridge and would be a direct route from the station to the centre of Norwich. The businessmen behind this venture formed the New Street Company and in 1859 the Norwich New Street Bill was presented to Parliament and was passed in 1860. The Corporation sold the land required to the Company for £3,260 and £2,000 of the purchase money was put towards the building of the new street, to be vested in it on completion. The remainder of the money was used towards widening the approach to the Cattle Market by Rose Lane.[39] The man behind the development of this new street was John Oddin Taylor who died in 1874. His obituary, published in the *Norwich Mercury* refers to the debt owed to him for the construction of this new street.[40]

Much of the land that was affected by the construction of the new street was owned by the Corporation and had been leased to a number of individuals for varying periods, but there were also a small number of private freeholders. Most of the property was on Upper King Street (the name Upper King Street only appears in the directories in 1859; before that it was called King Street, of which it is a continuation) and included Blackfriars Lane. A number of houses had to be demolished to allow access to the new road. Among those affected was William Brooke, who had a boarding school, house and garden on Blackfriars Lane. He was compensated as occupier, as was the lessee, Miss Charlotte Hudson. Mr Brooke's school is listed in the 1836, 1845 and 1854 directories. The 1851 census lists the occupants as the head master, a 'Mathematical' master, a writing master and an articled assistant as well as twenty-three boys aged between 7 and 16, all except one born in Norfolk or Suffolk. Miss Hudson, heiress and joint executrix of the estate of her father, Anthony Hudson of Harvey & Hudson's Bank, also had a house and garden on lease from Norwich Corporation. Harvey & Hudson's bank was also demolished and was later replaced by a splendid new bank – the Crown Bank - which was opened in 1866, later to become the General Post Office, afterwards Anglia Television.

The General Post Office

As well as the land belonging to the Corporation, there were also a number of freeholders including the Dean & Chapter of Norwich,

The Charity Trustees, the Norwich Guardians, leasing land for the Boys' Home from Norwich Corporation, and the auctioneer George Ives who had a dwellinghouse, office and garden on Upper King Street. There was also other leasehold property including small houses, gardens, paddocks and stables. All those affected by the development received compensation: freeholders, lessees and occupiers, although the amount of compensation offered was small for occupiers of garden ground.[41]

An undated rough plan of the area of the Greyfriars affected by the building of Prince of Wales Road gives an outline of the houses proposed for the new road[42] and shows buildings on both sides of the road from Upper King Street to St Faith's Lane (Cathedral Street). Most of these buildings are still standing. They are imposing terrace houses, with basements and small back gardens (the last no longer remaining). Although the design of the houses built seems to have envisaged residential use, a number of them were soon converted into offices and shops. *The Builder*, reporting on the Architectural Association meeting in Norwich in 1880, wrote about the good-looking private dwellings lining Prince of Wales Road and said 'it is pretty certain to be metamorphosed and lined with shops before many years are over'.[43] And this indeed is what happened.

Although Colman's 1877 Directory recorded a large number of private residents, as early as 1877 there were a significant number of businesses. Initially the quality of the houses had attracted many prosperous residents including the vicar of St Peter Mountergate, George Buckingham of the boot and shoe manufacturing firm of Buckingham & Sons, and the architect and surveyor to the Dean & Chapter of Norwich Cathedral. The directory entries show that numbers of private residents (as opposed to residents who lived over the shop) remained fairly constant between 1881 and 1900 even though the number of businesses increased markedly.

There were comparatively few provision stores on Prince of Wales Road and their number remained fairly constant, but instead a growing number of shops were established selling quality or specialist items. These included a firm of photographers by 1877, spirit merchants, a curiosity dealer, an antique dealer and a tailor by 1893. Because of the ease of access to the centre of Norwich, the business potential of Prince of Wales Road was recognised early and there were soon a number of solicitors' and several national insurance companies: the Industrial Assurance Company in 1883, the Commercial Union by 1890 and the Clerical Medical & General by 1900. The Liverpool Victoria Legal Friendly Society and the Church of England Temperance Society also had offices by 1900 and the Divisional Headquarters of the Salvation Army and the Midland Railway Company's Receiving Office both had premises by 1890.

Prince of Wales Road was also a convenient location for servant girls coming by train into the city for work, hence the continued success of the Registry Office for Servants run by Mrs Priscilla Causton who was in business from at least 1883. It was also a desirable location for those seeking either temporary or permanent accommodation. The 1871 census lists a number of boarding-house keepers and residents. The number of residents was very small, one had only four lodgers and the numbers are roughly similar in all the boarding houses. The lodgers were all respectable: the Vicar of Bawdeswell and the Vicar of Rougham lodged in one house; in another the Rector of Wattisfield. The 1900 directory lists four apartment owners and a large number of hotels: the Albert Commercial Hotel (on two sites), three Temperance Hotels and the Great Eastern Hotel.

The lower part of Prince of Wales Road near to Foundry Bridge had none of the fine buildings which were built between Upper King Street and St Faith's Lane and although there were no large-scale semi-industrial premises, there were a number of workshops, most of them behind a building with a large shop fronting the street. C.H. Rust, a monumental and stone mason, had premises on Prince of Wales Road in 1890 with offices, show-rooms, sheds, etc. An advertisement for T.C.R. King, lead and glass merchant, whose shop was built in 1864 and extended in 1882 states 'the shop is artistically arranged, and very beautiful offices are contained in the same, the whole being heated by hot water...there is a fine large yard...the workshops...are spacious and well ventilated...there are also large warehouses' where 'a large number of hands [are employed] in the various departments'.[44]

The premises of T.C.R. King in Prince of Wales Road, 1890

It is appropriate that many of the businesses in a new street should look to the future rather than the past: Henry W. Howes had premises in Prince of Wales Road and in 1890 was listed as a carriage builder and cycle agent (in 1875 he had advertised his services as a coach builder). The cycle manufacturer Walter Morris was listed in 1890 and the motor agents Hayes Thompson & Kahler in 1900. In addition, the firm of Arthur S. Howard of 'The Eastern Counties Depository & Pantechnicon Store Warehouses' had showrooms fronting Prince of

Wales Road and warehouses extending to Rose Lane. Nearby, on Rose Lane in 1883, there was a saw mill which extended to Prince of Wales Road. This business had disappeared by 1890 and the land appears to have been acquired by Arthur Howard for his warehouses. Howard's was a business catering for a new type of customer and he claimed in the 1907 *Official Guide to Norwich* to be able to give 'accommodation for gentlemen's carriages, motors, &c., requiring to be warehoused'.

At least one of the businesses on Prince of Wales Road near to the river between Foundry Bridge and St Faith's Lane owed more to the past than the future. The extensive premises of Hills & Underwood, distillers and vinegar manufacturers, was established long before the road was built and its original address was St Faith's Lane (it was in business at this address as Squire Hills & Son by 1830). And although there were no churches, the premises of the Railway Mission Hall was established in Prince of Wales Road in 1886 in what had previously been an engineering showroom, converted into a church for the railwaymen who lived nearby.[45]

Although the houses on Prince of Wales Road soon were no longer mainly residential, the businesses that took them over never competed with those that had historically been established in the commercial section of the City. What these new businesses and shops offered complemented the established businesses - a new service that was emerging as necessary in a more complex society with a growing educated population coming to terms with technological innovation and with the decline of traditional industry.

Central Norwich: Respectable Lodgings for Shop Assistants
As the drapery business expanded, the number of staff employed increased to such an extent that the owners had to provide lodgings for staff that came from the country. Given the long hours of work and the difficulty of travel before the advent of the railway, it was essential to provide boarding facilities. When shops were small, with few assistants, these could be accommodated within the family, but it was obviously impossible with larger shops. Separate lodgings for staff was not usual

until later in the century. Betts, a draper in the Market Place, was unusual in providing separate accommodation for staff as early as 1841, but as more and more prosperous shop owners moved into the suburbs, boarding houses were taken to provide lodgings for the young shop assistants from the country.

The Messrs. Bunting Boarding House for Young Lady Assistants has been mentioned and the 1881 census lists Garland's drapers shop in London Street as the residence of the proprietor's son, then aged 18 years, a housekeeper and one male and ten female assistants and a clerk. By 1900 Garland's shop assistants had moved and were lodged in a boarding-house in Castle Meadow.

The 1881 census lists a number of buildings in Gentleman's Walk and Haymarket which appear to be lodgings for drapers' assistants employed in the shops in Norwich as well as clerks, travelling salesmen and the like. In the Market Place there was a house with 40 young people in their late teens/early 20s listed as apprentices, clerks, drapery sales, etc. Their place of birth is given as Norfolk and Suffolk, with a small number from other parts of England. It had certainly become necessary to recruit staff from outside the City. For instance in about 1890 the silk mercers and drapers Chamberlin, Sons & Co. near the Market Place advertised a variety of services in-house including dress-making. They employed 600 assistants and the advertisement states that 'every precaution is taken to assure the physical and moral welfare of these [assistants]'.[46]

This paternalist concern for the 'physical and moral welfare' of employees has echoes throughout the country: in Robert Owen's New Lanark in 1819 one of the principal objects had been to 'have children educated in habits of industry and morality', in Titus Salt's model village of Saltaire in 1850 with a large chapel but no public house and in Port Sunlight in 1887 where W.H. Lever (later Lord Leverhulme) built a self-contained and model community. Although the scale of the above projects is not comparable, the manufacturers J. & J. Colman of Norwich expressed their concern for the 'material, social and general welfare of the numerous workmen and women', providing dining and refreshment rooms, a reading room, and dispensary for the workforce as well as a school for the children 'years before the Government undertook the management of this department.'[47]

Industrial Norwich

Away from the prosperous centre was the industrial heart of Norwich. In the Westwick and King Street areas were some of the manufactories that were making Norwich prosperous. In many ways the houses and the people living in St Giles, Surrey Street and All Saints Green mentioned above are not typical of the residents of Norwich as a whole. For in the 19th century Norwich was very much a working-class city with only pockets of wealth and prosperity and the professional men and wealthy merchants who lived in the City were greatly outnumbered by small shopkeepers and by working-class men and women. The majority of these were either outworkers or employed in the nearby manufactories, established throughout the nineteenth century, which, to a large extent, were enabling the workers to escape from the extreme poverty caused by the collapse of the hand-loom weaving industry. Despite adverse trade conditions, the woollen trade still employed a large number of people during the first part of the century and, although much reduced, it remained a significant source of employment. According to White's 1890 Directory, Grout & Co. employed between 600 and 700 people at their factory in Lower Westwick Street and there were numerous textile works on the other side of the river. By 1900, however, the major source of employment was the manufacture of boots and shoes. This had grown from a cottage industry; technical innovation had led to large manufactories being erected on both sides of the river. These were all situated in the city as were the food and drink, building and engineering and metalworking industries.

The coming of the railway also brought employment, as did the increase in insurance and banking although, judging by the census returns, the number of clerical workers resident within the walls was minimal. In the 1871 census a number of train drivers, porters and others engaged by the railway company lived near Thorpe railway station in Synagogue Street (Mountergate) and Orchard Street.

In the King Street area near to the river were iron foundries: one of them, the St Anne's Foundry of Thomas Smithdale, iron founder, was founded in 1871 and employed 65 men and 10 boys. It was situated in King Street but had ceased trading in 1885. Nearby was the Rose Lane Iron Foundry of Boulton & Paul which had grown from small beginnings and in 1879 employed 350 men. Morgan's (formerly Tompson's) Brewery in King Street was one of a number of breweries with a river location. The proximity to the river is reflected in the occupations of residents. The census returns reflect a diversity of occupations: boat-builders, porters, wharfingers as well as publicans, maltsters, dressmakers, labourers (unspecified), bricklayers, etc. as well as a considerable, although decreased, number employed as weavers, some working in Grout's Silk Mill.

In Lower Westwick Street, also near the river, there were more workshops and businesses big and small. The largest, Grout's Silk Mill, has already been mentioned, but the 1883 directory lists corn merchants and corn millers, coal dealers and maltsters as well as many other smaller businesses. The corn merchants Squirrell & Utting were a large concern which did business at the Norwich Corn Exchange and had premises also in Yarmouth.

And although London Street was the most important street for shopping south of the river there were more shops, indeed there were small shops in all the main streets. Upper Westwick Street had a large number of smaller shops and workshops. The 1783 directory lists a variety of occupations; as well as shopkeepers, there were small industrial premises. On this street there were few large shops, but many smaller ones, and grocers, butchers, clothiers, hairdressers and greengrocers are listed in the 1883 directory.

The changing townscape: Elm Hill

Although the parish of St Giles was one of the most prosperous in Norwich in the 18th and 19th centuries, this had not always been the case. Beatniffe, writing in 1773,[48] states that a number of tenements had recently been demolished and handsome houses erected in their place. One street that may have benefited was St Giles which had a large number of middle to late 18th century houses. This parish had been one of the poorest[49] in Tudor and Stuart times. Conversely, with the growth in the population and the large number of (mostly) older workers impoverished by the decline in textiles, the houses of wealthy merchants in previously affluent areas were being sub-divided and tenements built where there had previously been garden ground. As early as 1762[50] one such house on Ber Street, that of Sir Nicholas Bacon, was said to have been turned into tenements 'of an inferior kind.' In King Street, long the home of wealthy merchants, many of the once grand houses were in the process of becoming slums.

The entrance to Old Barge Yard in King Street, now the way into Dragon Hall

Elm Hill in 1929

Examples of the quality of the houses which have been lost can be seen in the few that remain. Elm Hill has had a long history of housing men of wealth and importance and its history during the 19th century is an illustration of the gradual deterioration of a street caused by the infilling of the numerous yards with small tenements. Although the quality of many of the houses was such that they were unaffected by the tenements close by, many of the buildings were neglected and photographs taken in the 1920s show a terrible degree of dilapidation.[51] Elm Hill has many important 16th century houses. Pettus House, once much larger and grander than it is today, was the family home of the Pettus family between 1550 and 1683. Thomas Pettus, a cloth merchant, was mayor of Norwich in 1590 and his son, Sir John, in 1608. The Paston family had a town house in Elm Hill. In 1783 the merchant Francis Columbine Esq. lived in Elm Hill. He was a member of an important Huguenot family which had fled to Norwich in the 17th century. He was a grocer and mayor of Norwich in 1776 and the son of the worsted weaver Peter Columbine (a memorial to Peter Columbine who died in 1770 is in the French church in Princes

Street, St Mary the Less)). The 1802 and 1810 directories show a mixed population of small shopkeepers and small specialist businesses including a clock and watch maker in 1802 and a cabinet maker in 1810.

In March 1812 the former residence of a Mr Columbine (possibly that of Francis Columbine who died in 1808) was sold at auction by S. Lovick.[52] The auction particulars show what may have been the beginning of a process leading to the deterioration of the housing stock in Elm Hill.[53] The property was divided into lots, of which 'Lot 1, Mr. Columbine's house', was advertised as being of the highest quality and very suitable for the use of a prosperous merchant or manufacturer with 'several capital cellars' as well as all the appurtenances for genteel living: sash windows, parlour, drawing room with marble chimney[54] and several bedrooms. According to the auction particulars, its large size made it suitable for conversion into two equally good dwelling houses. In addition, this Lot included a brick building which, according to the auctioneer, could be made into three 'good tenements'. By this means the canny buyer could have five buildings where before there had been only one. Lot 2 was also a good-quality house, although smaller than Lot 1. It too had sash windows and was advertised as suitable for the 'residence of a genteel family'. Lot 3 was another large house. Sash windows are not mentioned, but there was a large warehouse, work-rooms and granaries adjoining the river suitable for a manufacturer, corn merchant or any other business requiring large premises. The implication to be drawn from the wording of the sale particulars seems to be that Lots 1 and 3 were suitable premises for men in commerce, the former for a more prosperous merchant or manufacturer, the latter for a working manufacturer who was actively engaged in the business. On the other hand, Lot 2 would be the preferred option for a gentle-man of independent means. However, the probable breaking up of Lot 1 into smaller units raises questions about the future of all the houses in Elm Hill.

In 1812 the full effects of the industrial revolution were only beginning to be apparent, and the large warehouse and work-rooms would still have been used for their original purposes. There were a comparatively large number of manufacturers based in Elm Hill. Bayne[55] lists the most important, one of which was Wright & Son who at one time employed 1500 hand-loom weavers. The 1836 directory lists John Wright as a silk and worsted manufacturer and dyer with business premises in Elm Hill and a house in Middle Street (St George's Street). Wright is listed in the 1854 directory but not thereafter. The premises occupied need not have been very large and would have been required to store the raw materials to be handed to the weaver and to receive from them the worked cloth. In 1839 there were 4,054 looms at work, of which 3,398 were in the homes of weavers and only 650 in shops and factories.[56] It is likely that the majority of the hand-loom weavers employed by Wright were outworkers. The directories list other small businesses including that of Charles Cullington the boot and shoe maker who had a warehouse and is listed in 1836. Other boot and shoe makers in 1836 were Robert and William Harrison and Robert Tillyard. These were only very small businesses who would have handed out materials to outworkers and received back the finished work.

Other manufacturers with premises in Elm Hill include Shickle Towler & Campin who were silk manufacturers and shawl makers and were sufficiently large in 1836 to have an office in London. This firm was later known as Towler Campin & Co. and Towler Rowling & Allen. By 1864 the firm was also listed as occupying large rooms in a new building beside the St James's factory on the other side of the river.[57] The 1883 directory lists Allen J. Howse & Co. woollen and cotton goods manufacturers. He was listed earlier in Kelly's 1875 Directory, but had disappeared by 1890.

The census returns for Elm Hill (including its continuation, Church Street in the parish of St Simon, listed separately), give a more detailed picture of the residents than can be gleaned from the directories. The 1841 returns list, as well as a solicitor, an Excise

Supervisor and a surgeon. The other residents include a bookseller, a hairdresser, a musician, two parish clerks and two people of independent means as well as tailors, cordwainers, weavers, etc. The 1861 census records a shoemaker master employing four men, a coal merchant employing a female servant, a schoolmaster and a professor of music. The 1891 census records a draper and hosier who, according to the 1890 directory, had a shop on Prince's Street. One of the larger houses was occupied by an engineer and mill factor, and the census also lists a schoolmistress, teacher of music, insurance clerk, baker and pork butcher as well as a shoe and a boot finisher, a general labourer, a ferryman, a bricklayer's assistant etc.

The back of No. 18 Elm Hill

Although the deterioration of Elm Hill had reached an advanced stage by the 20th century, the census returns show that it housed people in a comfortable walk of life and that this continued into the 20th century. The 1900 directory lists a number of shopkeepers and small businesses and there are also a number of medium size workshops. Norwich, possibly because of its comparatively small size, has never had areas of absolute poverty and squalor as was the case in the large industrial towns. There always seems to have been at least one family, whose bread-winner was a skilled artisan or white-collar worker,[58] living in or beside a tenement building.

The returns for the yards at the back of Elm Hill show the degree of tolerance of substandard housing nearby. Judging by the census returns for Crown Court Yard, there was a large degree of over-crowding and squalor. Sale particulars of properties[59] show that by 1850 there had been some in-building in this yard. An indenture dated 31st August 1815 describes a messuage abutting the river and also the use of the yard and posts for drying linen, which suggests that the yard would have been of use to the textile trade. With the demise of this trade, the drying posts would no longer have been necessary, and indeed there is no mention made of them in the Abstract of Title for the property in 1850 which refers to 'three cottages or tenements together with a coal bin...recently converted into six cottages'. The census returns show the deterioration of the yard: in 1841 there were 69 people living in 18 tenements, in 1861 there were 75 people living in 19 tenements plus six said to be unoccupied. The 1891 census return, in which the number of rooms for each separate habitation was listed, show the living conditions: of the 17 tenements occupied, four had two rooms, seven had three rooms and two had four rooms. One larger tenement with five rooms was subdivided with two families living in two rooms and one room unoccupied.

Courts and Yards south of the river

Chapter 8 deals with the problem of the courts and yards but the worst ones were north of the river and I have focussed mainly on these. This is not to say that there were no slum dwellings south of the river, or even that slum dwelling only affected old derelict buildings, abandoned by their owners. Some slum property was new, probably the result of inadequate or non-existent buildings regulations. No part of Norwich was unaffected by the steady growth of slum property during the 19th century but the least affected were St Giles, Pottergate, Surrey Street, Tombland and All Saints Green, where traditional timber-framed buildings had been replaced in the late 18th/early 19th century and there was no encroachment on garden ground. The largest number of courts and yards were situated near to the industrial section of Norwich where old houses had been sub-divided and allowed to deteriorate and where traditional yards and gardens had been infilled with small cottages and tenements (the 1883 Ordnance Survey shows the convoluted nature of some of the yards and courts off the main streets). The 1891 census, which lists the numbers of rooms per house, shows the extent of the overcrowding. Nearly every house in the major thoroughfares such as St Benedict's Street had five rooms, but in the yards, houses with five rooms were a rarity. In Queen of Hungary yard, off St Benedict's Street, there were eight buildings with only two rooms (one of these had eight people resident), four had three rooms (one housed eight people). In Gaffers Yard, also off St Benedict's Street, there were four buildings, each with only two rooms. These are not isolated incidents, and the extent of the problem can be seen by the fact that in 1890 St Benedict's Street had twenty-six inhabited yards.

New slums were also being created in previously undeveloped parts of the city due to the lack of building controls. Coburg Street, as it name denotes, is not a particularly old street.[60]

It was originally a lane leading from St Stephen's Street to Chapelfield Gardens. Millard & Manning's 1830 map shows this street, then unnamed. Hudson's Buildings in Coburg Street were singled out as a particularly bad example of overcrowding by the Inspector leading the enquiry held in 1851 in connection with the Health of Towns Act.[61] The 1881 census return lists the residents of the 34 buildings and the numbers living in each cottage ranged from one to ten. Their occupations varied; the majority were employed in the boot and shoe trade, and there were also labourers, bricklayers and the like. The 1891 census additionally lists the number of rooms in each cottage as follows: there were two houses with two rooms, 29 houses with three rooms and two houses with four rooms. Thus out of a total of 34 houses, 33 were sub-standard and only one had more than four rooms. There were ten people living in one of the three-roomed houses. And yet, most of these houses had small front gardens. They would have been new-built during the first part of the 19th century and would likely have shared many of the qualities of the houses being built after 1815 in the so-called 'New City' outside the walls which the Inspector had condemned as looking 'well in front' (with small gardens) but which 'in reality are very unhealthy'.[62]

If any incentive were needed for the more prosperous citizens to leave the city centre, it must have been the increase in the numbers of people living in decayed slum property. The Inspector condemned Norwich because of its impure water, lack of sanitation and unhygienic and inferior housing stock in 1851, and this condemnation extended to many of the streets in the older parts of the city as well as to the newly-built suburbs.

Carrow Works beside the Wensum, c. 1890

The pattern of residence changed quite dramatically between 1801 and 1900, and yet the number of people living within the walls increased. According to the census returns in 1831, 30,833 lived in the parishes within the walls south of the river and in 1901 34,610. What had changed was the social composition of the inhabitants. Throughout the century there was a gradual movement to the suburbs as tradesmen became more prosperous. But there was a much more fundamental change than this. Norwich in 1801 was a city of self-employed workers, working at a trade that was in decline. Although the woollen industry was in decline, trade had diversified and was no longer dependent on one commodity. Work in factories was replacing the home worker and banks and insurance companies had been established and were achieving national success.

Notes

1. *Industries of Norfolk & Suffolk Business Review. A Guide to Leading Commercial Enterprises* [1890] p. 41 gives details of this business.
2. Hibgame, F.T. *Recollections of Norwich Fifty Years Ago*, p. 48 and Browne, P. *The History of Norwich...* p. 194 both praise the quality of the houses in St Giles Street. According to directory entries the street was variously named St Giles Broad Street (in 1789), Broad Street St Giles (in 1836), and the whole street was named St Giles and Upper St Giles in 1883.
3. The Norfolk & Norwich Savings Bank was first housed in the home of the founder in St Giles Street and moved to the Haymarket in 1845. It later became part of the East Anglian Trustee Savings Bank which today is incorporated into the Lloyds TSB. (See the *Norfolk & Norwich Savings Bank 1816-1900* Norwich, 1901).
4.. Much of the information about the residents of St. Giles Street has been gleaned from Sir Peter Eade, *Some Account of the Parish of St. Giles, Norwich* published in 1886. Eade was a surgeon who lived in St. Giles and who was also an amateur historian. He wrote a history of the Norfolk & Norwich Hospital and various other short articles on various medical subjects and also the history of his own house, Churchman House in St. Giles, which was published in *Norfolk Archaeology*.
5. See *The Mayors of Norwich 1403-1858* for further information about John Harvey. Brief details about Charles Tuck can be found in Mackie, Charles *Norfolk Annals* vol. 2. The building which today is called Gladstone House (after over fifty years as a Liberal club) was one of the offices of Norwich City Council and today is unoccupied.
6. NRO, SPE701 Sale by order of the executors of J.H. Cole deceased.
7. NRO, SPE705 Freehold dwellinghouses situated in the centre of St Giles Broad Street.
8. NRO, SPE704 Freehold messuage situate near the centre of and on the south side of St Giles Street.

9. White's 1890s Directory lists the Conservative Club in either the Norfolk Hotel or in a contiguous building.

10. Young. J.R. *The Inns and Taverns of Old Norwich*, pp. 23-24.

11. Eade, p. 45.

12. Eade, p. 24. Eade lists residents of St Giles and gives a brief history of each of the houses.

13. Mantle, Jonathan *Norwich Union. The First 200 Years*, p. 58.

14. Eade, p. 24 lists some past and present residents of Bethel Street.

15. NRO, SPE335 Parish of St Giles Bethel Street and Chapel Field.

16. Eade p. 27.

17. 1881 Census return for Norwich.

18. Eade p. 15.

19. Browne p. 158.

20. Wearing S. *Georgian Norwich. Its Builders,* pp. 34-35. Thomas Ivory (1709-1779) designed some of the most important Georgian buildings in Norwich including the Assembly Rooms in Theatre Street, the Octagon Unitarian Chapel in Colegate and a range of town houses in Surrey Street.

21. Mantle, Jonathan, *Norwich Union. The first 200 years,* p. 23.

22. Walter Rye in *Norfolk Families* states that Sigismond Boehm's forebears came from Strasbo urg and he assumed the name of Trafford the maiden name of his maternal grandmother and Southwell, the maiden name of his mother. He married the daughter of James Crowe and through her inherited the land in Lakenham (hence Trafford and Southwell roads in New Lakenham).

23. Kent 'The Houses of the Duke of Norfolk' *Norf. Arch.* XXIV pp. 73-87.

24. Wearing, p. 36.

25. *Norfolk Annals* Vol. 1 p. 279.

26. The Museum opened at new premises in 1833 (White p. 155).

27. *The Industries of Norfolk and Suffolk Business Review*, p. 28. There is also a large advertisement in Kelly's Directory 1900, p. 24.

28. *The Industries of Norfolk & Suffolk Business Review*, p. 62.

29. Chase, W. & Co. (printer) *The Norwich Directory*.....p. iv. Hint for Public Improvement No. 8.

30. Peck's Norwich Directory p. vi. In 1789 Cockey Lane ran from the Market Place to the junction with Back of the Inn and continued as London Lane. The entire street was called London Street by 1830.

31. Hibgame p. 5. In the preface Hibgame states that these were letters which were printed in the *Norfolk Chronicle* 'many years ago'. It was published as a book in 1919.

32. NRO, N/TC28/1 Paving Cleansing & Finance Committee.

33. NRO, N/TC28/3 Paving Cleansing & Finance Committee No. 4.

34. *Norfolk. Annals* p. 46.

35. Bayne, A.D. *A Comprehensive History of Norwich.....*, p. 590.

36. *The Industries of Norfolk and Suffolk Business Review,* p. 30.

37. *The House of Jarrolds 1823-1923* gives a history of the evolution of the store.

38. *Norfolk Annals* 2 p. 82.

39. *Norfolk Annals* 2 p. 241.

40. Norwich New Street - Book of Reference [Prince of Wales Road] n.d. The manuscript notebook is in the Library of the Norfolk & Norwich Archaeological Society.

41. Norwich New Street - Book of Reference

42. *The Builder* 18 September 1880.
43. *Industries of Norfolk & Suffolk Business Review,* p. 47.
44. Information in the Norwich *Evening News* 8th June 1995.
45. *Industries of Norfolk & Suffolk Business Review,* pp. 26 and 30.
46. Darley, Gillian. *Villages of Vision,* pp. 131 (Saltaire), 154 (New Lanark), 141 (Port Sunlight).
47. Beatniffe, R. *The Norfolk tour: or, traveller's pocket companion: being a concise description of all the principal towns, Noblemen's and gentlemen's seats, and other remarkable places.*
48. Slack, Paul. 'The Urban impact', p. 126ff. *The Impact of plague on Tudor and Stuart England.* Oxford, Clarendon Press 1985. Reproduced with corrections 1990
49. *History of the city and county of Norwich from the earliest accounts to the present time,* 1768, (printed by John Crouse), p. 454
50. The street was saved from clearance in the 1920s by the intervention of the Norwich Society.
51. *Norwich Mercury* 7th March 1812: Details of sale by auction by S. Lovick on 9th March 1812. Elm Hill had been the home of many prosperous mayors of Norwich (*Mayors of Norwich 1403-1835,* Cozens-Hardy,B. & Kent, E.A.)
52 See also other examples in chapter 4 'Norwich Over the Water'.
53. It seems likely that the house in Lot 1 was described as having sash windows and a marble fireplace in order to make clear that what was an old house had been modernised.
54. Bayne p. 581
55. Bayne p. 584
56. Bayne p. 592
57. See Chapter 8. Substandard Houses.
58. NRO, NPL10608, 20604-8 and 205968A Conveyance by the Trustees of the Loyal William Fox Lodge No. 4157 to Walter Rye 1st September 1903. (Crown Court Yard, Elm Hill)
59. Coburg Street is listed by White in the 1836 Directory. The name commemorates the house of Saxe-Coburg Gotha (*The Place-names of Norfolk Part One - Norwich.* Sandred, K.I. & Lindstrom, B. p.97).
60. William Lee, in his *Report of an Inquiry of the Sanitary Condition of the City and County of Norwich* published in 1850, describes Hudson's Buildings as being 'close and ill-ventilated' having cesspools close to the houses and that a woman living in one of the houses was always ill because her bedroom was over the privy (p. 56).
61. Health of Towns Act. *Report of an inquiry held before William Lee of the Sanitary Condition of the City and County of Norwich,* p. 56
62. Health of Towns Act. *Report of an inquiry held before William Lee of the sanitary Condition of the City and County of Norwich,* p. 56 Union Place.

Chapter 4. Norwich Over the Water

Introduction

Norwich Over the Water, bounded by the river Wensum to the south and the city walls to the north, seems to have been largely ignored by travel writers despite having many fine buildings and gardens. The high quality of the houses is evidence that this part of Norwich was popular with prosperous merchants and professional men who lived in Colegate, Calvert Street and Magdalen Street in the 18th and early 19th century; many of these buildings are still standing. However, in the 19th century this part of Norwich was affected by the expansion and growth of large factories and also by an increase in the number of substandard houses and tenements. There were slums in Barrack Street, Cowgate, Fishergate and in many other streets in the parishes of St James, St Paul and St Edmund, and conditions in these streets and in their yards and courts were condemned in 1850 by the Health Inspector in connection with the Health of Towns Act. It was not until the late 1890s that any serious attempt was made to deal with slum conditions and only in the 20th century was there wide-spread slum clearance.[1]

During the first half of the century, before the advent of the railway, the proximity to the river was an advantage to business. This had always been the case: Chase's 1783 directory listed numerous small businesses including a timber merchant who had a yard in Fishgate (Fishergate), the iron founders Ransome & Co. with a foundry near Whitefriars Bridge and a havel and sleamaker's workings also in Fishgate. These businesses were small compared to later ones such as Barnard Bishop & Barnards Norfolk Iron Works with large premises on Coslany Street and a showroom in London by 1890. According to the 1854 directory, this firm, at that time called Barnard & Bishop, was trading in a small way in Calvert Street nearby. In Colegate the boot and shoe maker Howlett & White, founded in 1846, prospered and expanded during the 19th century, building a large manufactory taking over much of the street by 1896 when it employed nearly 2,000 workers. There had always been small industrial works in this part of Norwich, but the growth of mechanisation necessitated the establishment of ever larger factories employing an increasing number of workers and this, in turn, led to the deterioration of the housing stock, with old large houses being divided up and substandard tenements built in already overcrowded courts and yards. Although the population growth of Norwich was small in comparison with that of many other towns of England, the census returns for each parish show a significant increase in each one.[2]

Colegate

In 1783 Colegate was largely residential, with a mixed population; the 1802 and 1810 directories list a variety of occupations including bricklayers, carpenters, painters, manufacturers, merchants and physicians and surgeons. Manning's plan of the Great Garden between Colegate and Golden Dog Lane [1832][3] with its large houses and garden grounds shows why this part of Norwich was popular with professional men and wealthy manufacturers. This plan covers an area bounded by Golden Dog Lane, Magdalen Street, Colegate and Snailgate (Calvert Street) and was the original site of the Dominican Friary. It was retained by the Dominicans when they moved across the river after the new church and convent buildings had been erected in the 15th century (St Andrew's and Blackfriars' Hall). The original church, dedicated to St John the Baptist, remained, and the whole of the site was acquired by the Crown at the Dissolution and then purchased by the City in 1540 (according to Blomefield this church was destroyed by fire in the 15th century).[4] Before the Dissolution, apart from a few small buildings, the main part of the land had been the garden ground for the Dominicans. By 1832 (when the plan was drawn) there were a large number of buildings on the site, as well as two chapels, one belonging to the Trustees of the Independent Congregation (The Old Meeting House built 1693) and the other to the Trustees of the Octagon Chapel (built 1754-6). There were two substantial houses with very large gardens, one of them the residence of William Dalrymple Esq. and the other that of Mrs Amelia Opie. There were also a large number of smaller properties, each with a garden. All of these properties were leasehold and the plan has a note of the unexpired portion of each lease.

The leaseholders were, in the main, people of substance: William Dalrymple had been elected Consulting Surgeon to the Norfolk and Norwich Hospital in 1812 and lived in Snailgate in 1810. Mrs Amelia Opie had inherited the property from her father Dr James Alderson and had lived there as a child.[5] Her father, who is listed as living in this house in 1810, was a man of some distinction, having been elected as Physician to the Norfolk and Norwich Hospital in 1772. Other leaseholders included one man styled 'gent.' who lived in Colegate in 1830 and a manufacturer who lived in Snailgate in 1810. Although the plan gives little or no detail of the houses, Mrs Opie's house was sold by auction in 1832[6] and the sale particulars describe the property as a freehold and leasehold estate in the parishes of St Clement and St Saviour consisting of a freehold house comprising breakfast, dining and drawing rooms and library, bedrooms, kitchen and domestic offices. There was a wash-house and laundry in a detached building, and a large garden with fruit trees. In addition there was a four-stalled stable and a coach-house under a lease from Norwich Corporation. Simpson's 1864 directory referred to this house as Opie House. Other prosperous residents of Colegate included merchants, clergymen and attorneys, as well as a small number described as 'gent.' and 'esq.'

One of the 18th century houses on Colegate (No. 18) has an interesting history. It was built c.1730 by the manufacturer Robert Harvey, Sheriff of Norwich in 1727 and another Robert Harvey is listed as living there in 1802 and 1810. There is a plan in the Norfolk Record Office which appears to be that of Robert Harvey's property. It is dated 1847 and is described as 'A plan of an estate in St Clement's Norwich to be sold by auction 24 May 1847'.[7] Although there is no mention of this on the plan, a card at the Norfolk Record Office states 'Endorsed Miss Norton's Estate'. Miss Norton is listed in White's Directory as living in Colegate in 1836, and in Blyth's in

1842 (according to the census return she was 70 years old in 1841 and at that time had one male and two female servants; it is likely that the estate was sold after her death). In this plan the estate is divided into two lots. Lot 1 has a frontage on Colegate, Lot 2 adjoining at the rear of Lot 1 has no frontage on the street and runs down to the river. A 6 ft passage divides the two lots from the property to the east. Lot 1 was a substantial dwelling-house with garden, and on Lot 2 were eight cottages and a good-sized garden with a 'summer seat' and stable. As it is unlikely that a garden and summer seat would be used by the tenants of the small cottages, it is probable that this was originally part of an estate which comprised both Lots consisting of garden ground and a good-quality house. The obligation on the purchaser of Lot 2 to erect a tall wall dividing the two lots supports this idea, as does the provision of a 6 ft passage to allow access from the road to the purchaser of Lot 2. The future proposed use for Lot 2 seems to be quasi-industrial, suggested by the words written in pencil 'drying ground' in front of the summer seat.

No. 18 Colegate, the house that was built by Robert Harvey and probably later lived in by Miss Norton, became the residence of John Jewson in 1868.[8] In the same year No. 20 Colegate (the large house beside No. 18, both of which are still standing) became the business office of Jewsons, the timber merchants. This house had also belonged to a member of the Harvey family and had been the home of the architect and surveyor Edward Boardman in 1864. The 1885 Ordinance Survey map shows a large timber yard beside the river. In 1883 John W. Jewson is listed as living beside the business; by 1890 he had a house on Unthank Road although the encroachment of large factories was making this an increasingly less desirable place to live. The 1883 Ordnance Survey shows that a brush factory was situated beside No. 18, the house then occupied by Mr Jewson; it remained in business there until at least 1908.

Colegate had always been a centre of industry, the river making it a desirable location for manufacturers. In 1802 there were scarlet dyers in St Clement's churchyard and in 1810 another dyer had premises in

St Clement's Church Alley. There were coal dealers in Colegate in 1802 and 1810 and Bolingbroke Enfield & Co., bombazine, crape and shawl manufacturers, had premises in St Clement's Church Alley by 1830 (called Bolingbroke Jones & Co. by 1883). Bolingbroke had gone out of business by 1890 and Edward Willett Nephew & Co. had its business on this site. White in 1890, writing about Willetts, says they 'are now the foremost producers of dress goods' with extensive premises in Colegate extending to the river where dyeing and hot pressing are carried on'. Willetts previously had premises in Pottergate and rented a floor in the St James's factory.[9]

The 1845 directory shows the firm of E. & R.W. Blake worsted spinners in Colegate and Lakenham Mills. The plan of Miss Norton's estate dated 1846 shows that the owner of land to the west and by the river side of her property was Robert Wiffen Blake. According to Blyth, in 1841 R.W. Blake had a house in Colegate and it is possible that he lived at No. 20 Colegate in premises that were afterwards held by Jewson's. The 1882 Ordnance Survey map of Norwich shows Jewson's timber yard and saw mill occupying land which in 1846 was said to be that of Robert Wiffen Blake. It is likely that in 1845 Blake used mainly outworkers and that the small business was carried on in his residence in Colegate as, according to the directory, by 1854 this business had moved to Fishgate Street (Fishergate) in the parish of St Edmund's and he retained his house in Colegate. (White in 1864 says 'R.W. Blake esq. possesses a large factory in St Edmund's and also Lakenham Mill spinning mohair and worsted yarn'.)

The proximity to the river, which made the street suitable for dyeing works, also allowed ease of access to materials for industry. Jewson's timber yard, already mentioned, is a case in point, as was the Norfolk Iron Works situated on Coslany Street, also beside the river. By the time Colegate was surveyed by the Ordnance Survey in 1883 there was more than one boot and shoe manufactory and there were also makers of fancy dress fabrics and numerous small tradesmen. The old houses remained, but many were no longer family homes, their size often making them more suitable for schools or business premises, and the large gardens and open spaces were built upon.

Dr Alderson's house had become a boarding school by 1847. Arthur Codling, who had run a small school in Magdalen Street in 1845, had moved to Dr Alderson's house by 1867 and established a boarding school. It was called Opie House School and the 1871 census lists 29 boys aged 9-15 living there. This boarding school had closed by 1890 and the house became the residence of the Revd Henry L. Norden, rector of St Clement with St Edmund. There were also a number of other educational establishments in Colegate: Miss Bennett had a ladies' boarding school in 1783 and there were a number of different boarding schools in the 1830s, 1840s and 1850s. Even though the names of the head teachers changed, it is likely that the premises used did not. Harriet and Amelia Coldwell's school is listed in the 1841 census at Church Alley, Colegate. The 1854 directory stated that the school took boarders, but only one pupil was listed in the 1851 census. The school is not listed in the 1864 directory but as Harriet Coldwell was 62 in 1851, she had probably retired.

There were also a number of charity schools. Blyth in 1842 mentions Miss Glover's school in Black Boys Yard which was supported by voluntary contributions.[10] Mrs Watts was the principal and 65 girls were educated there. The school is listed in the 1845 directory, but not subsequently. In Calvert Street the Unitarians (formerly Presbyterians) established a school for girls which, according to Blyth, had 70 pupils in 1842, each paying 1d. a week. This school, and a similar one for boys in King Street, was established with funds from the Joanna Scott Trust.[11] Another charity school on Colegate was Balderstone's school, founded in 1761 by Bartholomew Balderstone who had left money for the schooling of 20 children of poor parents belonging to the independent church or to other children with poor parents; it was originally housed in St Augustine's Street.[12] In 1845 there were 22 pupils. In 1842 a large school building was erected as a Day and Sunday school in Calvert Street with two rooms for boys and girls. This school was taken over by the School Board in 1872.[13]

In 1853 the Norwich Diocesan Training Institute for School-mistresses, which had been established in 1839, moved from the Lower Close to Colegate. The building chosen for the College accommodated 40 students and alterations and additions were made to two Georgian houses for this purpose. The College remained in Colegate until 1892 when, as the Norwich & Ely Diocesan Training College, it moved out of the City centre to a purpose-built building on College Road in the suburbs. The move from Colegate illustrates the change in public attitudes to what constituted acceptable living conditions. Although the situation of the College in Colegate was deemed satisfactory when the move was made, by 1883 the proximity to factories made its location unacceptable to the Education Department. The application for a building grant in 1852 had stated that 'no noxious or noisy trades [are] carried on near the proposed site', but during this thirty year period the size of the local industries had grown: the College's nearby neighbour, Howlett & White had built the 'Norvic' shoe factory in 1876 and in nearby Coslany Street, was the St Miles Foundry. The Education Department complained about the noise and smells; there was a greater appreciation of the importance of fresh air and exercise, and the students' accommodation was felt to be unsatisfactory.[14] In 1893 the former college building was occupied by the St George's Club and Home for Working Girls and the School of Cookery. The Working Girls Club had moved to Pitt Street by 1900, but the School of Cookery remained well into the 20th century.

On the other side of the College was the presbytery of Canon Duckett, a priest of St John's Roman Catholic Church. He had moved into a large house there in 1880. Because of its central position and size - stretching back to the river - this had originally been considered a possible site for the Roman Catholic church to be erected in Norwich by the Duke of Norfolk.[15] However this plan was abandoned when the site of the old prison on Unthank Road came up for sale, and by 1896 the premises of the presbytery were occupied by a small manufactory, Edward & Son, shoe manufacturers. (St John's Church, on the site of the old Norwich prison was completed in 1894.)

Colegate is notable for its churches and chapels. There are the medieval churches of St Clement and St George, and the 18th century Octagon chapel of the Unitarians and the 17th century Meeting House of the Congregationalists. The Baptists also had a chapel, St Clement's, built in 1814 on a site in Black Boys Yard. A Sunday School was built in 1850 with a library fitted out by Thomas Bignold.[16] (The chapel, long since demolished, was still in use in 1905.) As mentioned, Miss Glover also had a school on Black Boys Yard and it is unclear whether there were two schools here, side by side, or whether the school that Bignold built in 1850 was merely an enlargement or a replacement of Miss Glover's school.

The professional men had all moved away by 1901. However, many of the large houses still remained unspoilt and undivided and were occupied by wealthy manufacturers. The 1901 census return lists William Shave, a brush manufacturer, living near his brush manufactory, a shoe manufacturer Alfred Sexton whose business H. Sexton & Son Ltd was in Fishergate and Henry Barnes, a cardboard box manufacturer, who had premises in Fleece Yard off Colegate in 1900. All Hallows, a community of eight Church of England nuns, occupied a large house beside St Clement's Church. This had been purchased by the Community about 1900 after the order's move from premises in Palace Plain which it had occupied since 1882.[17] By 1900, although many of the old buildings remained in Colegate, the expansion of Howlett & White greatly reduced the number of domestic residences and a number of the properties that remained were used as business premises only. Nos. 22 and 24 Colegate are listed in the census as uninhabited; according to the 1900 directory these were the business premises of a cabinet maker and the English & American Machinery Co. Ltd respectively.

The expansion of the boot and shoe manufacturer Howlett & White had led to the early demolition of one part of the street. As Tillyard & Howlett the firm had moved to small premises opposite St George's church in 1856 and the first large factory was built there in 1876. As Howlett & White, the factory had almost doubled in size by

1896 and there were further enlargements in the 20th century.[18] In the process a number of small firms disappeared, including the boot and shoe manufacturer Thomas Rowland Ford which had premises in Colegate between Calvert Street and St George's Street (in the home of Henry Bacon, twice Mayor of Norwich, who died in 1567). Ford was in business in Bacon House in 1869[19] and is mentioned in the 1881 directory, but according to Jarrold's Directory, the premises were occupied by Howlett & White by 1885 when the building was said to be a branch of the factory. Even before the final building work in the 20th century, this factory was very large; in 1888 the whole workforce of 1,300 people was entertained by Mr White on the occasion of his son's 21st birthday.[20]

Magdalen Street

Hibgame[21] said that Magdalen Street was one of the streets that had changed the most and he remembered the time when there had been many desirable residences. He was 24 years old in 1881 and would have been thinking of the street in the late 1860s or early 1870s at a time when it still retained some of its former glory. It had been home to a number of prosperous merchants and bankers in the 18th century. Members of the Gurney family had lived there since early in the 18th century and John and Joseph Gurney are listed as living in Gurney Court in 1783. Part of this freehold property was put on the market in 1828.[22] According to the sale particulars it was then in the occupation of the proprietor, Mr Lewis Cooper. The 1810 directory lists Lewis Cooper & Co. as wholesale and retail linen-drapers in the Market Place. The property for sale consisted of one third of the house which was built around three sides of a court and was described as an 'excellent dwellinghouse' with a large garden at the back.

The plan of the Great Garden also shows houses of substance in Magdalen Street. Like the houses in Colegate, these were properties with long leases commencing 1769 and 1770. Thomas Martineau, Esq., a bombazine and camlet manufacturer, the father of Harriet Martineau, held a lease on one of the properties and lived there in

1810. He died in 1826 and Thomas Martineau & Son's business is listed there in the 1836 Directory. Another property was leased by the watchmaker Edward Russell, who is listed in the 1802 Directory and members of the Russell family continued to trade there until at least 1890.

Magdalen Street is situated in the parishes of St Clement, St Saviour and St Paul. The shops, businesses and residences of the inhabitants in the parishes of St Clement (including some property of what was the Great Garden) and St Saviour in the period 1841-1901 were larger and more prosperous than those in the parish of St Paul. However, this had not always been the case. According to the Poll Books of the 1802 Parliamentary election, out of 51 men eligible to vote in the parish of St Paul, no manufacturers or merchants were listed, but six were styled gentleman/esquire; in the 1830 election four gentlemen/esquires voted as well as seven manufacturers and one merchant.

The history of some of the properties situated in the parish of St Paul illustrates some of the reasons for its later decline and impoverishment. The brewery of James Beevor is listed in the 1783 and 1802 directories. The brewery and house were sold to John Patteson in 1794[23] and his son, John Staniforth Patteson lived in Beevor's house and was listed as resident by Pigot in 1830. However, the directory entry was probably out of date as there is a plan of this estate dated 1824[24] in which it had been divided into ten lots for sale. The plan shows house, yard, pigeon yard, dog house, 'Fowles house', lower garden, summer house, stable and harness house, another stable, chaise house and cottage. The division of the property into lots would have destroyed this large estate as even the house was to be divided into two lots. Apart from the plan, there is no other information about the property, but it seems likely that, with division into so many individual lots, a desirable residence was lost and the way cleared for the building of small tenements or manufactories. This sale suggests that as early as the 1820s, this part of Norwich was no longer such a desirable place to live. This situation would have been made worse by the subdivision of houses and the lack of any control of building. Another property in the same parish, divided into at least five lots, sold by John Gurney in 1791, shows how a large estate with extensive grounds could be replaced by small tenements and slum housing.[25] It was formerly the estate of John Wood, Citizen and Alderman of Norwich and was situated on Magdalen Street near its junction with Botolph Street and may have encompassed part of Bishop's Yard on Botolph Street. John Wood, who died in 1767, was sheriff in 1740 and mayor in 1746.

Unlike Colegate, Magdalen Street does not seem to have been popular with professional men. There were however a number of relatively prosperous small manufacturers and shopkeepers. Among the more substantial businessmen and manufacturers was the chemist and druggist Joseph Smith, who employed six men and had one apprentice living on the premises. The firm Smith & Sons, wholesale druggists and manufacturing chemists was still in business in Magdalen Street in 1900 although by 1890 only a junior member of the family, Joseph de Carle Smith junior, lived in a house on the premises, whilst the older Joseph de Carle Smith lived in Bracondale. According to the 1851 census Abraham Tillyard, a boot and shoe maker employing seven men, lived in Magdalen Street; according to the directory he had moved to Thorpe Road in the suburbs by 1854. Other larger businesses included a butcher, Robert Cobb, who in 1851 employed two men and one woman (by 1864 he had moved to Sprowston), a saddler employing two men, a baker employing three, a grocer employing seven, and a tin-plate worker and ironmonger employing three men and five boys.

The more prosperous businessmen may have moved to the suburbs, but according to the 1881 census it was still relatively rare for owners in this part of Norwich to live away from the premises. In this they differed from shopkeepers south of the river which suggests that their businesses were much smaller (this is confirmed by the 1910 Land Valuation Record which listed the valuation of houses, shops and businesses in Norwich).[26] The draper William Bullen had two female assistants lodging with him in his premises; the draper and hosier master, Edward Dixon had one assistant living in and James Loose junior, the son of James Loose, a dealer in high-class glass and earthenware, in business by 1883, lived on the premises. The corn and wine merchant James Baxter of the firm Boswell & Baxter, with premises in the Market Place and Magdalen Street, who employed eleven men and two boys, had a house near his business on Magdalen Street as did his son George; his other partner, James Boswell, lived on Thorpe Road.

In nearby St Saviour's Lane was Pendleton House, one of the few remaining large houses with garden ground in this part of Norwich. In 1881 it was the home of John W. Sparrow, solicitor registrar of the Court of the Guildhall Norwich, who had an office in Rampant Horse Street. He still lived there in 1890 but by 1900 the building was occupied by the cardboard box manufacturer D. Mansfield and was no longer solely residential.

A 16th century house in Muspole Street which had become a shoe factory by 1890

Although Magdalen Street had always had a large number of shops, by 1900 it was nearly completely commercial with a number of small businesses ranging from boot-dealers to pawnbrokers, grocers, bakers and butchers. A number of businesses occupied larger premises: A.F. Martin had a boot and shoe warehouse, George Morris was a carriage builder, James Tate & Co. a wholesale confectioner. There were also a few non-local businesses, the first of the multiples: the Danish Dairy Co, the Star Tea Co. Ltd, Maypole Dairy, the Norfolk & Norwich Co-op, Boots Cash Chemists, as well as a branch of Barclays Bank. However, the most notable thing about this street in 1900 was the large number of small shops. Although some of the original high-class buildings remained in what had once been the Great Garden, by 1900 most had also been converted into shops. A few quality buildings remained untouched: part of a property in Gurney's Court was the retirement home of John Theobald who had had a hosier and glover's shop in London Street in 1881 and a few persons are listed in the census returns as living on 'own means', but, although a number of wealthy manufacturers had made their homes in Magdalen Street early in the 19th century, most had moved away by 1901. In St Paul's parish was the Blind Institute; eleven blind adults and 45 blind children are recorded as living there in the 1901 census.

Courts and yards in Magdalen Street

The census returns of residents of Magdalen Street show that, at least in the period 1841-1901, there was a considerable difference between the status of the men and women living on the street itself and those living in the courts and yards. On Magdalen Street were the shopkeepers and small businesses; in the courts and yards these were a rarity and the residents were predominantly lower working-class, weavers, woolcombers, shoemakers, charwomen, labourers and paupers. This was especially true of those courts and yards in the parish of St Paul and, to a lesser extent, St Saviour. Although there were many unskilled and semi-skilled workers living in the courts and yards in the parish of St Clement, there was more variety of employment and fewer of the very poor.

The census returns show that, apart from a decrease in the number of men and women engaged as weavers and an increase in the number working in the boot and shoe industry, little changed in the sixty years 1841-1901. There seems to have been little overcrowding; most of the tenements housed at the most five persons, and very often there were fewer. However, there were a large number of residences in each yard, so each habitation must have been very small. In 1851 there were 17 tenements housing 88 people in Red Lion Yard in the parish of St Paul with one building sub-divided. Included in this figure were two families of ten but such a large number was unusual. The residents included ten weavers (in one family were five weavers), three dressmakers, two tailors and boot and shoe binders. The 1881 return for the same yard, records 22 households and 100 residents. The type of occupation of residents of this and other yards did not vary greatly.

Magdalen Gate from the outside, drawn by Ninham

In 1841 the census return of the occupants of another Red Lion Yard situated in the parish of St Clement recorded 38 people living in nine tenements and included three weavers, one shawl sewer, two employed in the shoe trade and a carpenter, a gardener, a labourer and a porter. According to the 1891 census there were 30 people living in nine tenements employed in the shoe trade, and as porters, servants and other similar occupations. The residents of the two Red Lion yards are typical of most of the other yards off Magdalen Street. The ages of the residents vary, with the old sometimes described as 'paupers' or 'hand-loom weavers'.

Red Lion Yard in St Paul's parish, near the junction of Bull Close Road and the other Red Lion Yard were only two of a large number of yards. The 1881 census records the following yards situated on Magdalen Street between Magdalen Gate and Cowgate: Cross Keys Yard, Beckham's Yard, Malt House Yard, Bailey's Yard, Whiting Yard, Barnes Yard, Zipfel's Yard, New Yard, Gilling's Yard, White Lion Yard and Two Brewers Yard. In Bayfield Yard, 37 residents lived in ten households. As in the two Red Lion yards the occupants were mainly unskilled workers. The occupants of some of the yards were older than the average: in Burrell's Yard there were 16 households and 43 people of whom 24 were over the age of 55 including four on 'parish relief'; there were three weavers, some out of employ, aged between 57 and 74 and a tailoress aged 88.

However, the common perception of the houses in courts and yards as slum property can be misleading. Although the majority of those living in the yards were unskilled or semi-skilled, a few properties were occupied by white-collar and/or professional men. A good example of this is Gurney's Court (later called Grout's Court, later still Gurney Court again) which had remained virtually unchanged since its occupation by the Gurney family in the early 19th century. The surgeon Charles Doyle lived in Grout's Court[27] in the parish of St Clement in 1881 as did the draper Thomas Cobbald of Fiske & Cobbald drapers and silk mercers in London Street. Marshall's Yard (later King's Head Yard) was the residence of a clerk at the Town Clerk's Office in 1881 although the occupations of the other residents were bricklayer, wire weaver, yarn filler, charwoman, monthly nurse, cooper, former servant/cook, silk winder and shoe fitter. In this it was not so different from the residents of Bayfield Yard in the same parish who included chimney sweep, labourer, factory worker, dressmaker, two shoemakers, labourer and a weaver, a widow aged 82. And in 1890 the boot and shoe maker, Robert Webster lived in Ling's Court in the parish of St Clement.

What types of houses became slums? The quality of the houses in the yards and courts seems to have varied, but a large number were poorly built, the sanitary arrangements basic. Many probably were like that of Sir Nicholas Bacon in Ber Street, high-quality timber-framed buildings in multi-occupation, the courtyard infilled with numerous small buildings. The history of the re-development of Willis Street in 1878 seems to confirm this (see Chapter 8) as local antiquaries lamented the demolition of 'singularly quaint half-timbered houses.'[28] It also appears that the uses to which an old-fashioned timber-framed house was put depended upon location. In Tombland, on the other side of the river, Samson & Hercules House was an antique shop in 1894 and had probably been saved due to its proximity to the Cathedral as well as its antiquarian interest.

This is confirmed by the 1910 Valuation of the properties in the courts and yard which range from £775 (one of the houses in Gurney's Court) to £30 (a property in Elephant Yard). The valuation of the properties in Bayfield Yard which range from £50 to £85 is rather above the average for the majority of courts and yards but below that of most of the small houses on Magdalen Street which are valued at about £150.[29]

Parishes of St Paul, St James and St Edmund

Other streets in the parishes of St Paul, St James and St Edmund had, in the main, very small houses whose inhabitants were engaged in semi-skilled and unskilled occupations and thus generally had much in common with the residents of the yards running off Magdalen Street. Most were poor: in 1851 St James's parish appears to have had more people employed as hand-loom weavers than neighbouring parishes and weaving was the most common occupation in both Cowgate and

Barrack Street for both men and women, the number of women weavers exceeding that of men; in Barrack Street there were 22 men registered as handloom weavers. In 1851, the boot and shoe industry was the second most common occupation. There were also a number of people styled 'pauper' although many of them were elderly and their number small compared to the number in employment.[30] Fishgate Street in the parish of St Edmund, had a similar social mix but also a few more prosperous residents: a corn and coal merchant with two live-in female servants, a tallow chandler employing two men and two boys and a timber merchant. There were quite a lot of small shops in Barrack Street and a lesser number in Cowgate and Fishgate Street. In all three streets there were a large number of public houses.

The 1851 census shows that the residents of the yards in these parishes, although not very different in occupations from the people living in the adjoining streets, included a larger number of poor and very poor. Seven paupers, and nine weavers lived in Long Yard, Fishgate Street, out of a population of 45 adults and many of these weavers were aged 50 and over. In Priory Yard, Cowgate, there was a preponderance of weavers, whether hand or power-loom is unspecified although some were listed as power-loom. The return for Bull Close in the parish of St Edmund records eleven hand-loom weavers (silk, shawl and unspecified) as against five power-loom weavers and four unspecified. Although the enumerators of the census were not always consistent in their recording of hand-loom and power-loom weavers, it is possible to guess roughly the proportion of hand-loom to power-loom weavers. White's 1845 Directory stated that there were 700 power looms in 1838 and Bayne[31] quoted the Royal Commission Report of 1839 in which it was reported that in the City and surrounds there were 5,075 looms, of which 4,059 were at work; 3,398 were in the houses of the workers and 650 in shops and factories. Bayne further states that in 1868 there were only 1,000 looms at work, half of them hand-looms.

The history of Priory Yard in the parish of St James can be traced from the census returns 1841-1901. The poverty and squalid living conditions of this part of Norwich were condemned by the antiquary and local historian Walter Rye in a lecture on the history of Pockthorpe (printed in the *Eastern Daily Press* on 28th November 1902). The tenements, situated on part of the site of the Whitefriars in Pockthorpe, had been condemned as slums and were due for demolition in 1902.

Numbers of households and residents in census returns 1841-1891

Year	Households	Residents
1841	30	139
1851	49	136
1861	41	133
1871	36	138
1881	37	170
1891	42	162

The 1891 census is the most revealing as the number of houses with fewer than five rooms had also to be included. There were three houses with four rooms, twenty with three rooms and seven with only two rooms. Except for a few houses with only two people resident, the majority of the houses in the yard were overcrowded: four people lived in each of five of the houses with three rooms, whilst a number of houses with only two rooms had more than four people resident. Clearance of these slum properties seems to have started by 1901 as ten houses are listed as empty.

Examination of the census returns shows how the pattern of employment changed during these sixty years. This was not very different from those of residents in other yards in the area. In the period 1841-61 the majority were weavers and there were comparatively few shoemakers. According to the 1901 census, the total number of workers in the boot and shoe trade was 7470. Hawkins, writing in 1912, calculated that in 1906 about 1,000 shoe workers were still not employed in factories, for despite the growth of factories there were still a large number of home-workers in the industry in 1900.[32] Employment in the factories was regular, wages varying little from month to month; outworkers, whose work was more seasonal and who lost time collecting and delivering the work of the garret masters, earned lower wages.

In 1881 the returns for both Barrack Street and Cowgate were very similar. The situation had changed inasmuch as the number of men engaged in weaving had declined, although the number of women so employed remained more or less constant. Presumably most of these women worked in the factories, although this is only occasionally stated in the census. The number of men and women working in the boot and shoe industry had not changed very much since 1851. However, the number of men classed as labourers had increased. In Barrack Street there were a few male brewery workers (although not as many as might be expected considering the Steward & Patteson brewery was nearby) and also a small number of agricultural workers. The number of shops on both streets showed little change, but by 1881 a small number of white-collar workers and men employed in more prestigious occupations are listed as living in Cowgate: two clerks, a stationer, a science artist, a musician, a letter carrier and a telegraph messenger, and in Barrack Street: two clerks, a telegraph messenger and a teacher, although overall their numbers were extremely low in this part of Norwich. Comparing the census returns of the city parishes with those of parishes in the suburbs, one of the most striking differences is the growth of white-collar workers living in the new parishes outside the walls compared to the small number in the City proper, especially north of the river, despite the number of schools built in the City since the passing of the Education Acts.

As the 1901 enumerators were required to give the employment status of those listed, it is possible to gauge the extent of the decline in home working. Only two silk weavers working at home are listed in Cowgate - a man of 67 and his wife aged 66. The number of women working in the silk mills was approximately half what it was in 1881, whereas the number of men and of women engaged in the boot and shoe industry had greatly increased. The returns for Barrack Street are similar to those from Cowgate in that very few of the men and women were self-employed. One of the small number of employers of labour was John Smith, the boot and shoe manufacturer who lived and worked on his premises in Cowgate. His business was large enough to be listed in Kelly's 1900 Directory. The other boot and shoe manufacturers listed in the census, William Barclay in Cowgate and Frederick Jarrett in Barrack Street, must have been too small to find it worthwhile to pay for inclusion.

There are no great surprises to be found in the census returns for residents of the courts and yards in these parishes during the period 1851-1901 and the returns reinforce the popular conception of poverty. Most of the tenements in the courts and yards and many of the houses have been demolished, subject to late 19th/early 20th century slum clearance programmes.[33] An earlier slum clearance resulted in the building of Willis Street[34] which was included in the 1883 Ordnance Survey map. This area had been a byword for poverty and squalor and in 1851 was especially mentioned by the Inspector in connection with the Health of Towns Act.[35] The 1901 census is of interest in showing slightly more variety of occupation in this new street: in addition to the dressmakers, shoemakers and labourers, a significant number of men worked on their own account, some of whom were employers. These included a coal merchant, cabinet turner, painter employing labour, and a greengrocer. In addition to the number of boot and shoe workers and dressmakers, there was also a printer, decorative painter, writer, sign painter, printer and book binder. The variety of employments is quite similar to the men resident in Magpie Road outside the walls. Many new houses were built here in the 1880s on land released by the Corporation for building, subject to covenants to ensure the quality of the houses built.[36]

The above is an attempt to describe a small part of the city north of the river. The streets chosen are in many ways typical of this part of Norwich. The good-quality houses in Colegate can be replicated in

Calvert Street, the shops in Magdalen Street have much in common with those in St Augustine's Street and the working-class streets of Cowgate and Barrack Streets have their counterparts in Coslany Street and Oak Street. Despite differences, in particular those resulting in the pre-eminence of a manufacturing process in a particular area, there is sufficient common ground for the streets studied to be considered 'typical' of this part of Norwich insofar as the number of residents grew considerably during the hundred year period and as a consequence a larger number of people were crammed into the same area and their quality of life deteriorated. In this respect, north of the river is very different from south of the river because although there were poor and very poor people south of the river and there were squalid courts and yards, there were also a considerable number of professional men who continued to live within the City or had prosperous businesses and shops employing many staff which were patronised by the growing middle classes now living in the suburbs.

How to explain the differences between the City north and south of the river? At the beginning of the 19th century they were not so very different. They both had a number of high-quality houses built in the 18th century. Wealthy merchants and manufacturers lived on both sides of the river. Although the parish of St Peter Mancroft had always been the wealthiest parish in Norwich, Norwich Over the Water was home to a large number of important manufacturers and merchants in the 17th and 18th centuries[37] and its decline in the 19th century mirrored the decline of the textile industry. And yet, while the commercial base of the City south of the river expanded, very little changed in Norwich Over the Water. Most of the prosperous residents moved away, the shops remained small and catered only for local residents. The history of this part of Norwich is a history of continuity rather than change. Unlike Norwich south of the river, it remained small-scale, much as it had been in 1800. It is only necessary to compare the number of jewellers in Norwich on each side of the river. Thirteen are listed in Kelly's 1900 Directory on the south side of the river and only one on the north.

There are many reasons for this disparity in fortune. The situation of the cattle and provision market and that of the Corn Hall and later Agricultural Hall south of the river gave an immense advantage and the influx of merchants and farmers from the county encouraged trade and the growth of large stores. Another advantage was that the development of the suburbs south of the river started much earlier than in the north. Moreover, when development came, with a few exceptions, mainly artisan houses were built in the northern suburbs. Finally, at the start of the century Norwich Over the Water had the benefit of being in the centre of the textile industry, but this was a dying industry and technological change came comparatively late to the boot and shoe industry.

Notes

1. See chapter 8 where the legality of proposals for clearance are discussed.
2. The number of residents in the parishes of St Augustine, St Edmund, St George Colegate, St James, St Martin at Oak, St Mary Coslany, St Michael Coslany, St Paul and St Saviour was 9,505 in 1801 and 15,908 in 1851. By 1881 there was a small decrease to 14,859. The parishes with the largest increases in the 50-year period 1801-1851 were St James which rose from 520 to 1538, St Paul which increased from 1395 to 2741 and St Saviour which was 984 in 1801 and 1457 in 1851. The population of the parish of St Clement increased from 853 in 1801 to 3230 in 1851 (this large increase was due to the development of the parish outside the walls).
3. NRO, BCH82. Plan of the Great Garden between Colegate and Golden Dog Lane [1832].
4. Harrod, Henry *Gleanings Among the Castles & Convents of Norwich*, p.72; Blomefield, F. *An essay towards a topographical history of the county of Norfolk*, Vol. IV. pp. 335-6 and 339.

5. Amelia Opie (1769-1853) who married the artist John Opie in 1798 was the author of many novels. In later life she lived in a house on Castle Meadow. According to Sandred, K.I. *The Place-names of Norfolk Part One – Norwich,* p. 122 Opie Street (which runs from London Street to Castle meadow) commemorates her.

6. NRO, SPE483.[Colegate Street] Sale particulars of Dr Alderson's house.

7. NRO, DS191(131) Plan of an estate in St Clement's, Norwich.

8. Jewson & Sons Ltd. (pub.) *Number 18 and Number 19 Colegate.*

9. Bayne, A.D. *A comprehensive history of Norwich, including a survey of the city,* p. 583. According to White's 1845 directory, the Norwich Yarn Company's factory in St James (built 1839) let off rooms to various manufacturer for weaving goods.

10. Blyth, G.K. *The Norwich Guide* [1842], p. 182.

11. White's 1845 Directory, p. 126. In 1709 Joanna Scott left £600 to be invested to establish and maintain a charity school for the poor children of Norwich's Unitarian congregation.

12. Blyth, p. 182.

13. White's 1883 Directory, p. 490.

14. Bull, J.(ed.). *1839-1981 The story of Keswick Hall Church of England College of Education. Norwich,* pp. 14-15.

15. *A Great Gothic Fane. The Catholic church of St. John the Baptist, Norwich. With historical retrospect of Catholicity in Norwich,* p. 111.

16. Jewson, C.B. *The Baptists in Norwich,* p. 104.

17. *All Hallows: Ditchingham. The story of an East Anglian Community* by Sister Violet, p. 47. All Hallows is a Church of England religious order of women which was founded by Lavinia Crosse, daughter of the John Green Crosse (1790-1850). Dr Crosse was the leading surgeon of the Norfolk & Norwich Hospital who lived in St Giles Street in 1830. The All Hallows Community was founded in 1854 and moved to Ditchingham by 1859.

18. Sparks, W.L. *The Story of Shoemaking Norwich, from the earliest times to the present day,* pp. 105-6

19. Bayne, p. 604.

20. *Industries of Norfolk & Suffolk Business Review.*

21. Hibgame, F.T. *Recollections of Norwich fifty years ago,* p. 47.

22. NRO, SPE134 Freehold estate in St. Saviour's - Gurney Court, Magdalen Street.

23. Gourvish, T. *Norfolk beers from English barley: a history of Steward and Patteson, 1793-1963,* pp. 14 & 17.

24. NRO, DS201(141) Magdalen Street.

25. NRO, TC63/1-9 62 Magdalen Street.

26. The 1910 Land Valuation Record was a valuation undertaken by the Commissioners of Inland Revenue in pursuance of the provision of the Finance (1909/10) Act 1910 in relation to the Duties on Land Values (NRO P/DLV).

27. Gurney court, the 18th century home of the Gurney family, had become Grout's Court by 1881 and reverted to its original name by 1893.

28. Hibgame, F.T. *Recollections of Norwich Fifty Years Ago*, p. 10

29. NRO P/DLV 1/41 Norwich North East.

30. The 1851 census return records 11 paupers resident in Cowgate, 22 in Barrack Street and four in Fishergate.

31. Bayne, p. 584.

32. Hawkins, C.B. *Norwich A Social Study*, London, 1912. p. 30ff.

33. See chapter 8 which lists the various committees involved.

34. See chapter 8 where the demolition of a large number of substandard houses in the parish of St Paul is described.

35. See chapter 8

36. See chapter 6 - NRO, TC785 Building sites on Magpie Road.

37. See Cozens-Hardy, Basil & Kent, Ernest A. *The Mayors of Norwich 1403-1836*, Norwich 1938.

Chapter 5. Growth of the Suburbs
1: Hamlets of Heigham, Lakenham and Eaton

Introduction

Browne described the hamlets of Norwich in 1814[1] as almost completely rural and little influenced by their proximity to Norwich. About a mile from the city walls and surrounded by fields was the parish church of St Bartholomew and a few buildings; the hamlet of Lakenham consisted of the parish church of St James the Apostle and one street of small houses, and Eaton was a single street of small houses near the parish church of St Andrew.

The hamlets were purveyors of the goods required by the City: the produce of the market gardeners and farmers was purchased by City shopkeepers as was the finished work of the worsted weavers commissioned by city merchants. Outside the City walls were brickworks and lime kilns, and tanneries on Heigham Street beside the river. Chase's 1783 directory listed a number of them: a lime-burner and brickmaker with works in Lakenham near Brazen Doors, a brickmaker and a lime-burner at Eaton as well as the tanners in Heigham. A number of gardeners are also listed: on St Benedict's Road (Dereham Road) and St Giles Road (Earlham Road) and two in Eaton. Farms were further away, including one at Eaton Hall and another at Earlham. The list is not comprehensive, only listing businesses sufficiently large to warrant an entry, but it gives a good idea of the variety of suppliers.

The Norfolk & Norwich Hospital was built outside the walls in 1776 and enlarged in 1808 and a number of medium-quality houses were built close by. Many of these houses were occupied by men working in the City. The directory also lists a small number of gentry in St Stephen's Road, Newmarket Road, Mile End, Eaton and Upper Heigham. A number of fine houses had been built in the 18th century including Town Close House on Ipswich Road, Tucks Wood House built in 1784 and Eaton Grove in 1805. Bracondale (technically in the parish of Lakenham, but contiguous to the City) was exceptional in being mainly suburban with semi-detached and terrace houses and a few detached country houses built along Bracondale Road late 1780-early 1800.

The poll for the 1784 election in Heigham[2], which lists the occupations of the electors, shows to what extent the residents were dependent on City trade in the late 18th century. The result, although by its nature selective, gives a good indication of the occupations of the people living in the hamlet at that time. Twenty-seven voted: two were styled freeholder (one an esquire), seventeen worsted weavers and a yeoman, bricklayer, tanner, woolcomber, carpenter, clerk and two gardeners. This is a very small number from which to draw any conclusions, but I think the large number of worsted weavers is significant; in the parish of St Benedict, the total number of voters was 32, of which 17 were worsted weavers. In the 1806 election in Heigham, out of a total of 37 voters, there were five gentlemen, one attorney, one merchant and twelve worsted weavers as well as other variously employed freemen. The inclusion of a hairdresser among the voters suggests that there was already some relocation of small tradesmen into this hamlet. The number voting in the other hamlets is too small from which to draw any conclusions.

This was the situation in 1801. By 1821 the population of Heigham had increased from 854 to 1,503 and that of Lakenham from 428 to 1,875. (The population of Norwich including the hamlets was 37,313 in 1811, 50,288 in 1821, and 68,706 in 1851.)

Expansion outside the City walls – working-class housing

The building of suburban houses commenced about 1815 south of the City wall in what was known as the 'New City' in Union Place. This was followed by building in the hamlet of Lakenham and also Crook's Place in that part of the parish of St Stephen outside the walls. These new houses seem to have been popular with newcomers to Norwich, and judging from the fact that the population within the walls rose during this period, much of the development of the hamlets seems to be accounted for by emigration from the county and, more rarely, from outside Norfolk. The 1851 census entries (the first time birthplaces are registered) for the earliest estates built in Lakenham, St Stephen and Heigham, reveal what proportion of the residents aged 40 and over were born in the county; well over half were born outside

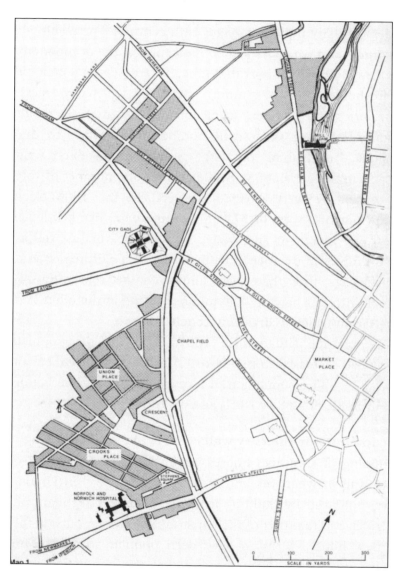

Based on Millard and Manning's map of Norwich, showing the South western expansion of the City outside the walls in 1830

Norwich. For instance, in Hudson's Buildings in the hamlet of Lakenham 57 were born in the county and beyond and only 24 in Norwich. The figures are similarly high in Heigham: for instance, the majority of residents in Short Queen Street were born outside Norwich as were the residents of Chapel Street in Crook's Place, Coach and Horses Street and Union Street.

Augustus Jessop, writing from 1881 to 1887, describes in detail the terrible housing of agricultural workers.[3] He was a clergyman attached to a country parish and describes the living conditions of the workers in a number of villages. Alan Armstrong's analysis of migration from rural Norfolk during the period 1841-1911[4] shows that Norwich was a net gainer by migration in the 1840s and the 1850s and L. Marion Springall[5] in her study of population movement in Norfolk in the 19th century described the circumstances prevailing in the county leading to emigration. While many of those living in the City are listed as weavers and hand-loom weavers in the 1851 census and many older people were paupers, the residents of the new estates were younger, very unlikely to be hand-loom weavers, more likely to be shoemakers. There is also a greater variety of occupation including gardeners and agricultural workers.

Crook's Place and Union Place 1815-25

Building began in 1815 when land formerly known as Crabtree or Clay Pit Close was divided into compartments and let to individuals as private gardens. This was purchased by Harman King and Porter[6] and then sold off in small plots, mainly to builders and carpenters for housing.

What came to be known as Crook's Place was built when a freehold estate in the parish of St Stephen, which had previously been cultivated as a market garden, was purchased by a Quaker doctor, J. Crook.[7] Building commenced in 1819 and the principal entrance was at St Stephen's Gate through a cast-iron arched gateway inscribed 'Crook's Place 1820'.[8] This was followed by the building of small houses in the parish of Heigham, in Julian Place and also in West

Pottergate (an extension of Pottergate Street within the City walls). Millard & Manning's 1830 map of Norwich shows the extent of the building.

The expansion of Norwich was a matter of pride: the new houses were described by Stacy[9] as being built 'in humble imitation of those countless erections which astonish the stranger on his approach to the metropolis of England'. Union Place was also singled out for praise by the author of *Excursions in the County of Norfolk* as containing 'several very pleasant and genteel residences'[10] and White's 1836 Directory speaks of the 'many new streets and handsome rows of houses [which] have been built on the site of, and beyond the City walls. The largest of these modern suburbs is the New City, extending from St Stephen's to St Giles Gate.'[11] The modern suburbs mentioned by White were probably Crook's Place, Union Place and Julian Place and the houses built in this part of the New City were mainly intended for artisans.

Although some houses erected in Union Place are described as 'genteel', the dwellings erected both in Crook's Place and Union Place were mostly very modest, some with only one living room and kitchen downstairs and one room above, others had front and back sitting room, kitchen downstairs and two bedrooms upstairs. The sanitary facilities were basic with most sharing a privy. In Manchester Buildings, Union Place, there were shared privies and water pump.[12] The use of water pumps and wells was common in all houses at that time, the only difference being that the number of households sharing a pump or well depended on the size and value of the house.

These early houses were intended for city dwellers not agricultural workers and there were restrictive covenants which prohibited the keeping of pigs, swine and live poultry (a necessary injunction if the majority of residents came from the country) although the long front gardens would have given the new suburb a semi-rural aspect. In Shadwell Street, Crook's Place,[13]Salford Street and Manchester Street,[14] thatched buildings were not allowed nor was the keeping of pigs, etc. An ordered and tidy urban landscape seems to have been aimed for as the properties had to be fenced (not more than four feet high) with a common building line. These stipulations were usual and show evidence of rudimentary town planning on the part of vendors. Streets were set out, and houses were required to conform to a pattern dictated by the vendor. In 1850 many of these houses were criticised by Mr Lee, the Inspector appointed under the Health of Towns Act[15] to look into the sanitary condition of the City and County. Writing about houses in Union Place, the Inspector's report said that the houses, which had small gardens in front, 'look well in front, but in reality are very unhealthy, being generally back to back'. It is possible that the original vendors had been more concerned with external appearance than with the actual quality of the houses to be erected, but changing standards may have played a part in the later condemnation. Most of the land sold was intended for low-cost housing and, in contrast to the covenants which were enacted later in the century regulating the type of building to be erected, the stipulations were only such as might be required by respectable urban dwellers: not to make or permit any nuisance and to share the cost of keeping the wells, roads, etc. in good repair.

None of these early houses now remain; those that were not destroyed during the Second World War, were condemned and demolished as slums. In fact there were already slum clearance orders made prior to the war, and those properties that had not been demolished then, were demolished afterwards. Although by present-day standards the houses were inadequate (and had been considered so as early as 1850, when they were first built), they would have been an improvement on the accommodation available at that time for the urban working classes. The imposition of covenants on the buildings, although it allowed a great deal of latitude to the builder, nevertheless was an effort to ensure that a certain standard was maintained. It would appear from Mr Lee's comments that the wording on the covenants was not specific enough to ensure the buildings did not deteriorate. It is possible that once the buildings were erected the landowners did not ensure that the covenants continued to be respected. (This still happens today.) These houses were built before the 1858 Board of Health Bylaws[16] with respect to new streets and new houses and before 1877 when Building Control Plans[17] had to be submitted and approved. The gradual improvements in the standard of living may have made these slums, but they were not built as such.

1820–1830 – West Pottergate in Heigham

Land between St Giles Road (that section of Earlham Road running from St Giles Gate to Heigham Road) and St Benedict's Road (Dereham Road) was being divided into lots; new streets were being constructed and houses built in the mid-1820s and 1830s. In 1830 a piece of land in Distillery Street[18] was divided up and sold for building purposes. Small dwelling-houses were planned subject to restrictive covenants as follows: they had to be built at a distance of 12 feet from the road and in parallel lines with other buildings in the street. There was the usual stipulation about the height of fences to be erected. What seem to have been required were dwellings in an urban setting: the new streets, the prohibition of pigs or poultry and the burning or digging of chalk, marl or brick earth on the land or the establishment of an offensive trade, show that the vendor was anxious to maintain the quality of all the buildings in much the same way as in Union Street.

There are numerous instances which show the vendors' concern for the future use of their property. Although many, probably most, of the houses built in the West Pottergate area in the 1820s and 1830 were small, the vendors tried to ensure that the houses built would attract respectable tenants. And this seems to have been what happened. The type of tenant that was envisaged is probably best summed up by the description of a property in West Pottergate Street for sale in 1847. The buildings were modest. There were six lots adjoining, each with two dwelling-houses and the sale particulars state that the houses had been built within the last 25 years and 'are of a type to be occupied by respectable tenants and this has been the case in the past'. These houses would most likely have been very basic with two rooms up and two down and the rental for these cottages – £14 p.a. for each lot of two – shows that they were of rather better quality than many of those built in Union Place.[19] The sanitary facilities would have been similar to those of another two houses in West Pottergate[20] sharing a privy and bin in a common yard, having use of the pump, well and cesspool as well as paying half the expenses of keeping them in repair.

In 1824, land[21] was purchased on the newly-made road of West Pottergate by Isaac Bailey. A number of buildings - called Bailey's Buildings - were erected on this site with the usual very basic covenants: the erection of a four foot wall and all dwelling-houses to be built in parallel lines with other buildings, the prohibition on burning or digging of chalk, marl or brick, on offensive trades being carried out and on the keeping of pigs or poultry. The prohibition on chalk and lime workings was common in this part of Norwich as such workings had taken place in historic times; this was a sign that vendors were selling land for housing and were not prepared to allow the land they sold to be turned into an industrial site. Bailey purchased other land in West Pottergate[22] in 1824 and the covenants to be observed were the same. The kind of property erected can be deduced from the description of two of the four tenements which were sold in 1857 and had to share two privies.

Some of the houses built on West Pottergate Street seem to have been of rather better quality than those in the streets adjoining. Sale particulars for two dwellings sold freehold in 1830[23] demonstrate this. The one on West Pottergate had front garden, back yard with washhouse, pump and offices, and contained parlour, kitchen, four bedrooms and another small room and two cellars. The rooms were panelled and neatly painted and the staircase finished with mahogany banisters and rails. The location of this house opposite the distillery (probably the one which gave Distillery Street its name) may have had some bearing on the quality of the house erected. The one in City Street (later Douro Street) only had a wash house, two sitting rooms, two sleeping rooms and an attic. The Distillery Street house sold for £450, the Douro Street one for £250. The sale in 1830 of four houses in Cross Street (Nile Street) and another in West Pottergate[24] shows a more common type. They each had front garden, two sitting rooms, two bedrooms, a part of the yard at back, use of privy, bin, pump, well and cesspit. Although there was a preponderance of smaller houses in the West Pottergate area, situation was important and the larger houses tended to be located on the corner and this was probably the case with one sold for £450 in West Pottergate.

Property in Lakenham

Land in the parish of Lakenham was also developed subject to restrictive covenants. These were minimal; lots sold in Trafalgar Place and Street in 1820[25] only stipulated that the ways and passages should be kept in good repair. The sale refers to additional land on this site which had already been partly occupied by houses. There is a certain amount of incidental information: pumps had been installed by the vendor and these were shared among the houses soon to be built on the vacant lots. There seems to have been no restriction on the quality of houses built in the remaining lots apart from the purchaser covenanting to share in the cost of the upkeep of the pump and the passageways. Perhaps it was assumed that the dwellings erected would be similar to those already built. These houses had parlour, kitchen, two chambers, wash-house and privy and a piece of garden ground in front and at the back. There were a total of five dwelling-houses in Trafalgar Street and each would share the pump.

The covenants imposed on purchasers of building land in a former orchard in what was later called Lewis Street, Grove Place[26] were considerably more detailed. The land was sold in 1825 and a 'sufficient paled fence,' parallel lines of houses at a specified distance from the road and the upkeep of the road were mentioned as was a prohibition on the keeping of pigs and poultry. The houses, intended as private dwelling-houses only, were to have no fewer than four rooms (similar in size to the ones already built in Trafalgar Street); the construction of public houses, baking offices or grocer's shop or any trade pertaining thereto was prohibited. Such detailed covenants regarding the number of rooms is unusual in such modest properties at that time. The stipulation that the building should have at least four rooms, suggests that it was not uncommon for very basic, low-grade tenements to be constructed with fewer rooms. As the 1891 census required the enumerator to list houses which had fewer than five rooms, it must be assumed that at that date all the above houses would have been considered substandard even though they had been acceptable when they were built and, judging by the detailed covenants, were desirable artisan dwellings.

There were large numbers of very small houses in Lakenham, some so insignificant that, as Rogers said in the 1859 directory *Norwich and Neighbourhood*, it was not unusual for people not to know the name of the street in which they lived, and in some instances the streets did not even have a name. This was the case with tenements which were built in Twenty-one Row off Southwell Road in Lakenham.

'Genteel' dwellings in Heigham and Lakenham in the early 19th century

The 1843 Tithe Apportionment map for Heigham shows the titheable land divided into numerous plots and still being used as garden, pasture, paddock, etc. Early building of artisan houses outside the walls did not encroach to any great extent on the mainly rural aspect of Heigham. This was the preserve of large estates. The houses built on the main arteries out of the City were large; they had gardens, pleasure grounds, coach houses, etc. - all the accoutrements of country living - *of* the country but not *in* the country. The owners of these large estates were mainly gentlemen, wealthy solicitors and manufacturers. There was a growing number of middle-class 'genteel' houses which were built on the major roads just outside the walls. The flight from the city into the suburbs was only just starting in the 1830s when houses were built in Heigham Grove, Chapelfield Road and Lakenham Hall Road. The main thoroughfares out of Norwich – Newmarket Road, Earlham Road and Unthank Road were still mainly the preserve of the large estates.

Development of so-called 'genteel' houses commenced in the early 19th century with the building of detached, semi-detached and terrace houses. These houses had small gardens and, as with artisan dwellings, the sell-off of land continued throughout the century starting slowly but gathering pace. This building land was also protected by restrictive covenants. The houses built in the Crescent[27] on Chapelfield Road were probably some of the first good-quality speculative buildings outside the walls. In 1821 a local builder, John Bunn, obtained an 80-year lease of a triangular plot of former garden ground. The land in question was subject to covenants which detailed the number of houses to be erected, their size and quality and even the materials to be used in the construction of the rooms. Eighteen dwelling-houses were to be erected within a specified time; they were to be decorated internally and externally and their rental value was also specified. The houses that resulted were of high quality and were home to a number of eminent persons over the years. They were popular with clergymen, five of them being listed as living in The Crescent in Mathieson's 1867 Directory. The houses built in The Crescent were quality suburban houses and no attempt was made to emulate the grand houses on Ipswich and Newmarket roads; they had more in common with the semi-detached and terrace houses built in Lakenham about the same time.

Houses were also built in Heigham Grove and St Giles Road in the early part of the century. The conveyance of land in Heigham Grove in 1835 where Craster House[28] was built states that the land sold should not be used to erect cottages; genteel dwelling-houses only should be built. Apart from a prohibition on burning chalk, lime or brick, or digging or taking any chalk or marl, the builders were left to interpret what was meant by 'genteel dwelling-houses'. Although the deeds examined refer only to Craster House, it is obvious from the wording of the conveyance that a number of habitations was envisaged. The area of Heigham Grove itself, although having a number of large superior-quality houses, is comparatively small. The 1883 Ordnance Survey shows that they all had large gardens some of which have since been lost. Most of these houses are about the same age as Craster House and would have been occupied by 'genteel' families. The Mathieson's 1842 Directory lists William Freeman esq. in Heigham Villa, Heigham Grove, and Henry Chamberlin, draper, of Chamberlin's large drapery store.

Lakenham also had a significant number of superior houses, many built before the great boom in artisan houses commenced. These included Windsor Place in Hall Road, which was built in 1821 and consisted of two large semi-detached houses, and Lakenham Terrace on City Road built in 1825. These houses are still standing, their dates of construction in the brickwork.

Bracondale and Richmond Hill

Bracondale, of which Bracondale Road and Richmond Hill are a part, is a hamlet of Lakenham. It is only one road and unusual in being built up earlier than the rest of the hamlet. It was already partly built up when Chase published his directory in 1783 and a number of residents are listed as living on Bracondale Hill. Browne writing in 1814[29] speaks of 'a row of well-built houses, one of which was honoured by the residence of His Royal Highness William, Duke of Gloucester, during the time he had command of the eastern district' (in 1797). There is the Manor House which was built in the 16th century; the remainder of the houses are of late 18th/early 19th century date. Their quality is consistently high: there are semis, terraces and detached houses. A number of the houses are large, with spacious gardens. A house, spoken of as a 'mansion-house', on Bracondale Hill, only partly finished when it was sold in 1820, had an entrance hall, three parlours, drawing-room, two kitchens, cellars, six chambers, three attics, together with a detached building intended for a stable, a wash-house and other offices. In addition it had 'an excellent patent pump'.[30] This was sold, together with two houses of lesser quality in Richmond Hill, which runs from Ber Street Gate to Carrow Hill where it joins Bracondale. These had parlour, kitchen, three chambers with privy and garden ground, both having the use of the pump at the back.

Land on Richmond Hill which was owned by Norwich Corporation was sold leasehold for building in 1849.[31] Richmond Place was described in the Supplement to *Excursions in the County of Norfolk*[32] in 1819 as having 'a range of respectable houses'. There were eight lots, to be leased for a varying number of years. One dwelling was already built, a former public house called 'The Richmond Hill Gardens'. This was Lot 1 and was leased for 40 years. Lots 6-8 were leased for 21 years as garden ground, whilst Lots 2-5 were leased for 75 years for the erection of superior dwelling-houses. The purchaser had to erect within two years either one dwelling-house with suitable offices, to be let at an annual rental value of £30, or two dwelling-houses to be let for £15 each. Houses had to be faced with white brick on the front or side facing Bracondale Road and to have uniform iron palisading fences on proper brick pinning next to the road; the bricks and all other materials used were to be of the highest quality, the plans and materials submitted for approval by the Corporation. Other conditions to be met were as follows: oak timber of English growth; fir timber to be good Baltic timber, the bricks well burnt, all materials, workmanship, etc., thickness of walls, dimension of timber and everything to be inspected and approved by the City Committee or its Surveyor. In addition each building had to be kept in good repair. There were also the usual prohibitions: no digging, burning bricks or lime on any lot, no chandling or bone-boiling office, no factory or steam-engine, no public house, liquor-shop, beer-shop (except Lot 1); only private dwelling-houses. With such detailed requirements, the city showed itself more exacting than many private vendors.

Further expansion

Union Place, Crooks Place, Julian Place and the West Pottergate areas were only the start of what was to become an ever-greater expansion of this part of Norwich. The building covenants changed over the years, reflecting the situation at the time of sale. Thus in 1820 thatched houses were prohibited, and even as late as 1842,[33] when property was sold on Dereham Road, the erection of cowhouses and pigsties was prohibited, but as the century progressed the urbanisation of Norwich south of the river grew and extended further and further away from the historic centre and the possibility of a rogue builder turning his land into a farm building vanished. The sale of land in Devonshire Street[34] in 1859 which refers to building land on 'The Gravel Pit Close' shows the spread of urbanisation. There was still agricultural land for sale, but this was much further away from the centre. In 1855[35] land in the triangle of the junction of Dereham Road and Waterworks Road which was described as arable land, was sold. Several lots were purchased by John Hotblack of Norwich; the 1854 directory describes him as a gentleman, living in Mount Pleasant. Hotblack Road, which runs from Dereham Road to Waterworks Road, presumably named after John Hotblack and encompassing his land, was not completely built up until much later – in fact many houses were not built until after World War I. Covenants on land sold for artisan dwellings in the middle part of the 19th century are all very similar and show that the land was for sale only because there was a ready market due to extensive urban development. However, the vendors were always aware of possible pitfalls, hence the restrictions: the doors or gates to open inwards, houses to be erected on building lines, prohibition on the digging or burning of chalk, marl or brick earth, no noisy or offensive trade to be conducted and no pigs, swine or poultry to be kept.[36]

The growth of Norwich outside the walls was always dependent on the willingness of the landowners to release their land for building. The development of land on Asylum Road (Park Lane) was delayed because it was the site of the Heigham Retreat, a private lunatic asylum, situated on a large estate entered from Unthank Road onto Asylum Road, but situated on land which later became known as Avenue Road. It is described in the 1842 Tithe map as: Plantation, Private Lunatic Asylum, Plantation and the landowners (and lessees) are Messrs Wright, Dalrymple and Cross. The asylum is described in Blyth's 1842 Directory of Norwich as being housed in 'a handsome building, commanding a most extensive and pleasing prospect.'[37] According to the 1841 census, there were fifteen patients (eight female, seven male) aged between 20 and 70. (This was not the only lunatic asylum in Heigham: Heigham Hall Asylum on Old Palace Road had eleven patients in 1841). Although that section of Asylum Road near to Unthank Road was not built up, there were a number of houses near its junction with St Giles Road of a quality commensurate with ones on St Giles Road itself: the 1841 census records residences of the auctioneer William Spelman and of Robert Muskett, a man of independent means.

The Unthank Estate in Heigham and the Eaton Glebe Estate

The sale of land in the hamlets of Heigham and Eaton gathered pace during the second half of the 19th century. The built-up area of the hamlets expanded as land off Dereham Road was parcelled up and sold for housing: West End Street, Adelaide Street and Nelson Street by 1852 and Northumberland Street by 1859. Small terrace houses without hall entrance were built, little better than those built in the West Pottergate area twenty years earlier. Better quality artisan houses had to await the 1858 Norwich Board of Health By-Laws with respect to New Street and New Houses etc., and the 1877 Building Control Plans.

The houses for middle-class and artisan occupants, built on Clement William Unthank's estate off Unthank Road prior to the building acts, were much higher in quality than those that had been built before and they were all, big and small, not unlike the so-called 'genteel' houses built in the early part of the century. They varied in size, larger houses suitable for middle-class occupants built near the junction with Unthank Road, smaller ones for artisans near to Rupert Street. According to the 1883 Directory, residents of Essex, Trinity and Cambridge streets included bank clerks, booksellers, etc. The haberdasher, William Alderton, lived in Trinity Street and had a shop in Swan Lane and George Tyce, cabinet maker and upholsterer, lived in a large house in Trinity Street on the corner of Unthank Road.

Some of the most precise and far-reaching covenants had been drawn up by Clement William Unthank for land in Heigham which he sold freehold between 1849 and 1883 in what were to become Rupert, Suffolk, Norfolk, Essex, Cambridge, Trinity and York streets. These covenants were important in guaranteeing that the quality of even the most humble of the houses was sufficiently high to obviate deterioration in the near future. The estate had been inherited by C.W. Unthank on the death of his father, the solicitor William Unthank, in 1837. Clement William Unthank married the heiress Mary Anne Muskett, daughter of Joseph Salisbury Muskett of Intwood Hall, in 1836 and had moved from his house, called Unthank's House by 1864, after the death of his father-in-law. Unthank's house was demolished when Onley Street and Bury Street were built in the 1890s.

Clement William Unthank's land in Heigham was sold in stages. The first sale, called 'Sale No. 1', started in 1849 and purchasers continued to sign a document accepting the restrictive covenants contained in it until 1870. Signatories were mainly bricklayers, builders and carpenters, but also included a number of small tradesmen and gentlemen. Forty-four people signed the covenant for the No. 1 sale and the prices paid ranged from about £30 to £300. Between 1852 and 1868 nineteen purchasers signed the document for sale No. 2. Again, the purchasers were mainly in the building trade and similar prices were paid. 'No. 3 Sale' included a parcel of land running from Essex to Trinity Streets. It was purchased by the Ecclesiastical Commissioners for £800 and Holy Trinity Church was erected here in 1860 and the rectory built beside it. The sale also included four parcels of land on which the rectory of St John Maddermarket was built. This was purchased for a total of £750 in 1864-66 and a large new house was built on the corner of Essex Street and Unthank Road with garden grounds extending up to Trinity Street. The size of house and garden was in keeping with other large properties built around the same period on Unthank Road and St Giles Road. (The rectory is now a hotel, although much altered, and the garden ground had given way to a garage by 1935. This was demolished in 2004 and a convenience store built.) There were 34 signatories to 'No. 3 Sale' and in general the prices paid were higher. Whereas a large number of the signatories to the 'No. 1 Sale' paid less than £100, the majority of the signatories to the 'No. 3 Sale' paid more than this.[38]

C.W. Unthank died in 1883 and the sale of land was continued by his son, Clement William Joseph Unthank, with land sold in Rupert, Leicester and York Streets as well as Unthank Road. In addition, houses were built on plots of land in Gloucester, Bury and Onley Streets, the site of Unthank's House and garden ground. Unthank's House is recorded in Millard's 1835 map and the 1843 Tithe Map of Heigham refers to 'the residence and garden ground belonging to C.W. Unthank, solicitor,' as follows: 'The Lodge and garden, house, gardens, etc. and The Lawn Plantation'. His estate also included land leased as arable land, pasture and garden ground. The sale of Unthank's land continued into the 20th century and the deeds for the sale of land fronting Dover Street sold in 1909 shows the covenants to be observed by the purchasers had not changed. There was the same attention to detail and there seems little to distinguish the requirements of the son from those of the father. However, the general effect is less good, the houses built in Dover Street are smaller and less impressive than the ones on the streets leading on to Unthank Road which were sold by Clement William Unthank. There is a preponderance of small terrace houses without a hall entrance in Dover Street as well as in Gloucester and Bury Streets, and these houses contrast unfavourably with the houses on Essex, Trinity and Cambridge Streets which were built near Unthank Road and with those on Mount Pleasant and College Road nearby. The terraces in Dover Street were built over a number of years. The deed of covenant refers to houses to be built in 1909 although another terrace of small houses without hall entrance in this street, Nos. 32-54 Weston Terrace, is dated 1889. The majority of the houses built on Unthank's estate still stand.

Cambridge Street c.1900

The covenants Clement William Unthank drew up in about 1849, when Sale No. 1 commenced, were agreed as follows:

1. Every building to be erected on the land sold shall be faced in the front and in the sides also if facing a walking way with good white bricks; shall be covered in the front and sides with good slate or tiles if the said Clement William Unthank his heirs appointees or assigns shall consent thereto (in which case the tiles shall be of such character and pattern as he or they shall select)

2. That every building shall have iron gutters in front and sides (except as to shop windows)

3. Except shops, that every building shall have sash windows only.

4. That every building shall be placed fronting adjoining street/streets/walking way.

5. That every building shall be placed in a straight line on the building line marked in the map or plan drawn on the contract.

6. That no privy, outhouse, workshop shall be allowed to front any street/walking way.

7. That the sides of the building not adjoining the walking way shall be coloured as nearly as possible like the front.

8. That no building shall be placed beyond the building line.
9. That the doors in the every building shall be arched and that no frontispiece, porch or other similar projection shall be allowed unless Clement William Unthank, his heirs, appointees or assigns consent but in such a case not to project more than 18 inches from the building line and to be made of wood or composition.
10. That no building should be less than 18 feet 3 inches from the floor line to the top of the wallplate and that the floor line should not to be less than 9 inches above the crown of the adjoining street or walking way.
11. That only division fences should be made or permitted to remain.
12. That no goods should be placed or exposed for sale
13. That no linen, etc. should be hung between the building line and the street.
14. That no building should be erected of a lesser rental value than stated on the individual contract of   purchase.
15. That no building should be used as a public house, or house for the sale of beer, ale, porter or spirituous liquors.
16. That no building should be more than two storeys high.
17. The purchasers should erect and maintain division fences not exceeding 3 foot 6 inches high on the sides of the land sold to them from the building line to the adjoining street and also a division fence not exceeding 4 foot high next the street or streets or walking way adjoining the land sold to them.
18. That these fences with the gates or doors therein should be of such character and pattern as should be selected by Clement William Unthank, his heirs, appointees or assigns.
19. That no division fence is required at front of shops.
20. That gates/doors to such fences should open inwards.
21. That purchasers should maintain and keep in good repair and condition streets, etc. adjoining land sold to them.
22. Purchasers should contribute and pay rateably towards the repair of footpaths, sewers, drains, channels and cesspools made and to

be made in proportion to the annual value of the property of each party including any buildings.

23. That purchasers must not dig for or burn or make bricks or lime on the land.

24. That purchasers should not place or use any Steam engine or chandling or bone boiling Office or Slaughter house, Mill or Factory thereon.

25. That purchasers should not carry on any noxious or offensive trade or business.

26. That purchasers should not make any drain or sewer or any Channel or Pipe for water from the land sold to them to fall upon or communicate with the surface of the adjoining street(s) etc.

A house in Cambridge Street, 2013

Although relating solely to the external appearance of the houses, the importance of these covenants was that they brought one standard which encompassed a wide variety of houses, built by a large number of builders, ranging from the very small to the medium large. This brought uniformity to each street whilst at the same time allowing a variety of different sized houses to be built by specifying the minimum rental value of each house. As a consequence the more prosperous occupiers of the larger terrace houses were assured that those artisans living in close proximity had houses which were in keeping with the general tone of the street and there was little possibility that the houses would deteriorate and thus become the residences of unsuitable tenants. The houses might be smaller, but they looked as desirable as the larger ones and would be attractive to respectable artisans. The degree of control that Unthank exerted over the land sold made the deterioration of this small planned estate all but impossible.

It is interesting to compare the covenants enforced on purchasers of land on the Eaton Glebe Estate[39] in 1890 with those of Clement William Unthank.

1. One dwellinghouse only with the necessary Offices thereto shall be erected & fully completed upon each plot within one year from the date of the Conveyance thereof to the purchaser & shall be of at least the annual value specified in such Conveyance And no building whatever shall be used for any other purpose than as a private Dwellinghouse without the previous consent of the Vendor.

2. All buildings shall be faced towards the front & on side roads & in such parts of the buildings as are plainly exposed to view with good red kiln bricks provided that other materials to be approved by the Vendor may be used for the purpose of decoration. The roofs shall be covered next the road or street which they face with Slates or Brosely Tiles unless otherwise approved by the Vendor.

3. Rights of way or drainage or other similar matters the same shall be referred to the Vendor's Surveyor for the time being whose decision shall be final.

The similarity in requirements is evident, but there is a difference in that all the purchasers of land on the Eaton Glebe Estate had an interest in all the land sold. The indenture stipulated that each purchaser 'Doth hrby for himself or herself & his & her heirs executors administrators & assigns Covenant with the vendor their heirs and assigns and also as a separate covenant with the others of the said purchasers & each of them their his & her heirs & assigns That each &

every such purchaser as aforesaid his & her heirs & assigns will observe abide by fulfil & perform All & every the Clauses & stipulations set forth in the Schedule....' Thus the houses to be built on land on what was later called College Road were doubly protected from inappropriate development. The houses still stand and the quality of both the bricks and of the houses is much superior to those built in the nearby streets. This is probably due to the extra control which the vendor had on development as, unlike Clement William Unthank, the covenants stipulated that plans of buildings to be erected had to be approved by each and every purchaser. The vendor, retained control of the remainder of the unsold part of the Eaton Glebe Estate and reserved the right to dig brick, earth, sand and chalk on land which had not been sold and also to make amendments to the plans for the unsold parts of the estate.

Havelock Road and St Philip's Road

Houses built in Havelock Road in about 1877 were also subject to restrictive covenants. The land for sale was part of the Park Town Estate and the deeds examined relate to No. 23[40] (there is no reason to suppose that there would have been any great difference in the requirements for the other buildings in this street) specify that the building erected should be fronted with good white brick and be roofed with slates, not more than two storeys high, placed on the building line and have a fence onto Havelock Road not more than 4 feet high. The rental value was to be not less than £15 per annum. Only a private dwellinghouse could be erected and there were also the usual prohibitions about building a shop, warehouse, public house, etc. These houses still stand and, although there are some differences in them, they are sufficiently alike to suggest, if not a single builder at least the same covenants.

Purchasers of land for sale in St Philip's Road in 1880 were also required to observe covenants which governed the appearance of the buildings. In general, there is a similarity in prohibitions: no linen to be put outside in front nor goods exposed for sale; only private dwellings; no brick or lime to be dug, nor farm animals to be kept. There is concern for the building line, the height of boundary fences and the distance of the buildings from St Philip's Road. The only significant difference was in the appearance of the finished houses: they were all required to have bay windows and to be made with good hard bricks and faced with stucco composed of Portland cement and washes.[41]

High-status country houses in the expanding southern suburbs

The houses built in The Crescent and Bracondale were mainly suburban - terraces and semis - with small gardens. However, easy access to the city was allowing wealthy industrialists to emulate the county gentry during the first half of the century; living in a semi-rural retreat outside the city boundary in a large house with pleasure gardens, stables and outhouses would have been idyllic. White's 1836 Directory lists houses in Newmarket Road and, as the pace of building in the suburbs quickened, in 1852 there was a proposal to build houses in part of the Town Close Estate, an area bounded by Newmarket, Ipswich and Eaton Roads. Plans were drawn up for a botanical garden surrounded by gentlemen's residences, each having extensive garden grounds. This would have been an integrated plan for a discrete area of quality houses in contrast to the *ad hoc* building which had been going on in the St Giles Road and Unthank Road area. However, the freemen of Norwich, as freeholders of the Town Close Estate rejected this proposal which was later developed with substantial but less ambitious houses.[42]

Most of the high-quality semi-country houses which were built late 18th/early 19th century on or near the main highways had garden-ground at the back and at the side and later in the century it was not uncommon for these gardens to be sold for building. The break-up of the large estates appears to have started early and, as was the case with agricultural land, the land sold was the subject of restrictive covenants. In the case of the garden ground surrounding large estates, the covenants were enacted to preserve the vendors' privacy. This explains the covenant by the purchasers of land in Paragon Street in 1832 to erect a brick wall six feet high along one side of the property[43] and why in Mill Hill Road and Earlham Road[44] land was sold in 1843 with a covenant as to the type of building to be erected and its situation on the plot. There were restrictions on land in Trory Street,[45] sold in 1852, in which a covenant ensured that outbuildings at the back would be concealed and not visible from the first floor window of Timothy Steward's house on the other side of Unthank Road. Even as late as 1897 when nine artisan cottages were erected on Bowthorpe Road, the purchasers covenanted not to erect any building which might be detrimental to the development of the vendors of the Dereham Road estate nearby, land where it was proposed to erect good-quality houses.[46]

The history of Timothy Steward's estate is a good example of changes that occurred to property in the 19th century, the only difference being that good quality houses were built on his land as this was not always the case. Steward lived in Heigham Lodge on Unthank Road and his property, as listed in the 1843 Tithe map, included Gaol Close, house, lawn, etc., Shrubbery, Home Close. He owned some of the land, some he leased and his property included what is now Grosvenor Road, Clarendon Road and Neville Road. Steward was a prosperous brewer, Sheriff of Norwich in 1855 and is listed as living in Heigham Lodge in the 1836, 1845 and 1854 directories. He died in 1858 but his house was still standing in 1883, as was part of the garden ground. However, by 1883 Salisbury House and Clarendon Villas had been built beside Heigham Lodge and there were high-quality terrace houses fronting Unthank Road on what seems to have been Heigham Lodge garden ground. In addition the 1883 Ordnance Survey shows building lots on the corner of Clarendon Road and Unthank Road. Thus the process whereby a comparatively large estate is carved up was already well under way. Heigham Lodge had been demolished by 1908 and Neville Street (originally called Neville Terrace) was marked with two rows of terrace houses on each side of what was then a short street. More houses were built later and the street was lengthened, running through the remains of the Heigham Lodge estate.

Many other large estates were broken up during the 19th century. The future of Clement William Unthank's house has already been mentioned. 'The Shrubbery' in Newmarket Road was another large house which had two acres of garden ground. It was the rectory of the Revd John Smith Perowne, Rector of St John Maddermarket in 1845, and is listed in the 1832 Norwich Poll as in the occupation of Francis Stone. In 1879 the property was acquired for an extension to the Norfolk & Norwich Hospital. And on Dereham Road a family residence in the occupation of the Revd J.C. Matchett was sold in two lots in 1849.[47] Lot 1 was a large house with entrance hall, principal and back staircases, drawing and dining rooms, study, seven bedrooms and dressing-room, kitchen, back kitchen, cellar and offices and, connected with the house, a kitchen garden and larder, brew-house and coal-house and chaise-house. Lot 2 was called a building site 'for a residence of the first class'. It was planted with shrubs and trees and adjoined Lot 1. The two lots together would have made a fine estate.

The 1883 Ordnance Survey shows the large properties on the major thoroughfares often interspersed with terrace houses, suggesting the earlier breaking-up of large estates. The majority of the houses that were built were quality terrace houses, suburban town houses, not country houses. Examples include terrace houses in St Giles Road: Grove Place dated 1827, Hamlet Place and Heigham Cottage. They are listed in White's 1836 Directory as is Heigham Terrace on Dereham Road. In 1847 Heigham Terrace was sold at auction.[48] The sale particulars describe the property: good-quality terrace houses with two sitting rooms, four bedrooms, one dressing-room, kitchen, scullery, store-room, yard and offices and a front and back garden. The rent was £15 p.a. This terrace is typical of the type of good-quality house built on the main roads during the 19th century.

The age of the large landed proprietors living on the outskirts of Norwich lasted well into the 19th century but these men and women lived on increasingly smaller estates. Although the number of dwellinghouses converted to schools increased during the 20th century, this process had started much earlier. Their size made them ideal for private schools: Paragon House on St Giles Road which had been the home of Charles Winter, owner of the shoe manufactory, James Southall & Co. Ltd., became a school after his death. The school was advertised in Eyre's 1883-4 directory as a boys' boarding and day school whose headmaster was Francis Wheeler. The 1891 census lists five schoolboys and an assistant master. Paragon House School had moved to Bracondale by 1900 where it was advertised in Kelly's Directory as 'Paragon House School'. (It was later re-named Bracondale School). Another school on St Giles Road was called Westbeech House School advertised in Eyre's directory as a boys' preparatory school.

Mr Ling's School, Unthank's Road c. 1864

Henry Ling's boys' school, listed in Mathieson's 1867 directory, occupied a large house on Unthank Road and, according to the 1861 census returns, had eleven boarders aged between 7 and 15. Ling was

56 in 1861 and had moved his school to Unthank Road after 1854 (the school is listed in the 1854 directory in Pottergate as the Pottergate Street House Academy). He is also listed in the 1871 census, but by 1881 a new school for girls, called Pembroke House School, occupied the building with headmistress, Mary Ann Steele and fourteen girls listed. (According to Jarrold's Directory, the school was still in business in 1935). Most small private schools seem to have had a relatively short life; Bracondale School survived the longest, closing in the 1980s.

By 1900 the number of large estates in the suburbs had substantially declined. Of the few that remained with their large grounds intact, a number had been converted to other purposes. In 1933 the governors of Norwich High School for Girls purchased Stafford House for the junior section of the school and Eaton Grove for the senior school. Eaton Grove had been built by Sir John Harrison Yallop who was Sheriff of Norwich in 1805 and Mayor in 1815 and 1831;[49] Earlham Hall, once the home of the Gurney family and a private residence in 1900, was purchased by Norwich City Council in 1925 and later became part of the University of East Anglia. And of the houses that retained their garden ground into the 20th century these, many were parcelled off and are still being parcelled off for building.

New building in Eaton and Lakenham

Despite the carving-up of the large estates, high-quality houses, especially in Unthank Road and Newmarket Road, continued to be built further and further away from the city centre. They were occupied by prosperous drapers, solicitors, merchants and also by retired businessmen. Those listed in the 1890 directory include: Clement Charles Spelman of auctioneers H.W. Spelman & Co. in 'Fern House', William Webster of Curl Bros. Ltd., Linen and Woollen Drapers in 'The Woodbines' and George White of Howlett & White, boot and shoe manufacturers. These houses are all on Unthank Road in the parish of Eaton, as was 'West View' the home of Henry R.W.

Garland of Garland & Sons Linen Drapers who is listed in the 1901 census return. These houses, although large, all have relatively small garden grounds. No longer are there the stables, paddock and meadow of earlier years.

The hamlet of Lakenham (New Lakenham) was not built up to the same extent in the 19th century. As mentioned, buildings were erected along both City and Hall roads early in the century, as well as in Southwell Road and Lewis Street, and the Peafield area nearby was built up with small tenements. The church of St Mark on City Road was built 1843-4 for this new suburb, but much of Lakenham remained as garden ground and nurseries. Manning's c.1833 map shows the Tucks Wood Estate and the Lakenham Grove Estate and the situation did not much alter throughout the century. The Grove on Ipswich Road had been part of the estate of James Crowe which passed to his son-in-law Sigismund Boehm (later Trafford) on his death. It was built in 1772 and remained the property of the family into the 20th century. It had been occupied by Alexander Chamberlin of Chamberlin's drapers by 1864 and later by his widow. The 1883 Ordnance Survey shows a large house with extensive garden ground and a lodge. There were also additional structures, possibly a stable and coach-house.[50] Jarrold's 1900 Directory lists very few roads in this part of Lakenham. There were a few houses as well as building sites on Sigismund Road, Trafford Road and Rowington Road, although by 1914 many more houses had been built. And along Ipswich Road, the Tuckswood council estate and the City College were built in the 20th century on the former great estate of James Crowe.

The development of the suburbs in Norwich south of the river brought an end to country-house living in large estates pleasantly close to the amenities of the City as gradually the land-owners released land for building. This had a domino-effect: as a land-owner sold up his estate, another near or beside it was sold as not only had the value of the land increased, but it was feared that the estate would be surrounded by

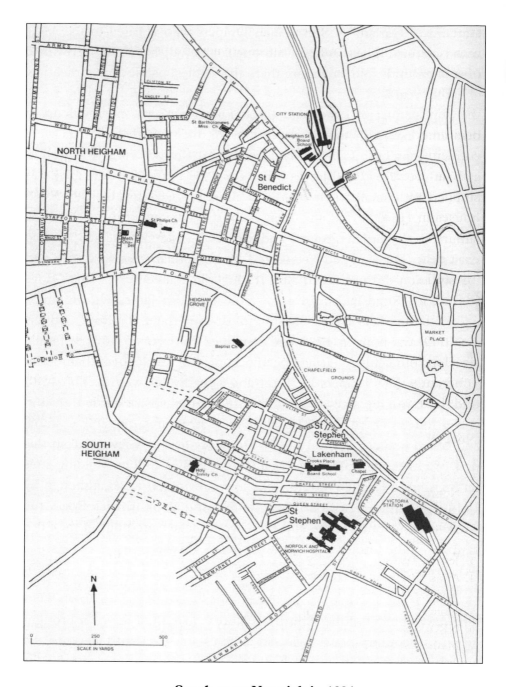

South-west Norwich in 1884

streets and houses. Attempts were made to deal with this problem, with restrictive covenants to protect privacy, but in the end the growth of suburbia was inevitable.

By 1900 the parish of Heigham was nearly completely built up, the few areas still awaiting development due to be built at the beginning of the 20th century, the earliest houses soon to be condemned as slum property. Indeed the 20th century had a good stab at demolishing much of the earlier housing stock, only being stopped by changing fashion. However, one way to characterise the houses in Heigham (apart from the very earliest) is that it is a mixed suburb - quality houses, middle-class houses and artisan houses co-exist near to each other. Whilst it is true that the grandest houses are on the main roads, the humbler artisan dwellings are very near them, indeed; in some places they are side by side.

Although that part of Eaton which is contiguous with Heigham was built up early, Eaton Village was too far away to be attractive to developers. As for New Lakenham, the hamlet was not developed as a coherent whole, large areas remaining as estates into the 20th century and there was little overall consistency in the buildings.

Notes

1. Browne, P. *The History of Norwich from the earliest records to the present time.* Norwich 1814 describes the parishes: Eaton p. 163, Lakenham p. 149, Heigham p. 201

2. Norwich was a so-called freeman borough, but had also a freeholder franchise giving the vote to people who possessed property in the city to a certain value (see Winstanley, Roy *Parson Woodforde – The Life & Times of a Country Diarist*, 1996, p. 195.

3. Jessop, Augustus. *Arcady For Better For Worst*, 1887. pp. xii, 23, etc.

4. Armstrong, Alan. *The population of Victorian and Edwardian Norfolk.* Centre of EastAnglian Studies, University of East Anglia, 2000, p. 33.

5. Springall, L. Marion. *Labouring Life in Norfolk Villages 1834-1914.* London, 1936

6. NRO, NRS 5794 18 D.2 Clay Pit or Crab Tree Close, Heigham

7. Muthesius, S. *Nineteenth Century Housing*, p. 100 suggests that this Quaker may have had a philanthropic motive wishing to improve the houses of the poor, in Barringer, Christopher (ed.), *Norwich in the Nineteenth Century*, 1984,

8. [Stacy, John], *A topographical & historical account of the City & County of Norwich*, *1832*, p. 66

9. [Stacy, John], *A topographical & historical account of the City & County of Norwich,* 1819, p. 42

10. *Excursions in the County of Norfolk...* Vol. 2 Supplement, 1819, p. 35

11. White's 1836 Directory, p. 153

12. NRO, Plan DS238, DS452(52) Manchester Buildings, Union Place.   Edward Powell's Estate

13. NRO, TC387 29, 31 and 33 Shadwell Street

14. NRO, TC184 15-19 Salford Street, 18-24 Manchester Street

15. Health of Towns Act. Report of an Inquiry held before William Lee of the Sanitary Condition of the City and County of Norwich. Norwich 1850, p. 56

16. 1858 Board of Health Bylaws

17. 1877 Building Control Plans

18. NRO, TC287 49 Distillery Street

19. NRO, SPE625 Freehold Estate in West Pottergate Street. In comparison, the rent of tenements in Union Place in 1846 was £9.15s. for two houses (NRO SPE555).

20. NRO, SPE286 27 West Pottergate

21. NRO, TC336, TC337 1-4 and 5-8 Bailey's Buildings, West Pottergate

22. NRO, TC286 27 West Pottergate

23. NRO, SPE303 Freehold dwellinghouse sold 23rd September 1830 [West Pottergate]

24. NRO, SPE285 Four freehold dwellinghouses in Cross Street and West Pottergate

25. NRO, MS18625/160 Trafalgar Place

26. NRO, TC8/3 Conveyance of a piece of land at Lakenham to W. Bales & E. Bales [Lewis Street]

27. Crescent History Group. *The Crescent, Norwich: listing of occupiers 1825-1978*

28. I am grateful to the late George Fenner for showing me the Title deeds to Craster House

29. Browne, p. 148

30. NRO, 18625/160 Richmond Place sold 8th May 1820 by Mr John Culley

31. NRO, ACC. Cozens-Hardy 21/3/1975

32. *Excursions:* Supplement, p. 33

33. NRO, SPE580 Freehold land on the Dereham Road

34. NRO, TC151 49 Devonshire Street

35. NRO, D.S. 1642 Sale of land in Heigham 15th August 1855

36. Urbanisation of the northern suburbs occurred later in the century and in the mid-1850s it was not uncommon for land still being sold for agricultural purposes.

37. Blyth's Directory of Norwich 1842, p. 210. The Asylum is listed in the 1851 census.

38. The Unthank papers have been deposited in the Norfolk Record Office

39. I am grateful to Gail Durbin for photocopying the title deeds for her house in College Road.

40. Jacqueline McCarney kindly photocopied the title deeds for her house in Havelock Road.
41. Ref. 9214 Norwich City Hall
42. Griffiths, Elizabeth & Smith, Hassell *'Buxom to the Mayor' A History of the Norwich Freemen,* 1987, p. 30ff.
43. NRO, TC119 2 Paragon Street
44. NRO, N/TC450 Land in Mill Hill Road and Earlham Road
45. NRO, TC277 30 Trory Street
46. Title deeds relating to 60-76 Bowthorpe Road in private possession.
47. TC52/6 Freehold properties in Union Place, Julian Place, Unthank's Road and Dereham Road
48. NRO, SPE644 [Dereham Road] Spelman auction 21st June 1849
49. *Norwich High School 1875-1950,* n.d., p. 25
50. See 'The Houses of the Dukes of Norfolk in Norwich' by Ernest A. Kent, *Norfolk Archaeology* 24, 1932, pp. 73-87.

Chapter 6. Growth of the Suburbs
2: The northern suburbs

Introduction

The northern suburbs of Norwich encompass that part of the parish of St Clement outside the wall known as St Clement Without (later known as Christchurch Catton or New Catton), part of the parish of St Paul outside the wall, and Lower Hellesdon. In the early 19th century, except for a number of small houses in the Philadelphia area and quality ones in the St Clement's Hill area, this part of Norwich was mainly agricultural with a few large estates. Today New Catton is notable for the large number of houses built in the latter part of the century, the majority of which are small-to-medium artisan dwellings in red-brick terraces with small gardens front and rear. Most of them remain, their continued popularity evidence of the improvements in building wrought by various local government acts. In 1858 Norwich Board of Health Bye-laws with respect to new streets and houses were published which led to greatly improved standards, and after July 1877 Building Control plans had to be submitted and approval given to drainage, leading to further improvements.

Development

Stacy described the parish of St Clement Without in 1819. He mentioned the Infirmary, and stated that 'more north [of the Infirmary] are a considerable number of buildings having the appearance of a little town'.[1] According to Browne[2] the Infirmary, originally a Lazar House, was then an asylum 'for old and decayed citizens and their widows' built on land leased by the Bishop of Norwich to the City which had 'lately' been enlarged and improved. In 1828 an asylum for 'pauper lunatics' was built beside this institution and enlarged in 1838.[3] These buildings, with additional ancillary accommodation, were situated on Infirmary Road (part of Waterloo Road). Sometime after 1863, despite the objections of the Corporation, the Asylum was declared to be unhealthy and unfit and was closed by the Lunacy Commissioners appointed under the Lunatic Asylum Act of 1853; a new asylum was built in Hellesdon.[4]

Apart from the Infirmary and related buildings, there were few houses, except for a number of small cottages built some distance from the walls near the boundary with Catton and Hellesdon in the area known as Philadelphia. This is marked on Manning's [1835] map of the suburbs of Norwich and later comprised Philadelphia Lane, Sun Lane and part of Aylsham Road. This may have been what Stacy meant when he referred to the considerable number of buildings which he saw as 'another proof of the increase in Norwich' as had been a number of small tenements that had been built here before 1826[5] although no widespread development as in the so-called New City in Heigham. Despite this early building, the expansion north was slow and it wasn't until the late 1880s that there was a significant increase in the building of roads and houses. By 1899 the network of streets linking the major roads to the different parts of the parish was all but complete. But this happened long after Heigham expanded outwards from the City walls; north of the walls, there was only sporadic development along the major roads and this part of Norwich retained its largely rural character nearly into the 20th century.

Although Millard and Manning's 1830 map of Norwich concentrated mainly on the area within the wall, that of Manning of c.1835 gives a good indication of the build-up outside. Apart from Philadelphia, mentioned above, and a few small concentrations of buildings on some of the main roads, the greater part of this suburb was given over to agriculture and market-gardening. There were also brick fields and lime workings, windmills and at least one saw mill. Near to the Infirmary was Chalk Farm with its related farm buildings. This belonged to the Corporation of Norwich and occupied a large area between Aylsham Road, Waterloo Road and Angel Road. Much of the land north of Bull Close Road was in the hamlet of Pockthorpe and belonged to the Dean and Chapter of Norwich and was partly in the parish of St Paul. There were no buildings there, nor on the land between Magdalen Road and Silver Road which was wood and heathland, crossed by some lanes.

There are a few large estates marked on Manning's map: Wren Park at the junction of St Clement's Hill and Constitution Hill, Point House on the corner of Spixworth and Magdalen roads, Sprowston Lodge off Constitution Hill and a few large houses on the main roads. There were few artisan dwellings. Unlike the parishes of Heigham and Lakenham, the land was not suitable for housing, being hilly with fairly steep gradients and scarred by former lime burning, brick digging and marl working. In the Manning map there are few roads apart from those that were necessary to give access to the villages and small towns north of Norwich: the Aylsham Turnpike (Aylsham Road), the Fakenham Turnpike (Drayton Road), Catton Back Lane (Angel Road) and the road to Wroxham (Sprowston Road). Infirmary Road was one of only a few roads of lesser importance marked, but not named.

The 1832 Poll Book for this part of Norwich indicates the built-up areas: there were houses on Infirmary Road and on Waterloo Place, Angel Road, Green Hills and Catton Road (these last two are today called Aylsham Road), St Clement's Place (St Clement's Hill), Sun Lane, Mill Hill (Miller's Lane). As voting was restricted, the list gives an incomplete picture of the number of residents but the addresses confirm that Manning's map was up to date. Compared to the returns for Heigham and Lakenham parishes, the number of those voting was small. References to Waterloo Place and St Clement's Terrace suggest an area only partially built up.

Christchurch, New Catton

As mentioned above, there were several superior houses and consequently a number of well-to-do residents living some distance from the City's medieval churches and this may explain why, despite the comparatively small number of parishioners, Christchurch was consecrated as early as 1841. This was the first Church of England church to be built in Norwich since the Middle Ages[6] and

Christchurch New Catton became an ecclesiastical parish out of the parish of St Clement in 1842.

This part of Norwich must have been very rural and thus the ideal location for high-quality houses. There were a number in the St Clement's Hill area near the large Wren Park estate. The 1841 and 1851 census returns record several persons of independent means, but very few men in the professions. Instead there were a number of wealthy merchants and manufacturers whose offices and factories were in the City. In 1841 the corn merchant Joseph Bolton lived there as did the silk and worsted manufacturer Francis Hinde, of Ephraim & Francis Hinde of Botolph Street and in 1851 residents living on St Clement's Hill included Joseph Greenhough, a worsted spinner who employed forty workers in the county of Yorkshire, who also had a business in Cowgate, and Frederick Pigg, a town councillor and mahogany merchant whose business was in Bridge Street, St George's.

Other parts of Christchurch Catton had good quality houses in or near Aylsham Road and here also were wealthy manufacturers with works in the City. In 1841 J.H. Robberds, the paper-maker of the firm Robberds & Monday with offices in St Margaret's Plain and a manufactory in Lyng, lived in Chalk Hill House, Aylsham Road. He had four female servants, and one of his sons was a solicitor's clerk, the other a post office clerk. William Press lived in Press's Lane (off Aylsham Road) in 1861. He was a paramatta manufacturer who employed eight people. Another prosperous Aylsham Road resident in 1883 was Samuel Denham of the firm Adcock and Denham. In 1881 Daniel Adcock lived in Salem Cottage, Press Lane. He was a tobacco and cigar manufacturer employing 48 people. In 1883 the firm Adcock and Denham had premises in Queen Street. After the death of Samuel Denham, the 1890 directory records the business as Adcock & Son, advertised in the *Industries of Norfolk & Suffolk Business Review* (c. 1890) as having retail premises in Back of the Inns and a manufactory in Queen Street where a large number of people were employed.

The industries located in this part of Norwich were predominantly rural. White's 1845 directory lists a number of gardeners and seedsmen and six corn millers: two in Philadelphia, one in Hellesdon, two in New Catton and one in Sprowston. The St Clement's Hill area was also chosen by retired farmers; two lived there in 1851.

In 1836 two saw mills are listed, one in Sprowston and one in Philadelphia as well as a lime-burner in New Catton. Land off Aylsham Road was mainly farmland and garden ground. The 1861 return gives a good idea of the extent of the holdings at that time: a farmer with 25 acres on Aylsham Road near to Hellesdon Mill and four gardeners (presumably market gardeners) each with substantial acreages, the largest with 15 acres, the smallest four. There were also thirteen agricultural labourers and seven gardeners.

Because Christchurch Catton was so near to Norwich, it combined country living with city convenience and this made it a very suitable location for one of Norwich's pleasure gardens as it was easily accessible to its citizens. These were very popular in the early part of the century and Green Hills Gardens situated outside St Augustine's gate had extensive grounds and was already well established by 1842 when it was said by Blyth to be one of the foremost gardens in Norwich.[7] The garden, marked on the 1883 Ordnance Survey map, had closed before 1890 when Green Hills Road was built and only the Green Hills Public House remained (today just one double-fronted residence on the street).

Despite the rural scene, the 1841 census of St Clement Without shows that although there were numbers of persons working in the mills and as gardeners and farm workers, employment was overwhelmingly dependent on Norwich with a large number of men employed as weavers, woolcombers and allied trades as well as carpenters, shoemakers and tailors. The 1841 and 1861 census returns indicate that suburban streets had already impinged on what had been a predominantly rural area. This is most evident in Philadelphia. In 1841 it had a varied population which included a butcher, surveyor and an innkeeper, as well as sawyers, carpenters, many weavers, tailors, charwomen and agricultural labourers. Apart from work associated with country living, most of the occupations were similar to those of the majority of people living within the walls and although there were a large number of agricultural workers living on Aylsham Road near to Hellesdon Mill, closer to the City were mainly weavers, labourers (unspecified) and some shoe workers.

With the exception of the houses in the St Clement's Hill area, there were few high-quality houses in this suburb in the early part of the century and in general the quality of the small artisan dwellings built before the building acts was greatly inferior to those built from 1880 onwards when the major part of this suburb was developed. The quality of many of these early houses can best be gauged by the census enumerator's reports of 1891 and 1901 in which the number of habitations with less than five rooms are listed. In Philadelphia Lane there were 27 houses with four rooms only. Although 14 of these had only two or three people resident, one had ten people, one nine and four had six people. In the 1891 census the residents were mainly employed as labourers and in the shoe industry (in 1841 the majority were weavers) and most wives were employed as laundresses, dressmakers and charwomen.

There were other very small houses on Denmark Road, Waterloo Road and Alma Terrace. In Alma Terrace, all seven houses listed in the 1891 census had four rooms. Miller's Lane had even smaller houses, many with only three rooms and in 1901 a small number of self-employed shoemakers are listed (and, as such, were probably less prosperous than those working in the factories). Many of the houses in Sun Lane also had only three rooms. Both Sun Lane and Miller's Lane are near Angel Road. Angel Road itself, while having a number of three and four-roomed houses in 1901 had a more mixed workforce including brickmakers, bricklayers, labourers and shoe workers as well as a few commercial travellers and clerks. In 1841, in this part of Christchurch Catton, the majority of the men had been employed as weavers, with only a few shoe workers and labourers and the 1891 and 1901 census returns show large numbers of labourers, shoe workers and other low-grade manual workers. The difference between the old and new parts of this suburb was that although labourers and shoe workers also lived in the newly built houses in the parish of St Paul outside the walls, there was much more variety of occupation there, with a number of clerks and skilled craftsmen.

Land Sales in the 19th century

In Heigham and Lakenham land for sale was almost invariably building land, but this was not the case in Christchurch Catton and in that part of St Paul's parish outside the walls where, apart from the areas already mentioned, until the 1880s, sale particulars described land for sale for agricultural purposes rather than house-building. A good example is the sale in 1846 of a leasehold estate in St Paul's parish fronting Bull Close Road and Magdalen Road.[8] Lot 2 was five small tenements fronting Bull Close Road and Lot 1 on the corner of these two roads was the Artichoke Public House which included a substantial barn and numerous outbuildings arranged as stabling, piggeries, etc. Lot 3 was a piece of land adjoining the barn in Lot 1 which was then occupied as garden and stock-yards. In neither case is there any mention of possible change of use. In fact the buildings in Lot 1 are said to be 'most advantageously situated for the reception of stock and for general business.' And this was land just outside the City wall. In 1834 freehold land near the Norwich and Aylsham Turnpike Road was sold at auction[9] either for building or garden ground which suggests that there was no demand in this part of Norwich for artisan terraces.

The urbanisation of this part of Norwich, which was fuelled by the owners of large estates discovering that their land was more valuable when divided into lots for building than if sold as a single unit, was only just beginning. This stage had not yet been reached in 1841 when some freehold land in St Clement and Catton was sold at auction.[10] This was a sizeable property of over 24 acres divided into three lots. Lot 1 was a gentleman's mansion house with coach-house, stable, orchard, garden lawn and there were also agricultural buildings and land amounting to over 11 acres. The purchaser was restricted from erecting any dwellinghouse or houses, factory, work-room except for erecting any dwellinghouse or houses, factory, work-room except for additions to the house and a lodge without chambers. Lot 2 was in the village of Catton, but Lot 3 in St Clement was arable land of over 8 acres with the same prohibitions on building, except that permission was given to erect one agricultural cottage with barn, stable and outbuildings, stipulations which ensured there would be no change of use. The description in the sale particulars states that the property is situated on a hill at Lower Whale Bone Close near to the Whale Bone Public House on Magdalen Road, near its junction with St Clement's Hill and some distance from the city walls. Although it remains open

to question, there seems little doubt that the property for sale is Wren Park (later called Clare House) which is marked on the Millard map. A handwritten note at the bottom of the sale particulars shows awareness of the future desirability of land of this type but also the realisation that the market is not yet ready for development of this kind. Among the present advantages the contiguity to the City was noted. As to the future advantage: the vendor was advised to 'Illustrate this by a retrospect of building

Houses in Magdalen Street

land and residences etc. in large cities - London, Manchester, Birmingham, Leeds *and even in this City*, at present less than others - but must *progress* and in time resume her Station with the Town in the Empire' (Estate Agent's italics). It is significant that in 1841, the vendor realised there was no hope of selling land such as this in smaller lots for housing development.

If the property for sale is in fact Wren Park, it was not sold in 1841 as on the 1845 St Clement Christchurch Tithe Map[11] the owner of Wren Park is listed as the Revd Thomas Cooper Colls and the lessee Revd Thomas Calvert. The Revd Calvert lived there and is listed in the 1845 Directory as the incumbent of St James's Church, Norwich.

Development

Morant's map of 1872 shows little had changed in the 40 years that had elapsed since Manning's map was published. There was still a preponderance of agricultural land and not many additional roads had been built. A number are marked on the map and there is some evidence that the development of the northern suburbs is starting, albeit slowly. Some buildings in Church Road (Denmark Road) near the church and Catton School had been erected in Sun Lane and nearby land was marked out for housing. Church Lane (Lawson Road) situated just off Magdalen Road had been built with small tenements along one side of the road and building plots on the other. Four good-quality terrace houses were built on Aylsham Road in 1852 near Green Hill Gardens not far from St Augustine's Gates. However, apart from the artisan terrace built on Long Row nearby, no other quality terraces were built and they must have appeared out of place in the country as they were surrounded by market gardens.

The 1883 Ordnance Survey of this part of Norwich shows a very gradual expansion. The Infirmary, said to be disused on the 1872 map, still remained, but part of its extensive grounds had now been marked into probable building plots. Chalk Farm, which was marked on the Manning map, was virtually unchanged, as was Wren Park. The Catton Recreation Ground occupied part of the open agricultural areas near Chalk Farm in 1899 (this became Waterloo Park in 1904) and by 1900 part of the farm was held by a market gardener. There had not been much road-building, but the housing density seems to have increased. In 1885 New Catton was still under-populated compared to Heigham, but there was a significant increase in building in the late

1880s and 1890s. According to the City Architect's 1899 map it would seem that nearly all the roads had been built, although the building of houses continued into the 20th century.

The extent and speed of building can be gauged by the following examples. In Bull Close Road where, according to the City Engineer's map of 1873, there had been terrace houses on only the city side of the road, by 1900 there were a number of small terrace houses on both sides of the road and the Bull Close Board School had been built near the Artichoke Public House. And on Angel Road the 1883 Ordnance Survey map[12] shows gaps in the housing, but by 1899 there was a nearly completely unbroken row of small terrace houses and Rosebery Road itself had been built, although the majority of houses were not built until the 20th century. In 1883 Denmark Farm on Sprowston Road was marked near the junction of Denmark Road as were lime works north of the farm. Denmark Farm was advertised for sale by auction in the *Norfolk Chronicle* on 23rd August 1884 as follows: 'Freehold estate, farmhouse with agricultural premises, eight cottages and 18 acres 20 perches of land in Pockthorpe and Sprowston parishes. Property has extensive frontages to the Wroxham and Silver Roads, Mousehold Heath and the land leading thereto.' The advertisement listed other advantages: five minutes' walk to the omnibus terminus and 'from its position [it] is particularly suitable for building purposes' and in 1900 plans were made to further develop the site by building a number of new roads.[13]

There was still some agricultural land left after the sale of Denmark Farm, but this advertisement was a portent of what was to come. What the vendors of property in St Clement in 1841 had described as a 'future possibility' by 1884 had become a reality and Jarrold's directories list new roads in course of construction: Bell Road in 1895, Northcote Road in 1893, Branford Road in 1895. These were south of Denmark Farm, and the east side of Sprowston Road, in 1883 open countryside, was rapidly becoming urbanised. Spencer Street was built by 1899 and so was the Silver Road tram depot. This was situated near the Silver Road/Sprowston Road junction. Churchill

Road was not on the 1883 map and is first listed in Jarrold's 1893 Directory when there were already a number of buildings, although there were still some building sites.

The 1883 Ordnance Survey map featured a number of large houses with garden ground, but these were to disappear and be replaced by new roads and artisan dwellings. The land between Magpie Road and the junction with Sprowston Road which included the estate of Edward Heath Esq. who lived in a house called The Beeches on Magdalen Road, gave way to Clarke Road, Shipstone Road, Stacy Road and Guernsey Road (all about 1890).

Numbers 24 and 26 Clarke Road

In 1897 Sprowston Lodge, which on the Manning map was said to be the estate of J. Cozzens Esq. was sold in 79 lots for building.[14]

Lots 1 to 43 inclusive were situated on Constitution Hill and were intended for private dwellinghouses with the building of stables and coach-houses allowed, the value of the property erected to let to be not less than £19 p.a. Lots 44 to 74 inclusive were on Denmark Road and 75 to 79 were on Sprowston Road. These were also sold for building but houses of lesser value were to be erected, to be let at not less than £10 p.a. The usual prohibitions about digging for brick-earth, etc., keeping pigs or cattle, building a mill or factory, selling alcoholic beverages etc. applied, but apart from the rental value of houses to be built, there were no other restrictions. The different valuation on the houses is explained by the fact that Denmark Road and Sprowston Road were already largely built up with small artisan dwellings whereas there were a number of good quality semi-detached and terrace houses with good gardens on St Clement's Hill as well as Clare House. The restrictive covenants, including those prohibiting the keeping of pigs or cattle, which had been included in land sales in Heigham and Lakenham some eighty years previously, demonstrate that New Catton could no longer be considered a semi-rural adjunct to the City, but part of the City - a truly urban environment.

Magdalen Road Estate

Apart from the quality houses built in the Constitution Hill/St Clement's Hill area, the houses on the new roads built in the late 1880s/early 1890s in this part of Norwich are all very similar. They are well-built red-brick terrace houses; some, but not all, have a hall entrance but they all have small gardens at the front and back and dining room, living room, kitchen and washroom downstairs (converted to bathroom in the 20th century) and three rooms upstairs. Their general aspect is neat and tidy. When first built there would have been a privy or water-closet in the garden. An example of the quality of the houses of that period are those built on what was known as the Magdalen Road Estate.[15] In 1890 land off Magdalen Road was released for sale and houses were built on what later became known as Northcote, Churchill, Knowsley, Beaconsfield, Shipstone, Clarke, Heath and Guernsey roads. The vendor went into great detail about the quality and type of building allowed and although the requirements quoted below refer to 28 and 30 Guernsey Road, there is no reason to suppose they differed materially from all the other houses on this estate. The following covenants were enforced: the buildings to be faced with good sound red kiln bricks with no salmon or badly burnt bricks: the roofs to be covered with black glazed pantiles and every building to have iron gutters and iron leading downpipes: all windows and door jambs in each front to be set in 4½" reveal and all windows facing Guernsey Road to be sash windows and no window or other opening except at the back or front of the building except if such openings face towards the piece of land hereby conveyed and not towards any property adjoining the property belonging to the vendor. No building to be higher than two storeys and the ground floor line to be not less than 18" above crown of Guernsey Road. Buildings should be on building line. Doors to be arches in brick or stone or made with a frontispiece which should not extend more than 12" beyond the building line. No public house, shop, tavern, beer house, club house or premises for the sale of beer, porter, wines, spirits, etc. No shops for sale of articles of any kind upon any part of the land and no goods whether for sale or not or linen or any article of show or trade should

Houses in Guernsey Road – built to requirements

140

be placed between building line and Guernsey Road. No boundary wall should be more than 6' high or less than 3'6". Iron palisade on a brick pinning or dwarf wall next Guernsey Road to be not more than 4' high. Private dwellinghouses only and each dwellinghouse should be at least of the annual value to let of £9 and should not exceed the annual value to let of £15.

This vendor, like so many others before and after, influenced the quality of the houses which were to be built on property previously owned by him and was guided by the type of house already built in the neighbourhood. Yet while it was usual at this period for the vendor to specify a minimum rental value for each house, in this case both a minimum *and* a maximum rental value were specified. The reason for this is unclear, the title deeds refer specifically to a number of building sites and these are marked on a plan. However, all the houses on this street, apart from the one on the corner of Magdalen Road are similar, and no doubt the same covenants would have applied to them. It is possible that by stating a maximum rental value the vendor may have been trying to encourage the erection of larger houses. If this was the case, he would have been disappointed as the houses are all small red-brick artisan terraces, just like all the others in this part of Norwich. The developers may have been unwilling to build more substantial houses which might have been difficult to let in this suburb with its overwhelmingly artisan-type dwellings. However, despite the very detailed requirements, the land-owner was probably more concerned with the external appearance of the houses built on his estate than with their sanitation, as houses built on Shipstone Road[16] in 1893 were each to be provided with a privy. In this he was no different from the majority of his peers who seemed to think it unnecessary for the working-classes to have water-closets - see Chapter 9. Although a few of the houses on the Magdalen Road Estate have a hall entrance, these in Shipstone Street are without one. However, they all have a small garden in front and a yard at the back.

Magpie Road

In 1814 Browne wrote about the buildings on the wall by St Augustine's Gate and said that 'on the outside it is nearly built up, with some of the best buildings which are to be found on the walls'. (Browne seems to be referring to houses built upon both sides of the city walls, and saying that those built on the outside are better than those built on the inside.) 'About half way from the gate is a public-house called the Pye'.[17] This would have been a reference to the Magpie public-house which by 1864 had given its name to the road. The public house is listed in Chase's 1830 Directory and in White's 1836 Directory; the address is given as Wales Buildings. However, it is possible that the address given for the pub is mistaken as in the 1841 census the public house and Wales Buildings are separate buildings; the landlord of the Magpie Public House is John Dunthorn and families of weavers lived in Wales Buildings. Blyth, writing in 1842, gives further details of the road at that time: 'The wall from St Augustine's gate to Magdalen Gate is partly built upon from within side and the towers converted to cottages.'[18] The Millard & Manning map shows a range of buildings on the walls on Magpie Road (although the road is not named in the map). These buildings do not extend the whole length of the street and there was only one building on the opposite side of the street, on the corner of Magdalen Road.

According to the census returns, the occupations of the residents of Magpie Road did not change very much between 1841 and 1861, but the number of people living on this road greatly increased in this twenty-year interval. Whilst in 1841 the inhabitants were mostly weavers, in 1861 although weavers of various kinds vastly outnumbered those in other occupations, shoemakers, bricklayers, washerwomen, and bricklayers are included in the return and the residents are mainly young - not many over 60. By 1881 the occupations of the residents were much more varied although still with a preponderance of shoe makers (seven men and five women), and included two men and four women employed as tailors or dressmakers, four women weavers and three women employed in laundry work. In a slightly larger house on the corner of Magpie Road and Magdalen Street lived James Chaplin a boot and shoe manufacturer who had a female servant and also employed six men, four women and three boys. The 1901 census returns show that the occupations of the residents had not materially changed, although at that time there were more men engaged in the shoe trade.

It is interesting to compare the quality of the houses built in 1890 on the Magdalen Road Estate with those built on Magpie Road. The houses on Magpie Road were built on land owned by Norwich Corporation which was released for building on a 72 year lease from 24th June 1880,[19] and the restrictive covenants imposed by the Corporation were very little different from those of private land owners. The required building standard was as follows: the rental value of the buildings should be not less than £7 p.a. although

Houses in Magpie Road

buildings of a higher value were allowed; 'sound foreign fir and English oak and well hard burnt bricks and all other requisite materials [should be] of the best description'. In addition, plans had to be submitted to the Corporation for approval. There were the usual prohibitions on the making or burning of bricks and lime, chandling, bone boiling, etc., as well as on public houses, beer houses, baking offices and shops. Only dwellinghouses were to be built. However, despite the Corporation's insistence on 'well hard burnt brick', the brick used was not of good quality[20] and in general the houses were not as good as those built on the Magdalen Road Estate, the rental value being smaller. A later deed included with these documents (probably relating to at least part of the original building land) dated 29th September 1883 and referring to Zig-Zag Terrace, 78-106 Magpie Road, shows that the houses shared a pump at the rear of the terrace. Salisbury Terrace, also on Magpie Road, with some fourteen houses, is dated 1869 and is also similar to those built on land which the Corporation had released for building in 1880. The houses are also similar to those built on Willis Street about 1881, some of which were demolished in the 20th century, the difference being that those on Willis Street do not have a front garden.[21]

Houses in Willis Street, built 1880

According to the 1883 Ordnance Survey of Norwich, Magpie Road was by then completely built up on the city wall side and although some land appears to have been marked out for building, there were only a very few buildings on the other side of the road. The early houses built on the wall had all been demolished by that time and replaced by rows of terrace houses and named variously Zig-Zag Terrace, Malvern Terrace and Salisbury Terrace. By 1901 there were houses on other side of the road and these were very similar to those built on the city wall side. Magpie Road today is a street of modest red-brick terrace houses with very small front gardens and without hall entrance. There are a few seemingly earlier white-brick houses near the corner of St Augustine's Street, and one or two of the houses have been demolished. The Magpie Public House, still in business, is a large, detached, double-fronted building, probably dating from the 1840s-1850s.

The residents of New Catton 1881-1901

According to the 1891 and 1901 census returns the occupations of the residents of the new houses in New Catton, although in many ways similar to those in the older parts of the suburb, were much more varied. Although in Philadelphia Lane and Sun Lane by 1891 boot and shoe workers had replaced the weavers, there appears to have been little social mobility; in 1901 a number of the more prosperous residents living in the recently-constructed houses in new streets such as Shipstone Street, Knowsley Road and Marlborough Road had higher-status jobs, being employers of labour, white-collar workers, teachers, etc. Although in nearly every one of these new streets the number of boot and shoe workers far outnumbered other residents, in Marlborough Road residents included a filing clerk and a brewer's clerk as well as a boot and shoe manufacturer with works in Cowgate.[22] In Shipstone Street lived a school teacher, decorative draughtsman and railway guard as well a boot and shoe manufacturer. There were also skilled artisans - carpenters, cabinet makers and the like. Possibly the biggest difference was that, unlike the residents of the Philadelphia Lane area, the wives of the workers in the new streets did not go out to work, which suggests that in general there was greater prosperity. The census returns 1881-1901 for this part of New Catton also show an increase in the number of white-collar workers. Most of them were the sons of working men, better educated as a result of the education acts and there were considerably more clerks living in New Catton than lived in the older houses in Norwich over the Water nearby.

As for the high-quality houses in the St Clement's Hill area, their numbers grew slowly. There had been some changes in this part of the suburb since 1841 as according to the 1881 census there were fewer persons of independent means and more successfully engaged in industry. The large mansion – Clare House[23] – was occupied by Philip Sewell from at least 1881, a retired civil engineer, together with his wife, daughter and a number of women servants: a parlour maid, sewing maid, laundry maid and kitchen maid. The census also records John Clarke, a boot and shoe manufacturer, who employed 20 men, two boys and nine women at works in St Stephen's Street, living on St Clement's Hill. Also listed in the 1883 directory was Thomas Bales a wholesale grocer of the firm Fisher & Bales who had premises in Colegate and Bridge Street and Charles Cunnell, a farmer with 244 acres who employed ten men and two boys. Both these men are listed in the 1883 directory as well as John Cunnell, a farmer and lime owner who had land at Church Farm, Eaton, and a brick and tile and flowerpot manufactory at Old Catton together with additional premises at the Corn Exchange and at Mile Cross, Hellesdon.

The quality of the houses in this suburb show very clearly the effect of the 1858 building regulations that came into effect from 1858 onwards, and as a consequence, very few of them have been demolished. This is a suburb which is unusual in its uniformity; where street after street has rows of small terrace houses which, although obviously the work of many small builders, are overwhelmingly artisan with minimal variation in size and style. There are few, if any large houses; most of them were built in the St Clement's Hill/Constitution Hill area, in the northern part of the suburb.

It is this comparative uniformity which makes it possible to suggest that the development of this part of Norwich was fuelled by the demand for houses by workers employed in factories as it coincided with mechanization and enlargement of the shoe factories. Whether this was cause and effect is uncertain, but the building of so many artisan dwellings relatively near to the shoe factories in Norwich over the Water would ensure a ready market for the new houses for a more affluent workforce, able to improve their housing on account of increased wages earned working in a factory.

House in Heath Road, formerly a baker's shop

Notes

1. [Stacy, John] *A topographical & historical account of the City & County of Norwich*, 1819, p. 61
2. Browne, P. *The History of Norwich from the Earliest Records to The Present Time*, 1814, p. 287
3. White's 1845 Directory, p.144

4. This proposed closure is mentioned by Bayne, A.D. *A Comprehensive History of Norwich*, 1869, (p. 441), and there are summary reports in *Norfolk Annals* Vol. 2 1873-5.

5. NRO, TC27/1-6: Philadelphia Lane. The Abstract of Title describes cottages on a private road that runs from the Aylsham turnpike to the Catton Road.

6. Norfolk Annals Vol. 1, p. 412

7. Blyth, G.K. *The Norwich Guide* [1842], p. 208

8. NRO, SPE553: Leasehold estate in St Paul's Parish (Magdalen Road and Bull Close Road)

9. NRO, SPE383: Freehold land near the Norwich & Aylsham Turnpike Road and a very short distance from St Augustine Gate

10. NRO, SPE514: Mansion house and land in St Clement and Catton

11. NRO, St Clement Norwich 887. The Revd Coll's property consisted of house, yard, lawn, garden, paddock and enclosure.

12. Ordnance Survey of the City and County of the City of Norwich. Surveyed 1883, published 1884-86.

13. NRO, N/EN 24/98 Denmark Farm Estate.

14. NRO, TC459: Sprowston Lodge Building Estate

15. NRO, TC726 This estate was sold for building by E. Heath in 1886. The property is 10 acres and 2 perches and described as house, cottages, stonemason's yard and garden ground.

16. NRO N/EN 24/9 Shipstone Road 25·th May 1893

17. Browne, p. 283. The *Oxford English Dictionary* states that the Pye (obsolete spelling) is 'now more usually called Magpie'.

18. Blyth, p. 5

19. NRO, TC785: Building sites on Magpie Road:

20. These buildings still stand despite the Council's intention to demolish them some years ago as being so badly built as not to merit modernisation (personal knowledge).

21. Willis Street was a new street built in the parish of St. Paul as part of the Corporation's adoption of the Artizans & Labourers' Dwellings Improvement Act 1875 - see Chapter 8 Substandard Houses and Slum Clearance.

22. Jarrold's 1905 Directory

23. Philip Sewell died in 1906 and bequeathed the Sewell Estate to the City of Norwich to become a public park (*The Sewell Connection. A Family A Community A Theatre* by Lorna Kellett [1979]

Chapter 7. Growth of the Suburbs
3: Thorpe Hamlet and Pockthorpe

East of the river are the parishes of Pockthorpe and Thorpe Hamlet. In 1801 the population of Thorpe Hamlet was only 74 and that of Pockthorpe 979 including the soldiers living in the Barracks. Pockthorpe encompassed a large area including Mousehold Heath, but the built-up portion was not much more than one long street - Pockthorpe Street (Kett's Hill)[1] - a continuation of Barrack Street within the walls which is marked on Millard & Manning's 1830 map. Pockthorpe, in the parish of St James, had once been a distinct village and had been incorporated into Norwich at any early date.[2] Thorpe Hamlet, originally part of the parish of Thorpe St Andrew, extended from Kett's Hill to Thorpe Road and encompassed the Dean and Chapter's meadows on the river Wensum. There are a number of large estates marked on Manning's c.1834 map, including the Mousehold Estate of General Sir Robert John Harvey, that of the Revd Sir George Stracey on Thorpe Road as well as that of John Harvey esq. John Harvey's house was in the village of Thorpe St Andrew, but he also had extensive holdings in Thorpe Hamlet.

The contrast between the two parishes could not be greater. Stacy, writing in 1819, described Pockthorpe: 'The street is uninteresting, it is thickly inhabited by the poorer class'[3] and Bayne, writing in 1869, described the inhabitants of Pockthorpe as very poor, and said that Thorpe Hamlet contained 'many handsome villas, which are mostly surrounded by gardens ... Many of the city gentry reside in this pleasant hamlet'.[4] He was repeating the information given in earlier directories, but elegant houses and large gardens remained a feature of many parts of Thorpe Hamlet throughout much of the 19th century (and into the 20th century). The Thorpe Hamlet described by Bayne was very probably Thorpe Road and Rosary Road where by 1869 there were a significant number of quality houses. However, when the author of *Excursions through Norfolk*, writing about 1825, described the 'several neat and respectable houses erected by the road-side'[5] he may have been referring to properties on Rosary Road near the junction with Thorpe Road. If Manning's 1835 plan of the City and County is accurate, there would have been relatively few houses on Thorpe Road in 1825 although their number gradually increased after the construction of Foundry Bridge in 1810. In contrast to the early country estates in the Thorpe Road area, the buildings in that part of Kett's Hill, also in the parish of Thorpe Hamlet, were poor and virtually indistinguishable from those in Pockthorpe of which it is an extension. The majority of the residents were similarly unskilled or semi-skilled.

The social composition of Pockthorpe and that of Ketts Hill and Plumstead Road remained virtually unchanged throughout the century: the 1830 poll shows that the majority of voters in Pockthorpe were engaged in the traditional trades of weaving, gardening, etc. The residents in the Thorpe Road area were mainly gentlemen or professional men. Later in the century, as more houses were built, the number of middle class and artisans living in this part of the parish increased, although they were fewer than those living in the other new suburbs and, in general, their occupations were more highly paid and/or more skilled especially after the opening of Norwich Thorpe Railway Station in 1844, large numbers being employed as guards, clerks, porters, etc.

Pockthorpe

The boundary of Pockthorpe is the site of the former Pockthorpe Gate on Barrack Street and the City wall and the hamlet extended to incorporate the northern side of Bull Close Road (north of the City wall) and the east side of Silver Road. Only Barrack Street (then called Bargate) and Pockthorpe Street are named in Millard & Manning's 1830 plan of the City, although Silver Road (one of the roads leading to Sprowston) is marked on the plan and listed in White's 1836 Directory as is The Paddocks (later called Silver Street).

Browne, writing in 1814, described the Horse Barracks on Barrack Street. This had been completed in 1794 at a cost of £20,000 and was much admired. It covered more than 12 acres and in 1814 there was accommodation for 250 officers and men. Apart from the remains of numerous ruined ecclesiastical buildings and the Barracks, he found little of note.[6] Patteson's Pockthorpe Brewery (later Steward & Patteson) founded in 1793, also situated on Barrack Street, was not mentioned. There had been a small brewery owned by Charles Grieves on this site which was sold to John Patteson II in 1793. Under Patteson, production expanded as the firm prospered (becoming Steward Patteson & Stewards 1820-31, Steward Patteson Finch & Co. 1837-95 and Steward & Patteson Ltd from 1895)[7] and small tenements were built in yards owned by the company. According to the 1851 census, there were eight yards: Bird in Hand, Little Brewery, Johnson, Griffin, George, Green, Robin Hood and Baker's and in three of them were public houses tied to the Patteson brewery.

The 1883 Ordnance Survey map shows the many tenements near the Brewery. These are, without exception, very small, some built back-to-back and many of them in yards. Only a few have gardens. The Light Horseman Public House on Barrack Street is mentioned in the 1836 Directory. This was owned by Steward & Patteson as were the seven cottages adjacent. The Griffin Public House, also on Barrack Street is also mentioned, as were a number of cottages in Griffin Yard. In this yard the privy and bin were shared, as was the right to take water from the pump. These cottages had been built by 1845[8] and were very small and crowded like so many of the buildings erected in the early part of the century. They were owned by the brewery and were some of a large number which it owned in Pockthorpe.[9]

By 1883 a number of new streets had been built and building plots had been marked out next to Barrack Loke and behind Silver Street in the 1883 OS map suggesting that building work would soon add to their number. There was dense housing in the Loke off Barrack Street and according to Jarrolds' 1892 Directory there were many small tenements in Anchor Street. Mousehold Street was built in the

20th century and the 1883 map shows the site of an old marl pit on what became Mousehold Avenue. A number of streets had been built by 1899 and are marked on the City Engineer's map. They are Harcourt Street, Balfour Street, Morley Street, Infantry Street and Cavalry Street, all in a small area between the brewery, Silver Road and Mousehold Heath. Very few residents are named in the various directories and the streets are listed as having 'small tenements'. Jarrolds directories give a good idea of the type of housing and the state of any buildings erected or to be erected. For example, Anchor Street is listed in 1893 as having small tenements, a building site and small shops as well as the Robin Hood Public House; all the building work had been completed by 1900. Morley Street had small tenements on one side of the street only in 1893 but was completely built up by 1900; Cavalry Street had small tenements in 1893 and two small shops. The 1905 directory states that in Harcourt Road, Balfour Street and Infantry Street no houses had yet been erected. The description of the new houses as 'tenements' suggests that the new houses were small, the owners unskilled and semi-skilled workers and that the status of residents had not changed during the century.

In the 19th century the poverty of the hamlet was universally acknowledged: the 1836 Directory speaks of several streets of humble dwellings.[10] Bayne, writing in 1869 says the parish is 'apparently wedded to poverty inhabited mainly by poor weavers and spinners,'[11] The 1841 Census return lists a large number of people living in Silver Street.[12] At that time the whole area was called Silver Street and the majority of the residents were very poor, with many men and women employed as silk weavers, some of them hand-loom weavers. There were small pockets of prosperity: the 1851 census lists William Dunn, a lucifer match maker who employed 48 labourers living in Silver Road and the listing of John Bussey, a farmer with 23 acres, is a reminder that the countryside was not far away. But in general the residents of Pockthorpe and especially of the yards leading out of Barrack Street were very poor. There were many paupers and labourers as well as weavers. In Baker's Yard eleven buildings housed 21 families and there was a lodging house in Griffin Yard with six lodgers. The tenements would have been very small, the 1851 census records eleven buildings housing 21 families in Baker's Yard.

The poor quality of housing in Pockthorpe had been confirmed by the report of the Inspector, William Lee, investigating the sanitary condition of the city in 1850. Mr Lee said Pockthorpe was 'found to be the residence of the worst characters in the city' (quoted by Walter Rye in a lecture on the History of Pockthorpe given in 1902).[13] Whether the poor housing conditions led to immorality, as was suggested by Mr Lee about Beckham's Yard in St James's parish, or whether a number of the inhabitants had criminal records is unclear. Conditions do not seem to have improved very much as a result of the Inspector's report. Walter Rye also spoke about the terrible conditions prevailing at Nickalls Square as an example of substandard accommodation (not a Steward & Patteson property but situated off Barrack Street) which had been condemned as a slum and was to be taken over for slum clearance by the Corporation. But the Corporation's expectations were low even when new buildings were erected: approval was given in 1894 for seven new houses on Silver Road between Wodehouse Street and Nightingale Lane where, despite the houses being connected to mains water with sinks connected to the sewer, all had earth closets at the bottom of the garden.[14] The situation was the same in 1900 when plans for six new houses in Mousehold Street were submitted for approval.[15] Although all houses had a kitchen sink connected to the sewer, they each had a privy at the back of the garden and the lack of water-closet was clearly indicated in the form which had to be completed by the builder. The form asks: 'Situation and dimensions of w.c.s and particulars of apparatus,' and the builder's written comment is *not water closets* (my italics). This also was approved. In each case these houses had been built to what was then considered an acceptable standard in conformity with the 1858 Norwich Board of Health By-Laws with respect to New Street and New Houses etc. and the 1877 Building Control Plans.

Kett's Hill and Central Area

Writers of 19th century histories and directories tend to copy each other and the fact that they continue to state that Thorpe Hamlet has 'many handsome villas' as late 1891 gives a false impression of uniformity which does not take into account the buildings in different parts of the neighbourhood. Although there certainly were some 'handsome villas' on St Leonard's Road, Rosary Road and Thorpe Road, the majority of the houses near Kett's Hill, where most of the buildings were originally located, were terraces, many of them very small. Those near the junction of Gas Hill and Bishopbridge Road had been built early in the 19th century for workers in the Gas Works, the lime works and the brick building trade. There were also many agricultural labourers living nearby. The proximity of the Barracks at Pockthorpe and Steward & Patteson's brewery may also have influenced development, although there is little indication in the census returns that many brewery workers lived here. A number of tenements had been built in what became known as Weeds Square[16] by 1823. These were small, and were built around a shared yard with shared bin, pump and facilities. These tenements adjoined the Gas Works which was erected by the British Gas Light Company on St Leonard's Hill (Gas Hill) in 1830. The 1901 Census returns of Weeds Square give an indication of the quality of buildings constructed. Listed are nine houses with only two rooms, six people living in one of them. In addition, there were also twelve houses with three rooms and fifteen houses with four rooms. Both the 1881 and 1901 census returns record many weavers, shoe-makers and labourers as well as laundresses, seamstresses and charwomen.

Many small artisan dwellings had been built on Kett's Hill near the Barracks by 1830 in an area called Little Spitalfield which backed onto St James's Hill in Mousehold. These houses no longer remain: none of the 51 residences listed in the 1901 Census had more than four rooms; one house was sub-divided and the residents' occupations were similar to those in Weeds Square. Some small sections of Kett's

Hill itself had similar poor-quality houses, although the majority had at least five rooms.

The census returns record changes in occupation of the residents in the western part of Thorpe Hamlet: by 1901 the number of houses and of residents had increased and their occupations were changing. There were fewer men with low-status jobs and very few farm labourers. The census lists electrical engineer, petroleum carter and a steam engine fitter and maker as well as some clerks. Although most of the clerks were very young, the sons of working-class men, their inclusion is significant in that it is extremely uncommon to find any office workers living either in houses on the main roads or in the tenements in the courts and yards in the poorer parts of Norwich, such as the parishes of St Paul or St James. The addresses for residents of this part of Thorpe Hamlet have to be treated with caution; as there were few named roads, very often the nearest large road was listed.

However, despite the buildings going up, much of the parish was largely unbuilt even as late as 1900. The gravel pit at the junction of Plumstead Road remained, and although a Mission Room was built on Kett's Hill in 1877, according to the Ordnance Survey of 1884 there were only a few buildings on the eastern side of the street. A number of roads had been built, but these were mainly near the Gas Works. The directory lists Albert Road in 1885 and Egyptian Road in 1890. On Rosary Road, the lime and brick works, listed in the 1841 Tithe Map for Thorpe Hamlet as being owned by George and Isaac Coalman, is still marked on the 1884 Ordnance Survey map. The 1875 directory had listed R.R. Ruymp as a lime burner and brick and tile maker on this site; the 1883 directory lists him as a brick and tile maker. The firm remained in business until 1934. Ruymp also had an interest in the construction of new streets and houses in Thorpe Hamlet. There is a plan dated 19th July 1886[17] in the Norfolk Record Office of proposed new roads and houses in an area which probably between St Leonard's Road, Rosary Road and Gas Hill. This was approved by the Corporation with a note 'roads only'; plots are drawn on the plan, but the work does not appear to have been carried out.

The Mousehold Estate

In 1821[18] General Sir Robert John Harvey's Mousehold Estate in Thorpe Hamlet which he inherited from his uncle, also Robert Harvey, encompassed a large area bounded by Telegraph Lane, Plumstead Road and Hearts Ease Lane. It also included land in Pockthorpe and off Kett's Hill and Gas Hill.[19] Sir Robert, Knight Commander of the Order of St Bento d'Avis, had seen active service during the Napoleonic Wars and many of the houses on his estate commemorated this fact: Magazine Cottages in Pockthorpe, St Bento, the Good Service Cottages and The Prize Cottages as well as the William IV Public House (also known as Mousehold Tea Gardens).

St Bento

Mousehold House itself was built 1820-2 and altered and extended 1829-36.[20] The North Lodge was enlarged by Sir Robert in 1822; this may have been the farmhouse that was mentioned in the Abstract of Title[21] to this estate, said to have been built in 1812. In 1841 Sir Robert lived in Mousehold House with his wife, two sons, three male servants and three female servants; a number of other male servants lived on the estate. Although some houses were built in the Mousehold Estate during the first half of the 19th century, land close to Mousehold House itself was not built upon until the 20th century. Manning's 1835 plan of Norwich shows only a few buildings on what appears as part of Harvey's estate. The nearest was the Black Mill which, according to Harvey's notes, was taken down and sold in 1831.[22]

Two albums of water-colour drawings, most of them dating from 1858 onwards, and also the Harvey Estate Plans and Drawings dated 1841-51, illustrate some of the houses erected on the estate.[23] The manuscript notes often refer to leasehold building land and the houses which were erected are illustrated, with a note giving a brief history with details of the properties. Judging from the drawings, each appears unique, and there is no suggestion of any systematised building plan of this estate as had occurred in most of the new suburbs where rows of houses were built along new streets. The drawings are of, at most, three cottages built in various parts of the estate. The streets or roads on which these lone houses were built were seldom named in the drawings but their location can be ascertained with the help of maps and directories.

The albums give some idea of the size and quality of the houses. Some of them were relatively modest: the Good Service Cottages were built on the site of a former Asphalt Manufactory near the gravel pits on Mousehold. There is a water-colour of these buildings with a plaque on the front with the date 1849 and 'Good Service Cottages'. A hand-written note states 'Good Service Cottages, late an Asphalt Manufactory, near the gravel pits on Mousehold, the property of Sir R. Harvey 1849 No. 1 "Called Good Service from Sir R. Harvey having a good Service Pension from the Queen".[24] The drawing is a bit difficult to interpret, but appears to show three cottages - two of them side by side and the third at the back of the first two. In Pockthorpe, two sets of three cottages are illustrated. These were called Magazine Cottages in about 1840, but in 1852 the names were changed to General's Cottages North and General's Cottages South. They were Sir Robert

Harvey's copyhold and were situated on Bishop's Bridge Road. Although these were very humble working-class residences, the 1901 census return records that each house had more than four rooms.

Good-quality houses built on St Leonard's Road included St Bento's. It is described on the plan as a 'look-out house on Mousehold Heath 1845 now called St Bento.'[25] The building had two cellars, a basement, kitchen, parlour, hall and passage, a wash-house and privy and bin. There were three bedrooms upstairs and an attic floor with bedroom and spare room. It shows a yard, stable and medium-sized garden and the date given is 1845. The plan also included an outline of three cottages which were called Kett's Camp and were situated on part of St Bento's yard. They had been built near to St Bento in 1853 and commemorated the place where Robert Kett was said to have made camp in 1549. These were very small cottages, just two rooms up and two down. The address of St Bento in Jarrold's 1889 directory is given as St Leonard's Road.

St Michael's Cottages,
(built c.1841 by General Sir Robert John Harvey)

Other houses illustrated in the albums include St Michael's Cottages built above the Gas Works about 1841, Wellington House built after 1859, Freneda Cottage 1856-9, and Surrey Cottages 1830-2. The 1851 census return gives some indication of the type of resident: an agricultural labourer and a schoolmaster lived in Asphalt Cottages (there is no indication of a resident in the third cottage); in St Michael's Cottages lived a woolman and a carpenter and in Press's House a labourer. Further up the social scale was a retired farmer who lived in St Bento Cottage, a master millwright who employed two men lived in one of General's Cottages and a wholesale grocer who employed 14 men lived in St Leonard's Cottage. There were two public houses on Harvey's land: William IV or Mousehold Tea Gardens, built in 1824, and Hearts Ease in 1836.

General Sir Robert John Harvey lived in Mousehold House until his death in 1860 and the house was afterwards occupied by his widow, Charlotte, aged 65, as landed proprietor and fund holder. She had a female companion and seven servants. After Lady Harvey's death, the census returns record various occupants: William Blackblock in 1881, Josiah Poyster in 1891 and Hugh Barclay in 1901. Blackblock was a non-practising barrister and a partner in the brewery of Morgan & Co; Poyster was a gentleman of independent means and Barclay a banker. The freeholder was Mr (later Sir) Robert John Harvey of Crown Point. He had purchased his brother Edward Kerrison Harvey's interest in the Mousehold Estate subject to the life interest of his mother.[26] Sir Robert Harvey died in 1870[27] and the property passed to his son, Sir Charles Harvey who is listed in the Altered Tithe Apportionment documents as the freeholder in 1874. Mousehold House remained a family home into the 20th century but was divided into flats in the late 1960s.

Thorpe Hamlet – the Bridges

Thorpe Hamlet is adjacent to Norwich but is divided from it by the river Wensum. In 1800 only one bridge crossed the river at Bishopgate. This narrow medieval bridge led to the hamlet and to the turnpike to Caister which was constructed in 1776 along Chalk Hill Road (later Rosary Road) and also gave access to the southern part of the hamlet. The map, included in Peck's 1802 Directory, shows there was a road from Bishopgate Bridge to Pockthorpe. Riverside Road, which links Bishopgate bridge to Foundry Bridge, was not built until 1890 and, apart from Rosary Road, the only access along the river from Bishopgate Bridge to Thorpe Road was what Morant in the 1872 map referred to as a 'towing path'. In addition there was a ferry across the river, Sandlings (later Pull's) ferry, which is shown on 18th century and later maps, and it is likely there was a footpath beside the river to what, according to Peck's map, seems to have been the site of the present Thorpe Road. On this map there is a drawing of a lane or path (in outline no different from the 'towing path' beside the river) but it does not go as far as the river. Foundry Road (also known as Foundry-bridge Road, later Thorpe Road) was probably built shortly after Foundry Bridge and ran from the bridge to the Yarmouth Road.

The Peck map shows habitations only near Kett's Hill and Bishopgate Bridge and nothing in the Thorpe Road area. Millard & Manning's map of 1830 shows a few large houses with extensive garden grounds in the area of what is now Thorpe Road and on Rosary Road, near to the Rosary Cemetery opened in 1821, the first non-denominational cemetery in England. The east side of Thorpe Road was meadow up to the river Wensum, the property of the Dean and Chapter of Norwich, and it was here that it was proposed to build a basin for sea-borne vessels as part of an only partly successful scheme to make Norwich a port.[28]

The building of Foundry Bridge in 1810 made this part of the hamlet easily accessible and the areas of 'meadow' in the Peck and Berry maps would have been prime building land. Foundry Bridge was a toll bridge, made mainly of timber. Browne, writing in 1814, makes no mention of it although he speaks of Thorpe St Andrew's good quality buildings and gardens. Before the bridge was erected there was no easy access from the Thorpe Road area to Norwich and even afterwards access may not have been easy. Once across the river, the route to the centre of Norwich seems to have been circuitous. The maps included in the Peck and Berry Directories suggest that there was only a narrow lane leading to St Faith's Lane (Mountergate). The traveller would then have had to proceed along Rose Lane until he reached King Street after which he would be still be some way from the centre of Norwich. By 1830 access seems to have improved as a road from the bridge to St Faith's Lane is clearly shown in the Millard & Manning map.

In 1810 another bridge was built crossing the Wensum at Carrow (Carrow Bridge) and a new road, called Carrow Road, opened up communication with the Yarmouth Road in Thorpe Hamlet. This was a link to the Yarmouth turnpike and to Great Yarmouth which had become accessible from Norwich since the building of a turnpike in 1800 that went via Caister-by-Yarmouth. The Acle turnpike (today called the Acle Straight) across the marshes was not built until 1834/5. However, there was no direct access from Carrow Road to Thorpe Road as there was only a towing path from Carrow Bridge to Foundry Bridge until late in the century.

The coming of the railway led to the replacement in 1844 of the wooden Foundry Bridge with an iron one when land to the east of Thorpe Road was acquired for Thorpe Railway station and goods yard. Once the station was up and running, improved access to Thorpe Hamlet became a necessity. Prince of Wales Road was built in the 1860s giving direct access to the centre of Norwich by-passing Rose Lane.

Thorpe Road[29]

The difficulty of access to Thorpe Road before 1810, even assuming there was suitable land for sale, would have made the Thorpe Road area unattractive to developers of low-cost artisan terraced dwellings. However, it was precisely this seclusion that had made this part of Thorpe Hamlet attractive to men of substance and led to the building of many superior dwellings and mansions with large gardens and pleasure grounds. In the early 19th century the advantages of living in the Thorpe Road area were many: near the centre of commercial activity and the intellectual and cultural pursuits in Norwich, yet partly isolated from the poverty, dirt and disease of the overcrowded city. Consequently, if the listings in the 1835 Poll are any indication of the generality of the residents, in Thorpe Road, Foundry Road and Chalk Hill Road, gentlemen, solicitors, clerks, clergymen and merchants were in the majority. Artisan development with its low-cost houses and squalor was well away near Pockthorpe and the rural industrial activity was confined there, in Kett's Hill and in the relatively uninhabited portions of the hamlet, away from the genteel residential areas.

However, during the century, the large estates in this part of the hamlet limited the amount of land available for building modest houses even when Foundry Bridge was built and this part of the hamlet became more accessible. One of the first large estates sold for building in Thorpe Hamlet belonged to the Revd Sir George Stracey and was sold freehold after his death in 1858. The property was divided into twelve lots for sale on 5th August 1858.[30] Stracey House itself was sold as a separate lot, but the terms of sale made it possible for the garden ground surrounding the house to be subdivided and built on. The area of this lot was large - 11 acres 1 rood 39 perches - and the sale particulars state that 'this lot is adapted as at present for a gentleman's residence, and from its frontage on the Foundry Road and proposed New Roads, the ground will admit of sites for several distinct Villas'. The remainder of the land was sold in eleven lots subject to covenants which made it clear that this was building land. There are a number of prohibitions: on the value of the buildings to be erected, with those on the turnpike to be of not less than £20 p.a. in value. Only private residences could be built and these, excluding the original residence, had to be placed on a building line. There were prohibitions on a variety of activities: no brick or lime to be made or burnt, no pigs kept, no trade or business to be carried on. The accoutrements of past country-house living would disappear with this sale. Lots 2 and 3 had been an integral part of the original building: Lot 2 comprised stables, wash-house, harness-room, barn, granary and other buildings and the plantation; Lot 3 the kitchen gardens, forcing pit and pump. The extent of the estate can be gauged by the road frontages: Foundry Road, Yarmouth Road, Carrow Road and the two new roads. The Stracey sale freed up much land for building and led to the construction of a number of new roads: Stracey Road, Lower Clarence Road and Clarence Road.

By the 1840s a number of more modest houses had been built on Foundry Road and Thorpe Road. Foundry Road Terrace and Thorpe Terrace are listed in the 1842 directory. They were not mansions, but high-quality terrace houses with gardens of moderate size which were built for 'genteel' residents, many of which were let to widows and single women of independent means. Other houses were larger, like the one sold by auction on 20th April 1831. This was an estate held under a 40 year lease from 2nd December 1824 at an annual rent of £7 from the Dean & Chapter of Norwich Cathedral.[31] The property sold was a newly built dwellinghouse then in the possession of the Revd George Day. It had about an acre of garden ground and adjoined Foundry Road. The Revd Day is listed as a Freeman in the 1835 Poll Book and in the 1836 Directory is described as the Vicar of Eaton Church.

The new parish

Thorpe Hamlet was only formally declared a separate ecclesiastical district as part of the City and County of Norwich in 1852, and the parish church of St Matthew, consecrated in 1851, was built on Rosary Road in the centre of the parish. Thorpe Hamlet Vicarage was built on Rosary Road near the church in 1863. This was an extensive parish, despite the comparatively small number of residents. Although Rosary Road was improved in 1776 when the turnpike was built, its *raison d'être* had originally been the chalk workings and there are few buildings marked on the 1830 map except for the houses which were built near the cemetery and the junction with Thorpe Road. St Leonard's Road, shown on the 1872 map, had a windmill and in 1867 was called Mill Lane. Quebec Road, Bishopbridge Road and St

Leonard's Road were not named on the 1872 map nor in contemporary directories but what in 1830 was marked 'footpath to Thorpe' was later called Telegraph Lane and 'footpath to Thorpe new Gas Works' became 'Gas House Hill' (these were roads to Thorpe St Andrew not to Thorpe Station) but by 1883 the roads were named and a few houses had been built. The 1872 map shows a chalk pit and brick field on Rosary Road, Newman's Chalk Pit and Lime Kiln on land that was to become Bishopbridge Road, Moore's Gravel Pits off Kett's Hill and Newman's Gravel Pits off Plumstead Road. The extensive Brick Works and Lime Kiln on Rosary Road, the gravel and sand pits on Kett's Hill and Quebec Road are also shown on the 1883 Ordnance Survey as is a saw mill on Kett's Camp Road. The survey shows further building, both of roads and dwellings, although the exploitation of the physical resources of this part of the hamlet has a long history and continued throughout most of the 19th century.

Although poll returns are by their very nature selective, it is interesting to compare those of the 1830 and 1835 elections. In 1830, the number living in Thorpe Hamlet was so small that the results were incorporated with those of Pockthorpe, but by 1835 the two parishes are listed separately. In 1830 the combined numbers for Pockthorpe and Thorpe Hamlet was 172; in 1835 for Pockhorpe alone it was 122 and 96 men voted in Thorpe Hamlet. As the number of men voting in Pockthorpe between 1830 and 1835 would probably not have increased significantly, this suggests that between 1830 and 1835 the number of voters in Thorpe Hamlet had increased by approximately 50. This was only a small increase given the fact that the number of eligible voters in 1835 had increased as a consequence of the 1832 Electoral Reform Act. The lists of voters in 1835 show a number of professional men, as well as so-called gentlemen and clerics in Thorpe Hamlet. Their names are listed in White's 1835 Directory and they are classified in the Poll Book as either freemen or occupiers. A number of freeholders are also listed, but most seem to have been non-resident as they cannot be found in the Directory and very few can be identified.

However, John Curr is an exception. He is in the Poll Book and also in the 1841 Tithe Apportionment Map List of Owners and Occupiers as holding a relatively large estate.[32] Resident freeholders include Sir Robert J. Harvey and the Revd Sir George Stracey who are listed in the Poll Book as freemen.

The population of Thorpe Hamlet in 1871 was only 2,714, in 1881 it was 2,864 and it had risen to 5,265 by 1891, but few roads were built until the late 1880s when the central portion of the parish was developed. The parish included a number of large estates in the area between Kett's Hill and Thorpe Road. The largest, as already described, was the Mousehold Estate of Sir Robert John Harvey. However, John Harvey, who held the Thorpe Lodge Estate in Thorpe St Andrew also held much land in Thorpe Hamlet on Thorpe Road itself and off Carrow Road. This included a house, shrubberies, yards, etc. occupied by Nicholas Bacon, premises occupied by Robert Browne and a mansion and grounds on Thorpe Road called Thorpe Grove which was occupied by William Foster bart. (Harvey's estate was sold after his death in 1841.)[33] Other relatively large holdings included the Hill House estate and the Aspland House Estate.

Much of this land was not developed until late in the 19th century and early in the 20th century. The number of large estates held back development, but a disincentive was the nature of the land itself, much of it hilly, scarred by the remains of former earth workings and by current industrial activity. Browne, in 1814, had written about very steep hills 'in some places inaccessible'[34] and it would probably not have been financially attractive to speculative builders; this in turn would have persuaded landowners to retain their land.

However, improvement of access to the hamlet, especially after the building of Prince of Wales Road, and the increase in the number of inhabitants in Thorpe Hamlet was not lost on landowners who were aware of the future economic potential of their property. Even as early as 1825 when a freehold estate was auctioned in eighteen lots[35] the land was described as 'eligible land for building'. The land for sale was between Bishopgate Bridge and Sandling's Ferry and may have been on Rosary Road, this being the only road near the river at that time. There is a handwritten note with the Sale Particulars which states that the land in question is 'desirable for Building upon - and ultimately must become valuable' which suggests that it held out hope, not for an immediate gain, but for a future profitable return.

The Hill House Estate

As mentioned, one of the estates marked on the Thorpe Hamlet Tithe Map was owned in 1841 by John Curr and the occupier was Robert Gilbert. This estate comprised mansion, shrubbery, plantation, paddock, etc. Its position on the Tithe Map is marked between Rosary Road and St Leonard's Road and it is likely that this was what was later known as the Hill House Estate. As John Curr is listed as a freeholder of property 'adjoining Rosary', it seems likely he was the owner. Robert Gilbert was not listed in the 1836 Directory, but in 1845 he was listed as a 'gent' living on Thorpe Road. (The different address is not significant as the directory compilers had difficulty in identifying properties in Thorpe Hamlet because there were so few roads). This estate had been advertised for sale by auction in the *Norwich Mercury* on 21st August 1841. The property, then said to be in the possession of Robert Gilbert esq., was described as a 'Villa Residence' with 15 acres and included, a large house with brew-house, a coach-house, stables, shrubbery, woodland, garden and paddocks.

In 1885 the owner of the Hill House Estate was I.B. Coaks. He is recorded in Kelly's 1875 directory as a solicitor with an office in Bank Plain, and commissioner to administer oaths in the Supreme Court and Perpetual Commissioner for taking acknowledgements of deeds by married women, etc. He was also secretary to the Norwich Corn Exchange Company. According to the 1883 directory, he headed the business of Coaks & Co. and was solicitor to the Norwich & Eastern Counties Freehold Land and Building Society. Although he held the freehold of the Hill House Estate, he was not resident. In the 1875 directory his address was given as Grove Road (today Cotman Road), Thorpe Hamlet, and in that of 1883 he was listed as living in Fern

Hill, Thorpe Hamlet. (As Fern Hill was situated in Grove Road, this was probably the same house). The 1881 census return records Hill House as the residence of James Southall, a boot manufacturer of the firm Willis & Southall.

The breaking up and selling of this estate brought about one of the most significant changes in the history of Thorpe Hamlet as it altered the social composition of this part of the parish by bringing a large number of lower middle class and artisan houses near to the larger and grander houses on Thorpe Road. There is a plan, dated 19th August 1885,[36] of five proposed new roads to be built: Marion, Florence, Ella, Ethel and Beatrice (named after the freeholder's daughters) which would divide up the Hill House Estate. In 1885 these roads were built from St Leonard's Road to the new road, Hill House Road (built about 1890) and Ella Road from Rosary Road to the remaining part of the Hill House property. The houses on the new streets were better than many similar houses built at that time in other parts of Norwich; they appear to have been intended for skilled artisans and lower-grade clerks as the 1901 census returns for Beatrice Road includes carpenter, clerk, insurance office superintendent, rail inspector and manager of a cutlery shop. The Building Control Plan for these properties describes terrace houses with four bedrooms and a water-closet upstairs.[37]

Hill House remained as a domestic residence into the 20th century. The size of the remaining property can be gauged by its description in the sale particulars when it was sold in two lots on 12th July 1932.[38] Lot 1 comprised a large house with basement and two wine cellars. There were four bedrooms and dressing room and two servants' bedrooms, back landing and back staircase. There were also two bedrooms on the second floor. This lot also included a cottage with four rooms. Lot 2 comprised building land with a frontage of about 130 ft to Hill House Road and extending to and having a frontage of about 120 ft on Ethel Road. There is a photograph of the property to be auctioned: it is a white-fronted brick house with slated roof and appears to have been built sometime between 1830 and 1850.

The Aspland Estate

The description of another large estate, bounded by the river Wensum, Wakefield House on Thorpe Road, Rosary Road and St Matthew's Road, as the Aspland Estate is a misnomer as it only became known as such in the 1870s when it was purchased by Robert Aspland Cooper. This property, which is marked on the Millard & Manning 1830 plan of Norwich, was originally held by John Kitson esq. Kitson was secretary to the Bishop of Norwich for 58 years, having been appointed in 1811. He was Registrar in 1825 and was Chapter Clerk and Registrar to the Dean & Chapter, and district registrar in Her Majesty's Court of Probate. He was the son of Mr Charles Kitson who lived in Tombland and had been one of the Chapter Registrars of the diocese of Norwich. John Kitson's address is regularly given as Foundry Road and he is listed in the 1835 Poll as an occupier and said to be living 'near Foundry Bridge'. Kitson is also listed as occupier of a mansion belonging to the Dean & Chapter of Norwich Cathedral in the 1841 list of owners and occupiers in the Thorpe Hamlet Tithe Apportionment Map and in the directories from 1830 onwards as resident in Thorpe Hamlet. Kitson died in 1869 and by 1875 Robert Aspland Cooper was recorded as owner of what then became known as the Aspland Estate. The address of the property as listed in the various directories was always Foundry Road (onto which the house backs). Although Robert Aspland Cooper was not at home on census day in 1881, his wife and sons were there. He had two sons, aged 28 and 27 and both were confectioners. Cooper was a successful businessman and in the 1885 Directory he is described as a wholesale confectioner with premises at 9 & 11 Queen Street, with works at Albion Works, King Street and Cooper's Restaurant in Bank Plain. (according to Mathieson's 1867 Directory, Jay & Sons, mohair and worsted spinners had premises in Albion Mills).

Part of the Aspland Estate was purchased for £3,022 by Norwich Town Council for the construction of Riverside Road in 1890[39] and Aspland Road was built by 1899. On the south side of the road there are white brick houses which were built about that time and building work had started on the opposite side of the road from Aspland House when the Jarrolds' 1905 Directory was published. The sale of Aspland House in 1923[40] gives some indication of the quality of the house. The property was sold at auction in three lots on 3rd August 1923. By that time Aspland House itself had been divided into two houses. The East half had six bedrooms and was said to be suitable for a boarding house or nursing home. The west half had five bedrooms.

The Thorpe Road section of this estate was sold for building high-quality terrace houses in 1893 when plans for four terrace houses were approved.[41] (Cooper did not sell the entire frontage on Thorpe Road and retained land on either side of the proposed development.) These houses had basement with kitchen, back kitchen and water-closet, ground floor with large dining and drawing rooms and study and first and second floors, each with three bedrooms. There was a bathroom with water-closet on the first floor. Although obviously intended as family homes, their proximity to the railway station led to them soon becoming apartments and three lots of apartments are listed in the 1900 directory. (This was similar to what had occurred on Prince of Wales Road on the other side of the river.)

Pockthorpe and Thorpe Hamlet in 1900

Pockthorpe and Thorpe Hamlet have been discussed together because one part of Thorpe Hamlet is a continuation of Pockthorpe and its development over the century has been very similar. In every other respect, they were, and continue to be, very different. By 1900 most of the large estates near to Thorpe Road had been sold and the land divided up with good-quality terrace houses being built in much the same way as they had been on Unthank and Earlham roads. The Kett's Hill area remained unchanged with many small tenements. A number of new streets were being laid down in the Thorpe Road area: Cozens Road was listed in 1899 with building work of 'many small tenements' still continuing in 1905; Chalk Hill Road (named after the original Chalk Hill later called Rosary Road) listed in Jarrold's 1899 Directory, built up by 1905, and Primrose Road listed in 1899 only partially built up with small tenements in 1903. But a large part of the hamlet remained nearly completely untouched: the Harvey Estate, a large country estate, was no longer in the country, but in the new suburb. Thus Thorpe Hamlet, unlike every other suburb that was built outside the walls in the City of the County was a largely 20th century suburb.

Chalk Hill Cottage (House)

Notes

1. Pockthorpe was the name given to the only street in the parish and this encompassed Barrack Street, and the name Kett's Hill (outside the City) seems only to have been current from the 1870s (in Morant's 1873 map of Norwich).

2. Browne, P. *The History of Norwich from the Earliest Records to the Present Time,* Norwich 1814 states that the parish was united with that of St James at the dissolution (p. 306)

3. [Stacy, John] *A topographical and Historical Account of the City and County of Norwich,* 1819

4. Bayne, A.D. *A Comprehensive History of Norwich,* p. 106

5. *Excursions through Norwich,* p.32

6. Browne, pp. 304-5

7. Gourvish, Terry *Norfolk Beers from English Barley. A History of Steward & Patteson 1793-1963* lists a number of public houses owned by this firm.

8. See BRI Steward & Patteson Ltd. Trust Deeds 30 July 1895 63.11.9 1885.

9. NRO, BR1146. Steward & Patteson Ltd. Trust Deed 30 July 1895 and Pockthorpe Brewery Deeds, N/TC/D1/659 ff.

10. White's 1836 Directory, p. 156

11. Bayne, p. 108

12. According to various directories and plans, this street was called The Paddock in 1836, Silver Street in 1884 and The Paddocks in 1899

13. Walter Rye's lecture on Pockthorpe and District was published in the *Eastern Daily Press* in 1902

14. NRO, TC/EN/12/2584 Properties on Silver Road and Wodehouse Street

15. NRO, N/EN/29/2/4016 Mousehold Street

16. NRO, TC780 1-3 Weeds Square

17. NRO, N/EN 24/7 Plan of new road leading from Rosary Road

18. NRO, BR46/7 'Rosary' Rosary Road. See also Rye, Walter *Norfolk Families*, Norwich 1913, pp.313-16 for information about the Harvey family.

19. NRO, Thorpe Hamlet Tithe Apportionment Map and 1841 List of owners & occupiers

20. NRO, MC 91/1/17, MC 91/1/18 Plans of Mousehold House

21. NRO, BRA46/7 'Rosary' Rosary Road

22. Norwich Castle Museum, *Views of the Mansion and Farm Houses ......belonging to Col. Sir Robert John Harvey TS 1830*, VOL. 1

23. There are two series of watercolours: one is in the Art Department at Norwich Castle Museum
and is entitled *Views of the Mansion and Farm Houses and Cottages, ...belonging to Col. Sir Robert John Harvey KTS 1830*, Vols. 1 and 2. The other is in the Norfolk Record Office reference
MC91 and contains a list of Harvey Estate Plans and Drawings 1841-1881

24. NRO, MC91/1/38 Good Service Cottages

25. Norwich Castle Museum, *Views of the Mansion and Farm Houses ......belonging to Col. Sir Robert John Harvey KTS 1830*, Vol. 1. This refers to both Magazine Cottages and St. Bento as well as the other named houses on the estate.

26. *Norfolk Annals* Vol. 2, p. 97

27. Sir Robert was responsible for the collapse of Harvey & Hudson's Crown Bank and committed suicide in 1870. *Norfolk Annals* Vol. 2, p. 203.

28. See Bayne pp. 361-5 which relates the history of the plan, where despite partial success, it was impossible to complete because of the opposition of Great Yarmouth.

29. Thorpe Road was originally called Foundrybridge Road or Foundry Road ran from the Foundry Bridge to Chalk Hill Road after which was called Thorpe Road.

30. NRO, SPE28 Estate in Thorpe Hamlet

31. The sale particulars are part of a collection of papers deposited by Cozens-Hardy in the Norfolk Record Office

32. The 1835 Poll Book lists John Curr as being a freeholder of property adjoining Rosary and he is also listed as such in the Tithe Apportionment Map 1841 List of Owners and Occupiers

33. NRO Thorpe Hamlet Tithe Apportionment Map and 1841 List of owners and occupiers.

34. Browne, p. 309

35. NRO, SPE1 Eligible land for building in Thorpe Hamlet

36. NRO, N/EN 24/1 19th August 1885 - Hill House Estate

37. NRO, N/EN/1/1774 Hill House Road, Thorpe Hamlet

38. NRO, BR241/4/984 Hill House, Hill House Road

39. *Norfolk Annals* 29 October 1890

40. NRO, BR 241/4/64 Aspland House: Rosary Road and Chalk Hill Road

41. NRO, N/EN 12/1/2406 Proposed four houses R.A. Cooper's Estate

Chapter 8. Substandard Houses and Slum Clearance

Norwich entered the 20th century with some of the worst slum property in England. On a smaller scale, it rivalled the slums of London and other large industrial towns. And yet early 19th century writers had praised its splendid houses and gardens. One of the reasons for the large number of slum dwellings was that many well-built timber-framed buildings - relics of Norwich's past prosperity – had been abandoned when wealthy merchants and traders started moving into new modern brick-built houses in the suburbs early in the 19th century. The buildings that they left were let; they were divided and subdivided, and small tenements were erected in their gardens and courtyards. The transformation of houses into slum tenements had already started in the 18th century as can be seen in Hochstetter's 1789 map of Norwich which shows the encroachment of small dwellings into the old courts and yards. The 16th century home of Sir Nicholas Bacon, on Ber Street beside the church of St Michael at Thorn, is just one of a number of houses that had been converted into small tenements. The quality of the mid-15th century Old Merchant's House on King Street was recognised only during the restoration of the building in 1979-88 when a splendid carved dragon was discovered in the spandrel of one of the tie-beams, hence the naming of the building as Dragon Hall in the 20th century.[1]

In 1819 Stacy had written about the large number of houses being built: the city walls had houses built along them, as did the area just outside the walls, and within the city 'each vacant space within the city, that circumstances permit, seems also about to be appropriated to the use of the builder'.[2] The author of the Health of Town Commission's Report 1845 attributed the deterioration of the health of the inhabitants partly to 'the custom of covering of gardens and unoccupied spaces with buildings, mostly cottages, closely packed together and numerously occupied by very poor persons'.[3]

Urban Slums

'To a Londoner, accustomed to what Norwich people no doubt refer to as East End slums, it is still something of an adventure to go through the unlighted nooks and corners of Ber Street or Pockthorpe after dark...' (Hawkins)

In 1910[4] the housing of the working classes in many parts of Norwich was so bad that even sophisticated Londoners would be shocked by what they saw. Although a start had been made in slum-clearance in the 19th century by the application of the Norwich Corporation Act 1889, there was still a lot to do. Overcrowded courts and yards in the city centre and poor quality houses built in the early 19th century, both within the walls and in the new suburbs, had left the city with an enormous number of sub-standard buildings, pasture and market gardens having given way to large numbers of very small houses (see chapter 5).

The houses and cottages built in the early part of the 19th century, their type and size, the method of sanitation and the availability of water had, to a large extent, been governed by what was acceptable at that time. Expectations of artisans and labourers were very much lower in the early 1800s than they were at the end of the century and even better-quality, so-called 'genteel' houses often had defective sanitation. The Health of Towns Act was passed in 1850 to deal with problems associated with inadequacies in the water supply and sanitation. Population growth had made the previous *ad hoc* arrangements unsustainable, a national problem which Norwich shared with other large towns.

There had been little control over the quality of houses prior to 1858 when the Norwich Board of Health Bye Laws were enacted following the city's adoption of the 1850 Health of Towns Act. There was further regulation of the quality of houses when, after July 1877, Building Control Plans for new houses had to be submitted for approval.[5] However, standards were low and only related to new buildings; the problems of building in the courts and yards do not appear to have been addressed until after 1889 when the Norwich Corporation Act was passed. Some early slum clearance had been possible by the Artizans' and Labourers' Dwellings Improvement Act of 1875 which enabled the Corporation to deal with the substandard older houses, although reports of the Courts & Yards Committee of 1897 and the Housing of the Working Classes Act Committee of 1890 showed how much there was still to be done. Slum clearance was always fraught with problems: difficulties in acquiring property and the financing of the work.

The City - the building of small tenements

Browne's tour of Norwich in 1814 found much substandard building. His survey took in the King Street area and he described Holgate (Mariner's Lane) and Skeygate (Horn's Lane) as 'steep, devious and disagreeable'. He reserved particular condemnation for Fuller's Hole describing it as 'a double row of buildings of the meanest description....part of which are level with the road, and others at the bottom of a deep defile which had originally been filled with water'.[6] Fuller's Hole was in the parish of St Martin at Oak and the 1861 census return lists 40 families and a total of 163 people living there. Although quite a number of the tenements housed only one or two people, there were two with ten residents, two with nine and two with eight. The tenements still remained in 1883 when the Ordnance Survey was made and there seems to have been little change when the survey was updated in 1905. In 1883 there was a tannery nearby and the area was said to be liable to flooding. Although it is possible that in the interim the buildings to which Browne had taken exception were replaced with other equally poor-quality tenements, this seems unlikely. Fuller's Hole, variously listed as off Coslany Street (in the 1861 census) and St Martin's at Oak Street (in the 1890 Directory), is near to Robinson's Yard in Oak Street; this part of Norwich was served with an improvement notice in 1904 by the Courts & Yards Committee and considered for demolition.[7] This was a large area on

Oak Street near to the junction with Sussex Street and very near to Fuller's Hole.

While property owners in the suburbs protected their land by means of restrictive covenants, land was sold in the city with few restrictions and consequently newly built houses very soon became slums. This may have been the fate of a freehold estate in All Saints and St Michael at Thorn parishes in 1833[8] which is described in the sale particulars as a good quality house being newly built and having a small sitting-room, dining-room, kitchen, cellar, drawing-room, three bedrooms, small front garden and a larger back one with a summer-house. It seems to have still been standing in 1883 when the Ordnance Survey was made but by then it was surrounded by a multiplicity of yards including Jubilee Yard, Malsters Court and Bakers Arms Yard, and could no longer have been a desirable place to live.

Land between Ber Street and King Street was also being sold: a large number of small tenements were built in 1826[9] between Thorn's Lane and Horn's Lane on land owned by the late James Alderton. Sale particulars refer to houses and streets 'which may hereafter be erected thereon' - probably Bartholomew Street and Garden Street. There were two properties already erected which were described as 'excellent dwellinghouses with convenient outbuildings, carpenters' shops, counting room, sheds, yard, garden and ground'. They were said to be 'exceedingly well calculated for carrying on the business of a builder'. These two houses were obviously intended for purchasers of substance, but there were no covenants to protect the land from further building and as the purchaser was only required to place any dwellinghouse or other buildings 'which may hereafter be erected' on the building line, the implication of the sale particulars was that they were unlikely to remain in their present form. Indeed the words 'any dwelling house' suggest that other buildings would follow.

Tenements in this part of Norwich were well established in 1850 when a number of small dwellinghouses were sold at auction.[10] These were probably either in Garden Street or Bartholomew Street, a total of eight houses in four lots. Six properties had a wash-house and four rooms - two up and two down. The other two were slightly larger, one having a large yard. As with many properties on sale at this time, there is no mention of sanitary provision, but all eight properties shared a single pump and well.

There were additional small streets in this part of Norwich, many of them first mentioned in Rogers' 1859 Directory: Compass Street, Julian's Alley, St Julian's Street, Russell Street, but the Millard & Manning map suggests that streets were in process of being laid out in this part of Norwich as early as 1830. The 1883 Ordnance Survey shows the numerous small tenements. The entrance to Russell Street, for instance, is through an alley communicating with Ber Street. Russell Place West is a terrace facing Russell Street, but Russell Place East faces onto a narrow passage. The map also shows many densely built-up areas including Lower Square, off Thorn Lane's, and St Julian's Alley which are covered with very small tenements with no access to the streets except through narrow passages.

There were even estates for sale which had no frontage on the street: the houses in an estate on St John's Timberhill was auctioned in

1848.[11] The entrance was from Scoles Green, but the road marked on the plan leads only to an 8 ft passage on which three of the plots fronted and the only requirement was that all buildings should be placed in line.

Beckwith Court, Quayside, c. 1900

The worst tenements were built before the Norwich Board of Health Bye-laws of 1858. As these related only to new houses and new streets, this did not affect older properties which continued to be divided and sub-divided throughout the century and the 1877 Building Control Plans also referred only to new buildings. And the Corporation's authority under the 1877 Building Control Plans related to new houses and new streets only to the extent of ensuring the provision of proper drainage and so the degree of control over the kind of buildings erected was minimal. As there was no control over sanitary provision, the situation was not much improved by the building regulations and the new houses built within the walls were often of poorer quality than those built in the new suburbs. For instance, plans were submitted for eleven cottages in Mariner's Lane in December 1878.[12] These cottages had four rooms: two up and two down, each with its own privy and ashpit. There is no mention of water being laid on and yet plans for nine cottages in nearby Horns Lane, submitted in July 1880 for similar cottages, had water laid on in the kitchen/scullery although they had no water-closets.[13] There appears to be no reason why some residents had water laid on and why some had to make do with obtaining water from a stand-pipe in the yard.

St Paul's

Although the implementation of Section 52 of the Norwich Corporation Act 1889 led to the start of large-scale clearance, it was not the first attempt to improve the housing stock. In 1877 the Corporation sent a petition to the Local Government Board that an improvement scheme be made under the Artizans & Labourers' Dwellings Improvement Act of 1875[14] with reference to a part of the parish of St Paul's which had been declared unhealthy and unfit for habitation by the Medical Officer of Health. In consequence, the parish of St Paul has the distinction of being the first one in Norwich to be the subject of slum clearance, with a large area near St Paul's churchyard being purchased by the Corporation and the buildings demolished. Although the Inspector's report in connection with the Health of Towns Act 1847 stated that St Paul's had some of the worst buildings, it is unclear why it was chosen in view of the large number of substandard houses in many other parishes which seem to have been just as bad.

The Millard & Manning map of 1830 shows that even though the parish was largely built up, there was still a considerable amount of garden ground and pasture. The octagonal tower of St Paul's church had been re-built about 1819 and work carried out on its interior, including putting in new pews in 1841.[15] In 1854 a harmonium was installed and in 1857 an appeal was made by the parishioners for funds to repair the church fabric. This suggests that at that time there was sufficient interest and money to keep the church in repair. In the 1830s there were a few good-quality houses. This is evident from the sale particulars of a freehold estate sold in two lots in 1835.[16] Lot 1 was a messuage with a large garden which was occupied by John Campling. The 1836 Directory lists him as a shawl manufacturer. Lot 2, a messuage with a large yard, garden and stable was occupied by James Basey, a bricklayer who is listed as such in the Directory. Both properties were in Cowgate.

The number of people living in this parish had nearly doubled between 1811 and 1871, having risen from 1583 to 2962. This was a very small parish and the increase in numbers could only have been achieved by building a large number of tenements and using all available vacant land including garden ground. The vendors of land in St Paul's were little interested in the future use of their property (probably because there were already substandard buildings on it). It is also true that the greater the decline in the market for such houses within the walls, the greater was the incentive to subdivide the large properties.

Sale particulars of properties in the parish of St Paul all refer to tenements or cottages already erected, but some include land which could be used for building. For instance, a freehold estate situated near the church of St James was sold on 23rd January 1827 in seven lots. Included are a public house - the Ship Tavern - and four tenements. Lot 6 is described as a 'piece of ground .... well calculated for the erection of a tenement or cottage'.[17] Like the other tenements for sale, it is situated in the Ship yard. The inhabitants of these tenements had to share the same water pump, privy and bin located in the yard. This property was recommended for investment purposes. Although no rental income was mentioned in these sale particulars, this was the exception for properties of this type.

In 1847 thirteen houses and cottages in Judd's Thoroughfare,[18] opposite St Paul's churchyard, were sold in seven lots. A considerable amount of detail is given: most of the dwellings were in Thoroughfare Yard and had no frontage on the highway and many were in multiple occupation. Seven families lived in the two dwellinghouses opposite the churchyard and what was called a 'cottage with low rooms' at the back of them. Three dwellinghouses in Judd's Thoroughfare also had seven families. This estate also shared a pump, privy and bin.

The Inspector's report of 1847 in connection with the Health of Towns Act, which specifically mentioned the sanitary facilities in St Paul's, had aroused some controversy. Reference had been made to White Lion Court, a court containing twelve houses, a stable and a slaughter house with a common privy, one of the residents being a gauze weaver. The report was mentioned in the *Norfolk Chronicle* in a series of letters one of which, on 19th January 1850, said it was not surprising that the Inspector found much to criticise when he inspected houses in St Paul's parish. What he had found there was not typical 'of the Norwich Weaver or his abode' because in St Paul's he would find the 'most wretched squalor and poverty... it is the resort of the lowest of the low, and the most idle, and the beggars of the city'.[19]

The Artizans Dwellings Committee had agreed on 13th December 1878 that application be made to the Local Government Board requesting the Board to exercise its powers under the 243rd Section of the Public Health Act 1875.[20] This gave the Corporation authority to purchase the land from the various freeholders which, once it was cleared, had to be sold for rebuilding. There were difficulties in carrying out the plan: although compulsory purchase was an option, the Corporation preferred to deal with each freeholder individually and come to a mutually agreed price. However, although the freeholders were happy to sell, in practice their valuations were often unrealistic. They were also unwilling to accept the independent valuations given and there were numerous appeals against the price offered. The land of the Revd T. Goodwin, who had the largest property, was the first to be purchased. Mr Goodwin said his land had been valued 'a few years ago' at about £4,000 and would not accept the Corporation's offer of £1460, the price fixed by the Arbitrator. Finally, in order to conclude the matter which had been running on for more than a year, the offer was raised to £1800 and this was agreed. The remainder of the freeholders had smaller holdings and many of them were also unhappy with the valuations given. Because of the many appeals ending in arbitration, the whole procedure was time-consuming and expensive, leading to a delay in re-building.

The Corporation not only had to pay the costs of the vendors' solicitors, of arbitration and of valuation, but also any extraneous damage such as that said to have been caused to St Paul's church by the building work, the vicar claiming that the church wall and church had been damaged in the course of alterations to the road. This matter was resolved by the Corporation purchasing a section of the churchyard to widen the road. The Corporation built the roads, sewers, water mains and purchased the land.

After completion, the property purchased was advertised for sale. Detailed specifications of the houses to be erected were given and on 12th February 1879 Mr Ambrose Winter offered to purchase the first ten building sites at £5 per rod. However, there does not seem to have been any great enthusiasm to purchase. The Minutes state that Mr Winter 'had been led to make this offer feeling that the scheme wanted a Start and from no thought of making any profit out of the speculation but that should any profit be made he had determined to give half thereof to the city Charities'.[21] Mr Winter was not alone in his lack of enthusiasm and the sale proceeded slowly; land was still being cleared prior to rebuilding a year after Mr Winter made his original offer. The final purchaser was Albert Waterton, a builder of St Clement's Hill, who bought 30 rods at £5 per rod to build 16 houses.

The 1883 Ordnance Survey of Norwich shows the parish after the demolition of the properties beside St Paul's churchyard. A new street had been built – Willis Street – with neat rows of houses running from Back Lane (part of Peacock Street) to Cowgate. The houses are small; there is no front garden and only a very small yard at the back of each house. (An interesting comment by an antiquarian is Hibgame's lament for the demolition of the 'singularly quaint half-timbered houses' in St Paul's and their replacement by what he called 'dozens of hideous red-brick cottages'.)[22]

Slum Clearance within the city after 1889

Apart from St Paul's, the Corporation did nothing about improving the houses within the walls until 1899 when a bye-law was agreed which led to the appointment of the Courts & Yards Committee,[23] empowered to order the paving of yards and to ensure that the water-closets were supplied with sufficient water for flushing or that a sufficient earth closet or privy be supplied and that there should be an ashpit furnished with proper doors and coverings.

A description of the yards and courts that the Corporation was endeavouring to improve or demolish in the Courts & Yards Committee report of 11th July 1898[24] is summarised below:

> *The approach to the yards is generally through a narrow covered passage. The yards are as a rule in two or more divisions.....The divisions farthest from the Street are sometimes approached through two other covered passageways, the surface of which is stony and in a very rough condition. The drainage is defective the closets which are often in close proximity to the fronts of the houses are either middens or pan closets.....Water in a large number of cases is supplied by a pump drawn from a well sunk in the soil.*

The provisions of this bye-law led indirectly to a significant amount of slum clearance. The problem was first considered in 1897 and the Committee drew up a list of yards to be dealt with first. Advice was sought from other councils which had taken action against slum dwellings after doubts were expressed about the legality of the Corporation's actions. Leicester and Liverpool replied that they had no powers other than those contained in the Public Health of 1875 but other councils - Newcastle and Sheffield - had had special Acts drafted.[25]

What was in doubt was whether the courts and yards were places open to the public and therefore highways, or whether they were private property from which the public could be excluded. The Town Clerk reported to the Courts & Yards Committee on 1st April 1898[26] that even though the courts and yards were cul-de-sacs, they were Public Highways and Streets at the passing of the 1835 Highways Act and according to the Public Health Act 1875 which defined a street as including 'any Square, Court, Alley or Passage whether a thoroughfare or not'.

The Committee, still being unsure of its legality, decided that the opinion of Counsel should be sought. The letter sent to Counsel which was reported at the meeting of 11th July 1898 gives a full description of the problem. It stated that the Courts & Yards Committee had been appointed on 15th December 1897 to investigate the condition of old dwellinghouses in the courts and yards and how the expense of improvement should be borne. There were about 650 of these, mainly in Ber Street, St Benedict's, St Martin's, Botolph Street, Fishgate Street, Cowgate Street and Barrack Street and the entrance to each yard was from these streets. It stated that they are generally 'of ancient character' and cul-de-sacs, some leading to the river, and none of the yards was lighted. These yards had never been sewered, paved or lighted; there was an insufficiency of water supply, closet or privy and ashpit accommodation and surface drainage and the owners were being required to comply with the provisions of the Public Health Act. The letter went on to describe the yards, stating that they did not seem overcrowded and the average rent was 2s. 6d. per week and separate rooms were let at 1s. In general the letting was in tenements of one room. The letter continued with the following proposals:

House at St Martin at Plain before and after restoration

(1) that the provisions of the Public Health Act as regards (a) insufficiency of water supply; (b) insufficiency of closet or privy and ashpit accommodation; (c) surface drainage be rigidly enforced.

(2) that power be delegated to the Committee in such yards as they at their discretion may determine to require the frontages pursuant to the Norwich Corporation Act 1889 to sewer level and pave the yards.

(3) That the Corporation contribute the expense of sewering under No. (2) recommendation

(4) that power also be delegated to the Committee to have such yards as they in their discretion may determine lighted at the public expense under section 161 of the Public Health Act.

Counsel's opinion[27] was reported to the Committee:

> 'the Corporation had only to shew a prima facie case that these yards, courts, etc. are private places not repairable by the inhabitants at large and it would be for the Owners to bring evidence to rebut it and that in respect to lighting the lamps, fittings, etc. [this] would have to be paid by the Owners and the Gas by the Corporation.'

As a consequence, it was reported to the Committee on 16th November 1898 that Mrs Dixon, the sole owner of Gaffer's Yard, St Benedict Street was to be served with a Provisional Apportionment on the following grounds: that the 16 houses in Gaffers Yard were without a sufficient water closet, earth closet or privy, that the street be sewered, levelled, paved, metalled, flagged, kerbed, channelled and made good, and proper means of lighting be provided. Mrs Dixon objected to the Provisional Apportionment on two grounds: that either Gaffer's Court was not a street, or did not form part of a street within the meaning of part 8 of the Norwich Corporation Act 1889 or, if Gaffers Yard was found to be a street it was a highway repairable by the inhabitants at large.[28] In view of the importance of the matter, the Committee decided that Counsel be briefed to appear before the Magistrates.

Although there is no further mention of Mrs Dixon's objection in the Minutes, it would appear that she was unsuccessful because on 6th March 1899 a deputation representing the owners of cottage property met the Town Clerk with some counter proposals as to the additional work which the Committee required to be done. In particular, the suggestion that a water-closet be provided was objected to. This was considered 'an unfair demand as the class of tenants there were in the yards, water-closets would always be out of order and choked up'. A privy bin system was suggested instead but the Committee would not accept this modification to the plan. It did make one concession however, and agreed that until the occupiers got accustomed to the water-closets the inspectors would look after the sanitary conditions in the same.

The Courts & Yards Committee, at its initial meeting on 15th December 1897 had named a number of yards off Barrack Street, Ber Street, Cowgate, Oak Street, St Mary's Plain and St Benedict's Street and a report to the Town Clerk on these yards confirmed that these required to be dealt with under the Act.[29] In addition to the above, properties in yards off Fishgate Street and Peacock Street were inspected and also found to be without 'sufficient water closet, earth closet or privy and ashpit furnished with proper doors and coverings'[30] and the work to be done was authorised by the Corporation. Knowledge of the quality of habitations in the courts and yards may have led to the initial inspections, but the lack of sanitation was not confined to them. Many of the houses facing the streets were also found to be without sanitary facilities of any kind including 3-11 Fishgate Street, 43-47 and 8-12 Peacock Street and 36-38 Barrack Street. This initial inspection confirmed that the sanitary facilities in many of the yards were also for the use of persons living in houses fronting the streets.[31]

As had been the case with Gaffer's Yard, there were many objections. Some of the land-owners objected to the apportionment, some ignored the order, some disagreed about the necessity of doing all the work, some asked to pay by instalments. In 1900 the owner of one of the properties in Priory Yard, Cowgate, asked the Corporation to purchase her property, the rents received were so low she could not afford to have the work done.[32] This purchase was complicated by the fact that there was more than one owner and the Corporation was only willing to purchase the whole yard for a housing scheme if all agreed to sell. This difficulty being overcome, the unrealistic valuations given by the owners led the Corporation to withdraw its offer. The sale was only completed by October 1902, and the site cleared by December of that year. Nickall's Square, Butcher's Yard and 49 and 52 Barrack Street were also purchased by the Corporation at the same time.

The scale of the problem facing the Corporation can be gauged by the Chief Sanitary Inspector's report given to the Courts & Yards Committee on 28th February 1899. There were:

> 4614 houses in 681 yards
> 6699 persons living in them under 15
> 9590 persons living in them over 15
> 106 yards with only pump supply
> 559 with Company's water
> 145 buildings used as workshops
> 1582 houses fronting the streets use yards
> 5801 people living in such houses
> Total population: 22,090
> Sanitary condition of yards: 69 fair, 445 bad, 167 very bad

The actions of the Courts & Yards Committee, although bringing a degree of improvement to these tenements, did not address the problem of unsatisfactory housing. The small size of the cottages and the large number of single room tenements, and in particular the large number of people living in overcrowded conditions was unsatisfactory. The clearing of the yards and courts was continuing slowly, and where necessary the people displaced were housed in the newly built areas. This was what was planned when the compulsory purchase and demolition of tenements between Oak Street and the river between Wensum Park and the New Mills Bridge as well as the Sun Yard area was agreed.[33]

However, the Corporation's policy changed after 1900 when a Special Committee, appointed on 29th May 1900 to consider the application of the Housing of the Working Classes Act 1890, decided that the purchase of land for housing in outlying parts of the city and County should be considered[34] (the work-force relying on the tramways for access to the city). At that meeting the City Engineer was asked to report on suitable properties and the members agreed to recommend to the Council that a scheme be authorised for the purchase of land to erect houses to be let to tenants at not more than 2s. 6d. per week. A number of suitable properties were inspected and on 17th October 1900 it was agreed that the Ecclesiastical Commissioners be asked the terms on which they would grant a building lease to the Corporation of their estate in Spencer Street near Mousehold. It was also agreed that land adjoining Angel Road and about 5 or 6 acres at the back for an entrance from Angel Road be purchased. The tenements which had been built off Angel Road (in Wilde Road) were not popular as the three blocks of twelve tenement buildings erected in December 1903 were not fully let by April 1904 despite their being advertised.[35] This unpopularity was well-known and was mentioned by Walter Rye in his lecture on the history of Pockthorpe on 28th November 1902[36] when he spoke about the making of 'spick and span new buildings into which the very poor [would] not go'. Their reluctance was not unusual. Godwin, writing in 1859,[37] mentioned the difficulty of persuading people living in slums to move, as did Hollingshead in 1865.[38] The reasons given include the time and expense of travelling to work and the necessity for casual workers to be near the workplace. In Norwich, it may have been a dislike of moving away. The people living in these overcrowded yards were nearly all Norwich-born men and women who had not left the parish in which they were born and even New Catton may have seemed like another country.

Suburban Slums

Many new streets and handsome rows of houses have been built on the site of, and beyond the city walls. The largest of these modern suburbs is the New City, extending from St. Stephen's to St. Giles Gate. (White 1836)

The development of the New City, as it was called, with its new streets and houses, seems to have been a source of pride to numerous Directory writers. And yet, about 30 years later, Mr Lee in his report on Norwich in connection with the Health of Towns Act, speaking of the same streets and houses, said of Union Place:

'*The construction of this part of the town is very peculiar, the cottages being erected mostly chamber height, from 40 to 50 feet apart, with small gardens in front. They consequently look well in front, but in reality are very unhealthy, being generally back to back, and therefore much confined.*'

How to reconcile the two different descriptions? They were the first houses to be built just outside the city walls on former agricultural land, and their model may have been that of country cottages, many of which have very long front gardens. As Mr Lee remarked, they looked good from the front and would have appealed to the writer's admiration for the picturesque.[39]

Tower and City wall in Coburg Street, houses built on the wall in the early 19th century

Although many of the new houses and streets built from 1815 onwards were the subject of restrictive covenants, these were mainly cosmetic, dealing with the outward appearance of the streets and Mr Lee's main concern of course was the lack of sanitary provision. But the report commented not only on this defect but on the houses themselves. Before 1839, when the 1825 Act was amended to include building outside the walls, the city had no control over roads and houses built in the suburbs. The 1825 Act for the better paving, lighting, cleaning, watching and otherwise improving the city of Norwich, had effected some small improvement to roads and other amenities within the walls, but was not intended to address the problem of substandard building, and the state of the housing stock would have been adversely affected by the lack of proper drainage and sanitary facilities. This would have been especially true with the increased number of people living in the suburbs.

The Sanitary Purposes Committee appointed by the Norwich Board of Health in 1851 attempted to improve living standards in the suburbs but, as was so often the case, it had to contend with landlords unwilling to spend any money on their properties. The following minute is not untypical: '...the Paving Committee be recommended to take all necessary steps...to compel the Owners of property in Lower Heigham Street, Peafield, Crooks, Union and Julian Places to construct House Drains from their respective properties connecting with the Common Sewer.'[40]

The difficulty of enforcing the regulations, despite summonses being issued, is demonstrated time and time again. Whether this was because there was not the will to enforce the regulations or it was due to the sheer size of the problem, is unclear. For instance, in September 1854 James Smith Rump esq. was ordered to cleanse and empty the stagnant trenches in his tan yard in Heigham. In October 1853 Mr Dawes of Crooks Place (ignoring the covenant prohibiting the keeping of pigs) was summonsed for keeping swine. In June 1855 Mr R.D. Holl was to be proceeded against for causing a public nuisance in his premises in Somerleyton Street.[41] A person against whom more than one complaint was made was Timothy Steward (of Steward & Patteson's brewery) because of offensive pigsties in 1851 and, summonses seemingly having had little effect, there were additional complaints made against him, including one in 1859. And yet Timothy Steward was a wealthy landowner living alongside other wealthy landowners, with a large house and garden on Unthank Road. Judging from the Minutes, it would seem that both landowners and tenants ignored the Corporation's attempts to regulate activities and it is not surprising that the houses built before the Corporation had the power to compel enforcement were condemned as slums.

The areas most affected by substandard buildings included Crook's, Union and Julian Place, part of West Pottergate, Lower Heigham, Peafield in New Lakenham as well as small parts of New Catton - Philadelphia and surrounding area - which had been built early in the 19th century; these were all mentioned by Mr Lee in his report. The facilities in other streets, most notably Bracondale and the Crescent were also condemned. However, as these were high-quality buildings, they had not been allowed to become dilapidated but their inclusion in the report suggests a general toleration of dirt and smells.

Although the Norwich Board of Health Bye-Laws 1858 with respect to New Streets and New Houses did not affect the houses already built, their implementation, together with Building Control Plans having to be approved from 1877 onwards, brought about a great improvement in artisan housing. It was not just that houses had to be built to a certain specified standard, but regulations made it impossible for the properties to deteriorate as the properties in Union Place had apparently done. It is likely that those writers who admired the houses in the New City were not deceived, and that the houses which had been built in the 1820s were a great improvement on previous habitations and exactly right for their law-abiding artisan inhabitants. The fond vision of a well-housed clean, cheerful and dutiful working-class was an upper-class commonplace and modernity its watchword. How else to account for Stacy's description of Union Place as 'now covered with buildings, and contains several pleasant and genteel residences'.[42] This suggests a mixed development and either selective blindness or, more probably, praise for cottages with well-managed gardens. The deterioration which had occurred between 1832 and 1850 may very well have been due to self-serving landlords, unwilling to spend any money on their properties and continuing to build additional cottages on any vacant space. What had started out as 'handsome rows of houses' would soon have deteriorated as buildings were added *ad hoc*.

The 1858 Bye-laws made it impossible for such a deterioration to occur again. Clause 11 specified that:

'...every building to be erected and used as a dwelling-house shall have in the rear or at the side thereof an open space exclusively belonging thereto, to the extent at least of 150 square feet, free from any erection thereon above the level of the ground, and the distance across such open space between every such building and the opposite property to the rear or side shall be ten feet at least' and Clause 12 states: *'Where any open space has been left belonging to any building when the sanction of the Board has been obtained for its erection, such space shall never afterwards be built upon without the approval of the Board.'*

The enforcement of these two clauses made the kind of structures complained about in Union Place impossible.

Lee's condemnation of many of the houses and streets he inspected seems absolute. And yet examination of the covenants imposed on new building suggests that some land-owners were aware of the consequences of not exercising control. In Lewis Street, for example, houses to be built on property sold in 1825 had to consist of not less than four rooms;[43] this seems to have been the norm for artisan dwellings at this period. The vendor's prohibition on houses with fewer than four rooms shows an awareness of many small inferior houses in the area. Stefan Muthesius describes houses of different sizes in his article on 19th century housing.[44] In 1984, when the book was published, there were few examples in Norwich of the smallest house - one up, one down - and he mentions only one, in Lion & Castle Yard,

Barrack Street. One other small house, which appears to have been part of a terrace, was put on the market in the 1980s. It had been much altered in the uses to which the rooms were put. Details of this property at 1 Esdelle Street are given in the sale particulars. It had one room down and one up and a shower room on the ground floor (probably where the kitchen would originally have been situated). There was no front or back garden. It had a small entrance hall at the side which seems a later addition. (This house was for sale in the 1980s, but appears to have been demolished.) Houses such as this were very numerous in the suburbs although many would have had a small garden.

In 1908 Lakenham had one of the highest infant mortality rates in Norwich. Hawkins wrote that the houses had been 'tumbled together without care or forethought, and in such a hurry that the streets have not even names to them'.[45] Peafield in Lakenham, sixty years before, had also been condemned for having in 1850 only eight pumps and two draw-wells[46] for a population of about 2,000. It would seem matters had not improved much in the interim period as in 1902 inspection of substandard properties in the suburbs by the Housing of the Working Classes Committee found many houses in Lakenham deficient in sanitary provision, etc.[47]

Although very few buildings in the suburbs were declared unfit for human habitation in the 19th century, a number were the subject of compulsory purchase, usually because of street widening. In such instances, the Corporation would sell any land not needed for housing, subject to any proposed buildings being approved by them. Both Vauxhall Street and Derby Street were subject to compulsory purchase for road widening in 1894 and in each case a number of the houses affected by the scheme were the subject of compulsory purchase.[48] Road improvements carried out under the Norwich Corporation Act of 1889 were also important and led to improvements in drainage. Among schemes of this kind was Bristol Terrace off Chapel Field Road which in October 1893 was ordered to be sewered, levelled, paved, metalled, flagged, kerbed, channelled and made good.

Seventeen houses were affected. Properties in Wingfield Road and a property on the corner of Aylsham Road were also ordered in January 1894 to make the same improvements.[49]

1900 and after

Clearance of substandard yards and courts proceeded slowly, and slum property was still being offered for sale in the early 20th century. This is illustrated by the auction held on 14th August 1903 of dwelling houses and tenements in St John's Alley and Farnell's Court in the parish of St John Maddermarket. The auctioneers (Irelands) stated that 'a considerable sum of money [has] recently been expended in putting the property in an excellent state of repair' but judging by the description, many would soon become the subject of slum clearance. Seventeen properties, described as dwelling houses and tenements, were for sale. Included was one larger and better equipped: a four-bedroomed house with large garden and water laid on indoors. This was in Farnell's Court, off St John's Alley. The remainder of the dwellings in the court were either small, or very small with two or three rooms. One - No. 7 – was subdivided: there were tenants in each of Nos. 7, 7a, 7b, 7c, 7d and these are described as sitting room, cellar, two sitting rooms and one sitting room respectively. The houses in St John's Alley were slightly larger. The tenants of the twenty tenements would have had to share the back yard at the rear of the properties and the four pan closets and the washhouse. They would also have had to share the tap in the yard, although this was for their sole use! The tenant of the house with garden was luckier as he or she would have had water installed in the house. Farnell's Court, was demolished in the 1950s and an extension to the Maddermarket Theatre built on the site in 1966. It was just one of many substandard buildings still remaining in 1910 when Hawkins reported that of the 749 courts and yards, 233 had been improved.[50] The majority of houses in the courts and yards, whether improved or unimproved, were demolished in the twentieth century. As for slum clearance of houses in the suburbs, these had to wait until the 20th century.

The process whereby houses were built for the working classes in the suburbs progressed slowly and Clearance Areas were still being declared in 1935. Although slow in implementation, the decision in 1900 to house persons displaced by slum clearance in the suburbs had a profound effect on the future development and expansion of Norwich with Corporation housing estates being built: the Mile Cross Estate was laid out 1918-20 in New Catton and the Angel Road Estate in 1919 (in addition to the earlier development in Wilde Road mentioned above). Council house building started again in the 1950s, after the war, and continued until the 1980s.[51]

Notes

Professor Muthesius (Muthesius, Stefan *The English Terrace House*, Yale 1982) has shown the difficulty in coming to any agreed definition of some buildings which are variously described as house, villa, cottage and tenement, etc. This nomenclature varies according to context, and also in different parts of the country. I have found that in describing houses in Norwich, the word tenement describes both a small terrace house and a large subdivided building. Thus, in the new suburbs tenement describes a small terrace house, whereas within the city itself, with large areas of former garden ground built over, it often describes either a house in multiple occupation or inferior buildings put up on former garden ground.

1. Pevsner, Nikolaus & Wilson, Bill. *The Buildings of England. Norfolk I; Norwich and the North-East.* London 2nd edition 1997, pp. 303-5.
2. [Stacy. John] 1819, *A topographical & historical account of the City & County of Norwich*, p. 42
3. Health of Towns Commission: Report from Commissioners 1845 - Second Report of the Commissioners for Inquiring into the State of Large Towns and Populous districts - Appendix Norwich pages 280 to 286, J.R. Martin. The copy referred is a typescript obtained from the Norfolk Local Studies Library.
4. Hawkins, C.B. *Norwich A Social Study* 1910, pp. 74-75
5. NRO, N/EN 12/1 ff. The Norfolk Record Office has a large number of Building Control Plans dating from 1877 onwards.

6. Browne, P. *The History of Norwich from the Earliest Records to the Present Time*, pp. 147 and 272-3
7. NRO, N/TC54/3 Robinson's yard, Oak Street; N/TC28/19 Courts & Yards Committee
8. NRO, SPE257 Freehold estate in All Saints and St. Michael at Thorn
9. NRO, SPE14 Freehold estate next the Thorn Lane in the parish of St. Michael at Thorn
10. NRO, 18625/138 Spelman Auction Particulars 26th June 1850
11. NRO, TC52/6 Plan of freehold building ground in St. John's Timberhill for sale by auction by Mr Wilde 7th June 1848 and freehold estate in St John's Timberhill to be auctioned by Dennis Barnard 5th February 1851
12. NRO, N/EN/12/1/142 Plan of eleven cottages Mariner's Lane 31st December 1878
13. NRO, N/EN/12/1/384 Nine cottages on Horns Lane
14. NRO, MS4382 Artizans Dwellings Committee
15. This is recorded in White's 1845 Directory. The appeal by 'An old Parishioner', which also asked for extra police supervision because of vandalism, was printed in May 1857 by J. Davy, Printer, St Clement's Church Alley.
16. NRO, SPE447 Freehold estate in the parishes of St Paul, St Augustine and St Clement sold by William Spelman 7th December 1835
17.. NRO, SPE207 Freehold estate situated in St Paul's near St James's church
18. NRO, SPE601 Thirteen dwellinghouses and cottages in Judd's Thoroughfare and opposite St Paul's churchyard
19. Sited by Pound, John 'Poverty and Public Health in Norwich 1845-1880' in *Norwich in the 19th century*, ed. Christopher Barringer
20. NRO, MS4382 - Artizans Dwellings Committee Minute 13th December 1878
21. NRO, MS4382 - Artizans Dwellings Committee Minute 12th February 1879
22. Hibgame, F.T. *Recollections of Norwich Fifty Years Ago*, p. 10
23. NRO, N/TC 28/19 Courts & Yards Committee 1899-1902
24. NRO, N/TC 9/7 Courts & Yards Committee
25. NR0, N/TC 9/7 Executive & Sanitary Sub-Committee 17 November 1897

26. NRO, N/TC 9/7 Special Committee Minutes - Courts & yards Committee - 1st April 1898

27. NRO, N/TC 9/7 Minutes of the Courts & Yards Committee 11th July 1898

28. NRO, N/TC 9/7 Courts & Yards Committee - Reported at the meeting 27th January 1899

29. NRO, N/TC 9/7 Minutes of the Courts & Yards Committee 15th December 1897

30. NRO, N/TC 28/19 Minutes of the Courts & Yards Committee 18th July 1899

31. NRO, N/TC 28/19 Minutes of the Courts & Yards Committee 11th July 1898

32. The 1891 census lists 162 people living in 42 tenements in Priory Yard. There were three houses with four rooms, twenty houses with three rooms and seven houses with two rooms.

33. NRO, N/TC 54/3 Robinsons Yard, Oak Street

34. NRO, N/TC 9/7 Special Committee Minutes - Housing of the Working Class Committee

35. NRO, N/TC 29/1 Minutes of Housing Allotments Committee 21st March 1904

36. This lecture was published in the *Eastern Daily Press*

37. Godwin, George. *Town Swamps and Social Bridge*. 1859. Reprinted Leicester University Press, 1972, p. 8

38. Holingshead, John in *Today's Essays and Miscellenies II*, 1865, p. 306. Referred to in Dyos, H.J. & Reeder, John. 'Slums and Suburbs', p. 368 in Dyos, H.J. & Wolff, Michael (eds.) *The Victorian City Images and Realities Vol. II. Shapes on the Ground/A change of Account.*

39. The cottages in Silvergate, a hamlet of the parish of Blickling, are a good example of the type. Many of the cottages on this estate have very small or no back yards and long front gardens. The directory writers may have shared the then current romantic view of country living. This, and the practical reality, are summarised by John Burnett in *A History of Housing 1815-1985*.

40. NRO, N/TC 4/11-13 Minutes of the Sanitary Purpose Committee 7 November 1854

41. NRO, N/TC 4/11-13 Sanitary Purpose Committee

42. Stacy 1832 p. 66

43. NRO, TC8/3, TC9/5: Conveyance of a piece of land at Lakenham to W. Bales & E. Bales

44. Different sizes of houses are described by Stefan Muthesius in 'Nineteenth Century Housing in Norwich', p. 108

45. Hawkins, C.B. *Norwich: A Social Study,* p. 88

46. Health of Towns Act. *Report of an inquiry held before William Lee of the Sanitary Condition of the City and County of Norwich,* p. 56

47. NRO, N/TC 28/19 Minutes of the Courts & Yards Committee 18th December 1902

48. NRO, N/TC 9/7 Streets Improvements Committee. Vauxhall Street Improvement 27/11/1894, Derby Street Improvement 19/7/1895

49. NRO, N/TC 54/1 Street Improvement Committee

50. Hawkins, p. 74

51. A description of Norwich council houses since the war is given by Horsey, Miles & Muthesius,
Stefan. Provincial Mixed Development. Norwich Council Housing 1955-1973. Norwich 1986.

Chapter 9: Towards a Clean and Decent City: Local government 1801-1900

Introduction

How did the city authorities cope with change and expansion? It had to counter an inherent distrust of any interference in what were considered purely domestic and personal affairs and the belief that the state should interfere as little as possible seems to have been behind much of the opposition to improvement. In 1803 Alderman Browne had spoken against a proposed bill for the better paving, lighting, watching and cleaning the city on the grounds that the 'wisest policy in all States [is] to be governed by as few Laws as possible' believing the probable increased powers of magistrates would be 'a degree of tyranny'.[1] These sentiments were behind much of the opposition to change. In addition, the need to keep the rates low was a powerful motive for inaction and a rise in the rates was an important consideration in a city where the number of poor was large and its financial base small.

The Acts

In 1800 a proposal to pave, cleanse and light the city, to be funded by a toll on horses and wheeled vehicles entering the city,[2] had been dropped because of the opposition of a Committee of Country Gentlemen. However, in 1803, after an increasing number of complaints had been received about the state of the city, another proposal was made for a Bill to be presented to Parliament for the better paving, lighting, watching and cleansing of the city. Again there were many objections. The *Norfolk Chronicle*[3] reported the controversy at some length. Those in favour of the Bill spoke about the increased trade and the number of strangers that improvements would bring into the city, a claim derided by objectors as a 'fairy-tale'. Although a majority was in favour of the Bill, because of the strength of opposition, the proposal was deferred.

Alderman Browne was again in the forefront when another, slightly amended, Bill was brought forward in 1806. Although his name is not in the advertising counter-petition which was printed in the *Norfolk Chronicle* on 11th January 1806, it is likely he was the prime mover behind the opposition:

Paving Bill - Counter Petition
Whereas it is expected that as soon as Parliament meets, a Petition for 'An Act for better Paving, Lighting, Watching and Cleansing, the City of Norwich will be presented, and as there is great reason to believe that a large majority of Owners and Occupiers of Estates, consider the proposed measure as inexpedient, and that if an act were obtained, it would be partial and unjust in its operation; such persons are requested to meet at the Hall in the Market, on Tuesday, the 14th day of January, precisely at 10 o'clock in the Forenoon, to promote the most efficacious means of opposing the said Petition.

Norwich 10th January 1806

The meeting of the Counter-Petitioners was reported in the *Norfolk Chronicle* on 18th January. There were objections because of the great expense in carrying out the provisions of the Bill and a large subscription was raised to oppose it. On 1st February a second Counter-Petition was printed where it was stated that 1601 people had signed the first Counter-Petition. Edward Rigby, the Chairman of the Committee formed to conduct the application to Parliament for the Bill, replied to the Counter-Petitioners on 8th February. He spoke about the necessity for improvement, and the respectability and status of those who supported the measure: a large number of citizens had raised money for the expense of the application to Parliament, one gentleman offering £500. (One factor militating against improvement was that, until 1877, the cost of bringing a Bill before Parliament had to be met by individuals and could not be offset against the rates.)

The resistance continued with a further Counter-Petition published in the *Norfolk Chronicle* and a letter from 'A Citizen' addressed 'To the Inhabitants of Norwich' dated 31st May which stated that 'despite reports that the Bill had either already been passed or was in the process of being passed, opposition should be continued'. However, despite all the opposition, the Bill entitled 'An Act for better paving, lighting, cleaning, watching and other wise improving the city of Norwich' (46 Geo. III c. lxvii) received Royal assent on 13th June 1806. The high status of those opposing the Bill can be gauged by Alderman John Browne's eminent position: he was sheriff in 1794, Alderman 1798-1833, resigned April 1834, Mayor 1798, Auditor 1807-30. He was an ironmonger, ironfounder and colourman at 19 St Peter's Street and had a country residence in Hethersett.[4]

The provisions of the 1806 Act were wide-ranging. It laid down the qualifications for the Commissioners to be elected, the officers to be appointed, and made it lawful to enter into contracts for paving, flagging, repairing, cleansing and lighting. It also ruled that all the dirt, dust, dung, ashes, etc. that was swept up should belong to the Commissioners (one of the objections to the Act had been that this would be detrimental to gardeners). It authorised the appointment of paviors and carters and the purchase of horses. The Commissioners were also empowered to new pave, flag and repair the streets; the principal streets were to be greatly improved, narrow passages widened and all nuisances removed. Proper cesspools, drains and watercourses to drain the streets were to be made. It also ruled that street signs be put up, streets named and houses numbered. The Commissioners were also empowered to arrange for lamps to be set, appoint watchmen for night times and establish Watch Houses and Watch Boxes. However, the work of paving, cleansing and lighting the city was a mammoth operation which the Act was only partially successful in carrying out.

It brought about some improvements: the paving of St Stephen's Street commenced; Berry's 1810 Directory speaks of the lighting being brighter and the streets better paved.[5] Further improvements followed and Acts were passed enabling the building of the Norwich Foundry Bridge and the Carrow Bridge in 1810. There were a number of proposals for improvements, not always implemented, but in general not very much was done, and in 1815 the Norwich Quarter Sessions Grand Jury recorded that the pavements were still defective and the streets inadequately cleansed and lighted. The improvement of Norwich was a very expensive business as the whole city needed to be repaired, cleansed, lighted, etc. One result of the Act was that the cleanliness of the streets deteriorated as the inhabitants, whose duty it had been to clear the filth outside their properties, no longer did so. Scavengers were employed to clean the streets, the profit to go to the Commissioners, but their efforts were less satisfactory than those of the householders. The watching does not seem to have been very effectively carried out either as in 1812 the Mayor called a meeting of the Magistrates and delegates of the parishes to consider ways to make it more effective. The inhabitants of Bracondale had already appointed an armed watch because of an increase in crime.[6]

In 1824 the Paving Commissioners applied to Parliament for permission to bring in a Bill for amending the 1806 Act and for raising additional funds. Just as in 1806, this encountered much opposition. The principal objection was to the proposal to impose a tonnage duty on items coming by river into Norwich. This, it was feared, would hurt industry as many of the raw materials - e.g. coal and sand (for the iron industry) which came by river were bulky and heavy but low in value and would thus be disproportionately affected, paying much more than low weight high value items such as wine. A heated correspondence ensued, carried out in the pages of the *Norfolk Chronicle* with both sides going into great detail about the effect on prices of the tonnage duty. The opposition formed a Committee and opened a subscription to fight the Act. However, they do not appear to have objected to the Act in principle if the additional levy needed for carrying it into effect was raised by assessment of rateable property in the city.[7] The Bill was presented in its original form but was later amended to remove the offending clause. It is interesting that those opposing the Bill accepted the necessity of paving the streets and only objected to the proposed method of paying for improvements. Unlike the objectors of the 1806

Bill, they did not seem to have felt that this was an attack on their freedom.[8]

The Act for the better paving, lighting, cleaning, watching and otherwise improving the city of Norwich Amended 1825 (6 Geo. IV, c. lxxviii) which was passed in June brought in its wake a number of improvements to the streets including repairs to St Stephen's Street and Duke Street in 1830, the widening of Brigg's Lane (Brigg Street) in 1839-42 and the widening of Tombland in 1843. Improvement was gradual, not helped by the length of time it took to accomplish anything (see London Street, the state of which was first raised by the Committee in 1830[9] which seems not to have been considered again until 1848). Regarding street cleaning, the position was reversed: whereas in 1806 householders were forbidden to sweep away the dirt in front their property, the 1825 Act laid down that this was now their responsibility. This reversal of policy seems to have been either ignored or not understood for, despite the Act, the dirt was not always swept away and in 1831 the Paving, Cleansing & Finance Committee ordered that notices be sent out to the inhabitants to remind them of this duty.

In addition to street improvements, other measures were enacted which would, if complied with, have contributed to the well-being and comfort of the citizens. These were intended to modify the behaviour of people and would be cheap to implement. The most important sought to influence behaviour in the streets: not to fodder, shoe, bleed or farry any horse, nor to clean or exercise it; not to kill any animal or to allow its blood to flow onto the streets; not to throw any rubbish into a common sewer or throw any dead animal or offal, etc. into any well, pump, water-course or reservoir for water. These are just a few of a long list of prohibitions. A number of these, especially those relating to the killing of animals and allowing blood to flow into the streets, were also included in the 1806 Act which suggests that it was not easy to enforce a change in customary behaviour. The state of the city in 1806 can be gauged by the attitude to hygiene and the probable improvements that had come about between 1806 and 1825 when it was thought no longer necessary to prohibit the inhabitants from [causing] 'any privy or necessary house within the said city to be emptied, except between 11 p.m. and 5 a.m.' (although judging by the comments of the Inspector in connection with the Health of Towns Commission in 1850, this belief may have been over-optimistic).

However, even with the increased rates received as a consequence of the 1825 Bill, the amount of work necessary was impossibly large. Committee minutes for the 1830s and 1840s include reports of work necessary or proposed as follows: the improvement of a common sewer that was causing inundations in Rampant Horse Street, proposals for gas lighting in the city, for the macadamising of numerous streets, for the repair of kerbs and footways and for the flagging of streets. The Committee ordered the laying of a common sewer from the corner of Brigg's Lane in 1832 and until 1853 a number of sewers were laid as and when, but mostly in response to complaints about flooding. In the same way, pavements were re-laid and roads improved, but again, this was not done systematically, but piecemeal.[10]

In 1839 there was a proposal to bring in a new bill to extend the provisions of the 1825 Act to include the hamlets. Predictably, this was received with great hostility. Once again a lively correspondence was carried out in the pages of both the *Norwich Mercury* and the *Norfolk Chronicle*. Only in very select parts of the hamlets, such as in Newmarket Road, was there any lighting and even within the city itself the lighting of the roads was uneven. The unsatisfactory state of lighting in the city had been publicised in a letter written to the Editor of the *Norwich Mercury* on 9th February 1839 complaining about the dangerous state of 'The Black Horse Road' (the Black Horse Public House is listed in White's 1845 Directory on St Catherine's Plain) where there was need for an additional gas light and where there had been a number of accidents and a fatality. The letter-writer stated that his complaint had been received in an 'offhand' manner by the Paving Committee and their response had been that 'nothing need be done in the matter'. Its author was Captain Ferdinand Ives, living in St Catherine's Hill, his address showing him to have been a man of substance. A further letter from the Captain, printed on 16th February, stated that he had heard again from the Committee to the effect that the streets and roads in Norwich were properly lighted. Bayne, in his *History of Norwich* writes about the bad state of the city in 1839 as follows: 'a great part of the city remained undrained and the pavements continued in a bad state.'[11] He seems not to have noticed that the state of the city had improved after 1806 and had been improved continuously since 1825 as would have been the case if many previous acts had been successfully implemented.

The new Paving Act which was brought into the House of Commons by Mr Beckwith and Mr C.S. Gilman,[12] was discussed at the meeting of the Paving Commissioners on 12th February 1839. As well as lighting the hamlets (itself a contentious issue), there was much in the proposals that could be guaranteed to provoke hostility. There were objections on the ground of increased expense because of the proposal to form a new Fire Department with new Board, officers, engines etc., and to erect a new gas manufactory if there was not sufficient power to bring lighting to the hamlets. The Committee poured scorn on proposals which would benefit the hamlets by bringing them within the provisions of the Paving Act. It was said that the reason places such as Union Place were not paved was because the owners were not willing to pay for this to be done. The suggestion that the Corporation should build a gas manufactory was dismissed with the words: 'were the Commissioners to become a jobbing Gas Company?' The Committee voted £300 to oppose the Bill and mounted an energetic campaign against it.

The opponents of the Bill drew up a petition which stated that the city had been paved, lighted, cleansed and watched for thirty years and they believed that a majority was satisfied with the situation. Its adoption was unnecessary and would only lead to an increase in expenditure; in any case the hamlets could be lighted under the provisions of the Municipal Act. However, as the promoters of the new Bill pointed out, although the 1835 Municipal Corporations Act reformed local government, the new borough councils had little additional power because a special local Act was required each time. As this had not been done, even Exchange Street, an important commercial street which housed the Corn Exchange was unlighted and could not be made a public street because it had been built after the passing of the 1825 Act.[13] Although those in favour of the Bill were willing to drop some of the more contentious clauses, they continued in their belief that the hamlets should be paved, cleansed, etc. in the same way as the city and were anxious to remove anomalies which had arisen due to expansion beyond the walls since 1825.

Because of the great opposition the Bill failed. The rejoicing of the opponents was reported in the *Norfolk Chronicle* on 13th July 1839. However, this was not the end of the matter. In November of the same year a notice in the *Norfolk Chronicle* by the solicitor Charles S. Gilman notified the public of his intention to make application to Parliament to amend the 1825 Act. The clauses were much the same as the previous Bill. As before, there was much opposition and, at the Town Council meeting on 14th December, Mr Gilman's character was attacked. He was called a 'jobbing lawyer' and his motives for bringing forward the Bill were questioned. There was also much indignation about the costs incurred by the Council (over £1,000) in defeating the previous Bill and its opponents were angry at having to pay such a large sum to oppose what was considered an unnecessary Bill.

As before, promoters of the Bill proposed a whole range of measures which included widening Brigg Street and extending the 1825 Act for the better Paving, Lighting and Improving the city to the hamlets, although the main thrust of their efforts appears to have been towards lighting the hamlets. The opposition continued to maintain that the Council already had sufficient powers to deal with the lighting and paving. As for the cleansing and sewering, they admitted that this was a problem, but stated that the Surveyor, who had the power to cleanse and keep open drains and watercourses, etc. could be referred to if necessary. At a meeting at the Guildhall to consider (and oppose) the new Paving Act held on 25th February 1840[14] one speaker said that it was not fair that the city should be charged for improvements to the suburbs, people went to live there so as not to have to pay such high rates and therefore had no right to complain and in any case it was not the Council's fault that builders built houses and streets without proper drainage!

In the end Mr Gilman's Bill was defeated by the action of the Town Council which brought forward its own Bill under section 87 of the Municipal Reform Act of 1835 (5 & 6 Wm. c. iv) which allowed it to incorporate a specific section of Norwich outside the walls (not included in the 1825 Act) and to provide it with lighting. Those who argued that the only way to make improvements was to obtain a new Act of Parliament said that the Council was taking these measures solely in order to defeat the Bill. This seems extremely likely: there had already been two attempts to bring in a new Bill, opposing these Bills was an expensive business and the Council, by its action, ensured that there should be no third attempt. And later events showed that the statement of Councillor George Seppings[15] 'that the only object of the order [to invoke the Municipal Reform Act] is to defeat the Bill now brought into Parliament and that the Hamlets cannot be lighted without an Act of Parliament' was correct. (When Mr Lee's Report on the Sanitary Conditions of the City and County of Norwich was published in 1850, the parlous state of the hamlets was blamed on them not being included in the 1825 Act).

The resolution passed by the Town Council meeting on 10th March 1840 was as follows:

'That ..... it is desirable and essential that certain parts of the limits of this Borough and City should be included in the provisions of such local Acts of Parliament now existing for regulating the lighting the other parts of the limits of the same Borough and City should be included in the provisions of such local Acts And that the Council ought therefore forthwith to exercise the power and authority given to or vested in them by the 87 Section of the Municipal Act and to order that certain parts of the Borough and City not now within the provisions of such local Acts, as require to be lighted, shall from and after the sixteenth day of March *instant be taken to be within the provisions of the said two local Acts respectively so far as related to lighting.'*

What was proposed by the Bill was lighting the southern side of the city for a distance of 500 yards from the city boundary from King Street to St Martin-at-Oak gate. This would include all of Bracondale Hill, Peafield, Crooks Place, Union Place and West Pottergate Street. It was also proposed to extend the lighting of Newmarket Road. It was reported that the city had also made a contract with the Gas Company which had offered to lay down the mains, erect the standards, supply the lamps and light for an additional payment.

To the objectors it seemed doubtful that the Gas Company would provide gas lighting to all parts of the suburbs and not just the best parts (the request by the inhabitants of Suffolk Street for gas lamps made more than ten years after the Act was amended suggests that the objectors were justified in their suspicions). The Act proposed to extend the lighting of certain streets, such as Newmarket Road, and the Lighting Commissioners, meeting on 30th March 1840, spoke of 'lighting only that portion of the Hamlets pointed out to Mr Steward' (of the Norwich Gas Company) which suggests that street lighting would be confined to affluent areas. In any event, even before the Bill came into effect, those with enough influence were able to get street lighting in parts of the city and suburbs over which the 1825 Act did not apply. Post Office Street (Exchange Street) which was built after 1825 seems already to have been partially lighted but had additional lamps installed after the residents complained that the lighting was inadequate.[16]

The Tonnage Act which levied a toll on all goods coming to Norwich along the river past Thorpe Old Hall was repealed in 1839. In addition to the repair of the main roads, bridges and walls, the Act had provided for the widening of streets and roads leading into the city, the repair and renewal of St Andrew's Hall and the Guildhall and the formation and maintenance of a river police. The most important aspect of the Act was the repealing of the proposed clause in the

Eastern Counties Railway Act which had given the Corporation power to impose certain dues on merchandise brought into the city. This was a most damaging clause as the railway was unwilling to come into the city if it were enforced.

Water and Sewage

Browne, writing in 1814, praised Norwich for its provision of running water, this being sufficiently uncommon in the early 19th century to evoke comment. However, he was only partially correct in saying that the waterworks supplied the inhabitants of Norwich with water brought to the houses by pipes as was done in London[17] as not everyone, even in better-quality houses, would have had water on tap. It very much depended on the part of the city in which they lived.

In 1790, an Act had been passed for better supplying the city of Norwich and parts adjacent with water (30 Geo. III c. xxi). There had been a system in place since Elizabethan times which was improved in 1699, but the new Act envisaged increasing the supply so that all parts of the city would have sufficient water. The Corporation already owned a number of buildings necessary for this purpose, but required permission to erect and/or repair buildings, to make reservoirs and ponds and to lay pipes. In order to do this, pavements would have to be dug up, and posts, kerbs, sewers and drains installed and passages widened where necessary. The Act gave the city the power of enforcement and anyone damaging the pipes that had been laid, or found to have polluted the reservoirs or the river Wensum, up-stream from where it was proposed to draw water, would be prosecuted. Under the Act, the Corporation would charge for the water, the inhabitants being allowed to bring it into their own homes on payment of a charge. Stacy[18] described the process: the water was to be sent from the New Mills, which had a 99 year lease from the Corporation from 1793, to a reservoir in Chapelfield and Tombland.

However, despite all the work that was done, many parts of the city were still unable to receive water. That this objective had not been achieved is evident from the Report written by the Engineer, Robert

Milne, in March 1798, on the work then being carried out to implement the Act. This stated that although the work should have been finished by 10th October 1798, very little had been done and completion by the specified date would be impossible as very few of the requirements in the Schedule drawn up in 1794 had been met. It listed them, item by item, and either the work had not even commenced or, if it had, the plan drawn up had not been adhered to. In addition, the reservoir was a great deal smaller than that specified. His report makes his dissatisfaction clear: 'The Work, called a Reservoir, formed on one side of Chapel-Field, is so small, and so different in all respects from that in the agreed Drawings, that I am totally at a loss what to say on this head, but to observe, that it seems to be the produce of an obvious intention to abandon the most essential Stipulations entered into.'[19] There were other reasons for dissatisfaction including the failure to lay the main pipes in the principal streets. In the event, that part of the Schedule which referred to the reservoir was never carried out satisfactorily and Milne's criticism, that Ber Street and the adjoining area would not be able to get water, was confirmed by the report written in connection with the Public Health Act of 1848.

Although part of the city was supplied with running water, this did not mean that everyone who was able to receive the water was actually connected to the mains. The water had to be paid for. The owners of small tenements had to pay to be connected to the Corporation's water and to install a common stand-pipe in each court and they were seldom prepared to do this. The success of this Act can be judged by examining the findings of the Inspector's enquiry into the Sanitary Condition of Norwich in 1850.

In tandem with the inadequate provision of water, there was the almost total lack of adequate drainage and sewage disposal at the beginning of the 19th century. The extent of the problem can be appreciated by Hardy's description of Cockey Lane. He was born about 1793 and, writing about Cockey Lane in his youth, said 'conceive two inclined planes, at an angle of 45 [degrees], paved with large heavy stones called cobbles. At their meeting at the bottom, ran a kennel or gutter. The owners of the houses on each side emptied all their refuse on the streets, which on the first shower was washed into the gutter, fell into the drain below - the main drain of the system - and was carried into the river.'[20] At the beginning of the 19th century, Cockey Lane (later London Street) was nearly as important a shopping street then as it later became. Writing his memoirs in 1888, Hardy felt a great deal had been achieved in the intervening years. No doubt it had, but the improvement he mentioned was comparative and it was not until the following year (1889) that the Municipal Reform Act provided the basis for the making of the modern city.

Mr Lee's Report

The 'Report of an inquiry of the Sanitary Condition of the City and County of Norwich' was published in 1850. The enquiry was held in May 1850 before the Inspector, William Lee, and his report made clear the deficiencies of the system then being operated. It stated that there was not sufficient height in the Water-Works system to bring water to the highest parts of the city[21] and that in some parts of the city there was no supply at all. In 1850 only 5,619 out of a total of 17,008 houses were supplied with the Company's water.[22] However, the figure given of the number of houses that actually were supplied may not have been a true reflection of the number that could be supplied. This was especially true in the case of slum dwellings as landlords may not have been willing to pay for installation. In more prosperous areas' owners with a well and a good pump and employing servants to do the work, might not have wanted to pay for the water supplied by the Water-works which might be intermittent, only three or four times a week for two or three hours a day.

In 1850 there were about the 1000 wells which were used by those who were without Company water but this, because of the poor state of the drainage, was often contaminated with foul water. A typical example of the very basic facilities commonly provided can be deduced from the sale particulars relating to five dwellinghouses sold in three lots situated on a new road 'leading out of St. Michael at Thorn Lane to Horn's Lane'.[23]   These were for sale in 1850 in four lots with a pump in the yard to be shared among all five dwellings. The facilities provided were probably better than most dwellings of that type at the time: there were two dwelling houses in each of Lots 3 and 4, each house having two rooms up and two down with shared wash-house. The other lot comprised one house, also with two rooms up and two down and wash-house and a large yard. All these houses had a share of the pump in the yard. These were the lucky ones. At least the residents had a share of a pump and did not have to get their water from the river as did the residents of Shuttle's Yard, Lower Heigham Street.[24] This property, comprising six tenements was sold on 15th September 1841, the residents having the right to use the out-house in the yard in common with other houses and of going to the Mill River to draw water. (This yard was situated off Heigham Street and there were tanning yards at either side of it).

Although the small tenements in courts and yards were the most badly served by the lack of proper water and sanitation, other streets with larger houses were without proper drainage and Sussex Street was referred to in Mr Lee's report as being a street, with a respectable type of house, having no water pipes and contaminated wells.[25] Outside the walls, Bracondale Hill, with good houses, had no proper drainage and the report states that a sewer ran down the road.[26]

The scale of the problem was huge and many other high-quality houses were shown to have defective sanitation. Houses in the Crescent had been inspected and found wanting: 'Very good houses....All of them had cesspools near the back doors with open bins and privies. Some of them had water-closets going to these cess-pools.......when these cesspools were full they were not of much use.'[27]

Mr Lee's findings had confirmed a previous inspection made in March 1850 by Mr Stevenson, a Civil Engineer appointed by the Earl of Carlisle, his Majesty's Chief Commissioner of Woods and Forests, to make an examination and survey of the district which would be affected by the proposed New Water Works Bill. He is said to have reported that 'this city is as badly supplied with water as any place he ever was in.'[28]

New Waterworks Bill

Despite the many deficiencies reported by the Inspector, there was considerable opposition to the Norwich New Waterworks Bill which was introduced into Parliament early in 1850. The introduction of the Bill had led to a vigorous debate on its merits even before Mr Lee's enquiry had begun and comments printed in both the *Norfolk Chronicle* and the *Norwich Mercury* were quoted in his final report. The objections seem to have been of two kinds: those that thought it would not do any good as owners would not take water unless compelled to do so, and those who believed that the supply of water should be under the control of the Corporation, not of a private business. Those against a new waterworks of any kind spoke of compulsion. Councillor Osborn Springfield, one of the objectors, hoped it would not be compulsory to take the Company's water as 'persons living next the river ought not to be taxed for water when they could take from the river.'[29] Other objectors felt it unnecessary for a constant supply of water to be available at all times, a few hours a day would be sufficient. The necessity for the universal supply of water was questioned because there were about 1,000 wells in Norwich and people, who at that time were able to take the Waterworks water often did not do so. They could not be compelled to be clean, and often those who were offered water refused to take it. As proof of this assertion it was stated: 'On Saturday last we visited several yards and courts in one of the worst parts of the city. We found many of the houses perfectly neat and clean and nothing whatever offensive....while others with the same advantage were complete receptacles of dirt and filth.... The former required no sanitary interference, whilst no measure that could be adopted could improve the latter.'[30] The probable expense was touched upon by the objectors, as were the merits of a recently established new Water Works Company which, it was suggested, could provide the city with water more cheaply than the Corporation, and the Nuisance Removal

& Diseases Prevention Act was cited as being sufficient to deal with the present and future state of the sanitary system. But as Mr Lee had stated in his Report, this was just a temporary Act which would only enable Local Authorities to remove dirt for periods of six months and could not be renewed.

Many who opposed the Norwich New Water Works Bill did so because they did not think the supply of water should be a profit-making business and that the Corporation itself should take over the supply. Despite the opposition, the Norwich New Water Works Bill was read for the third time on 3rd June 1850. There seems to have been a genuine desire on the part of the promoters to rectify what was coming to be perceived as a great need; their only interest was in getting the work done and they would have been quite happy for the city to take over the project if it were able to guarantee to do the work. As for a possible increase in charges, Mr Chamberlin, a large water user, speaking at a Town Council meeting on 5th February 1850 said that he would not object to paying two or three times as much for water if it would benefit the inhabitants. The promoters agreed to the amendments proposed to safeguard the rights of the Corporation and guaranteed not to increase the price of water, but they were unwilling either to drop or defer the scheme. And in the end the Corporation withdrew its opposition and despite all the reports and arguments, the Norwich New Water Works Bill (13 & 14 Vict. c. lii) was passed because, as was noted 'although the Corporation had the power to remove the evils complained of, yet they had done nothing for a great number of years'.[31]

None of the interested parties in the dispute about the water works seem to have considered that an inadequate water supply, whilst it affected the health of the people, was also a handicap to manu-facturers and hence to those employed in the new factories. In 1839 Grout & Co. had applied for water to be supplied to its silk works by the Norwich Water Works but the application was rejected on the grounds that, if the request was granted, two or three parishes would have to be deprived of water. At a meeting of the Council on 12th

November 1839 it was stated that other manufacturers had sunk a well and suggested that Grout do likewise. Grout responded that well water was not suitable for the very delicate coloured silks it proposed to dye. The Company already had some wells, but needed extra water and it reminded the Council of the large number of people it employed. The matter was resolved in Grout's favour in March 1840. The Water Company had been under an obligation to supply water under the terms of the lease, but their inadequacy can be seen by its reaction to this request (as also can the fact that other manufacturers depended for much of their water supply on wells).[32]

Public Health Act 1851

The Inspector's report had spoken about the probable contamination of the well water by the numerous privies, and observed that the river water taken by some inhabitants was also contaminated by industrial and animal waste and by raw sewage. Despite its damning nature, the report did not immediately lead to the application of the Health of Towns Act to Norwich. The passing of the Norwich New Water Works Bill by-passed the provisions of the Act although, to counter opposition, the promoters had pledged that the water provided by the new company would be constant and pure. The first general meeting of the Norwich Water Works Company was held on 15th October 1850 and a new reservoir constructed by the Norwich Waterworks Company at Lakenham was opened in 1871.

After much soul-searching Norwich Corporation adopted the Public Health Act in August 1851 and a Board of Health was established. At a meeting of the Paving Commissioners on 24th June 1851 there were worries about the expense of implementing the Act and its possible compulsory powers, this worry only being dispelled on receiving written confirmation that the General Board of Health had no power to compel a local Board to carry out any works. This fear of compulsion was voiced again and again, not only by the Paving Commissioners, but also by the Corporation itself.[33]

The powers which the Public Health Act gave to the city were far-ranging. They concerned not only the provision of water and sewerage but also the fitting of gas and water pipes, the providing, cleansing and emptying of sewers, the disposal of the dead, the provision of slaughter-houses, the levelling and widening of streets, the drainage of ditches, etc. and ordered the provision of water-closet, privy and ashpit in all houses. The Act also gave the city the power of removing nuisances, proceeding against those allowing privies etc. to flow onto the streets and against people living in filthy and unhealthy houses. It outlawed the occupation of cellars except in exceptional circumstances, fixed the number of lodgers in common lodging houses and allowed the city to prohibit the establishment of certain businesses such as soap-boiling and blood-boiling. However, these powers were not compulsory, only permissive, and they did not have to be carried out within a certain time-scale. The only part of the Act that was compulsory was that which related to sewerage, but again there was no time-scale involved. The provision of sewerage would be expensive, but it would be possible to borrow money for this purpose but only with government approval.

Despite the compulsory nature of improvement in sewage and waste disposal and the appointment of the Paving, Cleansing, Sewerage and Lighting Committee in 1853, nothing much changed and the city continued to allow sewage to pour into the river. A plan in August 1856 by the Paving Committee to drain the northern part of the city was only accepted in January 1858 after it had been rejected on the grounds of cost. In June 1865 the City Engineer reported that it was impossible to provide pure water to the city so long as the drainage was not improved and matters came to a head in April 1866 when the inhabitants of Thorpe St Andrew, situated down river and consequently also suffering from Norwich's impure water, threatened to bring proceedings against the Mayor and Corporation to stop them from emptying sewage into the river. The matter assumed some urgency because of this threat and the Norwich Board of Health reported on 14th July 1866 that it proposed to hire about 1,300 acres of land at Whitlingham - the Crown Point Estate - for the purpose of irrigating the sewage. Despite opposition, the Corporation agreed to the proposal. Those who were against it had argued that the town of Croydon had used this method unsuccessfully (this was refuted), and the argument that there was no suitable land was also refuted. The Committee was told that Blackburn had used a similar excuse, but that this had not been accepted and the government was taking out an injunction against all large towns that were holding out.

The Act for sewering the city of Norwich and for applying the sewage to the irrigation of land and for the making of Trowse Road (30 & 31 Vict. c.ii) was passed, but there was still considerable opposition to its implementation and it was not until 1872 that a part of the Crown Point Estate was purchased for sewerage and irrigation purposes. However (probably because of a desire to keep costs down), the new system was a failure. This was because the old sewers were used. There were two sewers: a higher one and a lower one, which were to be used with the new system of irrigation to take the sewage to the Crown Point Estate instead of running it into the river. However, the lower sewer had too low a fall to do this in a satisfactory manner and the problems (and the proposed solution) arising because of the unsuitable sewers was reported at a meeting of the Norwich Board of Health on 11th February 1873.[34] In the end, because of the unsatisfactory state of the system it was decided in 1887 to replace the old low-level sewage pipes and to construct new ones. This was the start of a long process which continued until 1899 when the City Engineer reported the work completed.

The delay in implementing the sewerage scheme was to a large extent caused by the opposition. In 1867 a 'memorial' to the Board of Health entitled 'Norwich Drainage' deplored the proposed expenditure and the adoption of the Earth System was advocated. According to the Memorialists this had been approved by the Indian Government. Although this may now seem eccentric, the proposal was taken very seriously and, in response, a leaflet dated 7th January 1868 entitled 'Earth Closets. To the Ratepayers of Norwich' quoted biblical precedent to counter the arguments of the proponents of the earth system and examples given of failures with earth closets in other English towns. The author, who entitled himself 'Anxious Ratepayer' also refuted the Memorialists' contention and quoted evidence from Winchester and Leamington, both of which had considered and then rejected the possibility of adopting the earth system. The suggestion that a profit could be made from the sale of night soil was rebutted by the information that Glasgow was losing £7,000 a year and Manchester £8,000[35] from its collection and sale.

Sanitary facilities in Norwich

Despite proposals for slum clearance and the implementation of the Public Health Act, the 1858 Board of Health Bye-Laws and 1877 Building Control Plans (see Chapter 8), the general view of the housing requirements of the poorest members of society did not materially alter and the sharing of privies and later, of water-closets, continued into the 20th century. Only this can explain the decision of the Corporation regarding improvements to Bailey's Buildings, West Pottergate.[36] The houses themselves had been built sometime shortly after 1824 and, naturally enough, had no proper facilities (it is unclear from the document what were the facilities to be replaced). In 1909 the Corporation ordered the landlord to make 'a sufficient water closet' for four of the houses, but said that two would be sufficient for the four buildings and the sharing of water-closets continued as late as 1912, when sale particulars for 68-74 Trinity Street[37] describe small houses with two water-closets and two bins for the four houses although all had the Company's water and gas.

By the 1890s, nearly every house, even the smallest, had a sink and the Company's water. The almost universal provision of piped water is evident in its availability to the inhabitants of the three brick and tile cottages in Cossey's Yard, Botolph Street which were sold in 1893.[38] These cottages would have been outside the range of the old Waterworks. But there seems to have been little or no provision for water-closets, especially for small tenements. The special report by the

City Engineer, published in *The Norfolk Chronicle* on 4th November 1893, summarised the situation. He reported that out of 23,111 houses in the city, only 4,100 water-closets were in existence and, for those unacquainted with the apparatus, described the midden closet with which he assumed a large number of the above houses must be provided:

> *'It consists usually of a roughly bricked hole in the ground, in many cases having no proper bottom or cemented sides and is situated at the end of the tenement portion of the cottage. The centre portion is provided with a door through which all the ashes and garbage of the house are thrown, while on either side is situate the seat of the closet, through which the excreta fall and in time are covered up by ashes, etc. and so lost to view, although not to smell....'* In overcrowded sections of the city, this is often the back door of the cottages.*

> *With a view to the emptying of the privy bins the Sanitary Authority have divided the city into 15 districts and the work is let to various contractors who are expected to empty every privy or midden once every month or, in the case of privy pans being used, twice in every week, but no cleansing whatever of the pans takes place beyond the mere emptying. The removal is conducted during the night and entails the scooping out of the filth from the bins into receptacles in which it is conveyed, frequently through long passages, and then emptied into large waggons in the streets....As soon as it is gathered (about 39,000 tons a year) it is removed to a depot, which, according to the terms of the contract, must be outside the boundaries of the city; and then it is sold to farmers and market gardens for manure.'*

The City Engineer added that as the contents contained not only human excrement, but also ashes, kitchen waste, broken bottles, etc., there was not much goodness in it and it was sometimes difficult to get farmers to take it. This was a national problem, although as there was so much agricultural land locally, it was not so acute in Norfolk as in some cities in the Midlands, etc. Nevertheless he was confident that once the sewer system was up and running, the use of middens and privies would quickly decline as had been the case in other parts of the country.

However, Building Control Plans for houses built between 1893 and 1900 show that, in the case of small terrace houses, it was a matter of chance whether or not a water-closet was provided. Five houses built in West End Street in 1898[39] had a water-closet at the back of each house entered from the yard whereas 18 houses built on Waddington Street and Armes Street in 1899[40] each had an earth closet attached to the house, entered from the yard. It is interesting that in the case of the 18 houses, the original plan was not approved, not because of the lack of water-closets, but because of the combined drainage of all the houses (Waddington Street connects West End Street to Armes Street). In 1900 approval was given for six houses in Mousehold Street[41] each having a privy at the back of the garden. All the above houses had a sink and the Water Company's water. They were all basically the same type of small terrace house without a hall entrance, with three bedrooms upstairs, two living rooms and kitchen on the ground floor and a small garden at the front and a slightly larger one at the back. This type of house, suitably modernised, is still very common in Norwich.

In general, there was not much improvement in sanitation despite improved sewage provision; the facilities which each house enjoyed depended partly on its size and status. However this was not invariably the case and there were often great differences in the facilities provided even in houses situated one beside the other. In 1894 the estate of Mrs George Ling was sold.[42] This consisted of a number of houses in All Saints Green and other parts of Norwich. All the houses sold had the Company's water but only three out of a total of six houses in All Saints Green had a water-closet: Mrs Ling's own house (No. 31), the house beside it (No. 29) and another house some distance away (No. 11). No. 31 was the largest house with a water-closet on both ground and first floors, carriage house, harness-house, stable, greenhouse, garden, etc. No. 29 was smaller and had one water-closet in the rear garden, whilst No. 11 had a water-closet on the first floor. However,

Nos. 23, 25 and 27 which were smaller, each had only a privy. Mrs Ling also held property in the suburbs and the facilities provided for Nos. 32 and 34 Earlham Road were very different. For sale in 1894, they were identical houses, each with four bedrooms and had both front and back stairs. And yet No. 32 had a water-closet at the back, whilst No. 34 had only an earth-closet and a privy.

The love-affair with earth closets was a long time dying. Moule's Earth Closets were patented in 1905 and were advertised as affording 'absolute assurance of freedom from the dangers inseparable from every other form of closet; there can be no sewer gas, no cesspit evils, no contaminated wells, no wasteful expenditure of water, and no frozen pipes in winter'. And, so it was said, they can be set up inside or outside a house and are cheaper and simpler than modern water closets. They were advertised in 1905 by *Country Cottages & Week-end Homes* by J. H. Elder-Duncan, a quality publication with plans of houses ranging from £200 to £3,500.[43]

Norwich Corporation Bill

The Norwich Corporation Act of 1889 (52 & 53 Vict. c.clxxxvii) empowered the Corporation to exercise its statutory borrowing power by means of the creation and issue of stock. This was a very far-reaching Act which enabled money to be borrowed for the construction of efficient sewers. There were a range of other measures including sanitary and building regulations, the management of infectious diseases, police regulations, the regulation of hackney carriages and the employment of children, increasing the library rate and freeing Carrow Bridge from tolls. The Corporation would also be responsible for the repair etc. of all streets and this expense would be a charged to all the inhabitants through the rates. Private streets would be the responsibility of those who lived in them but the Corporation would be able to order their repair if in a dangerous condition and to charge the owners of the property on the street. Additionally, it would be able to adopt private streets and would afterwards become responsible for them.

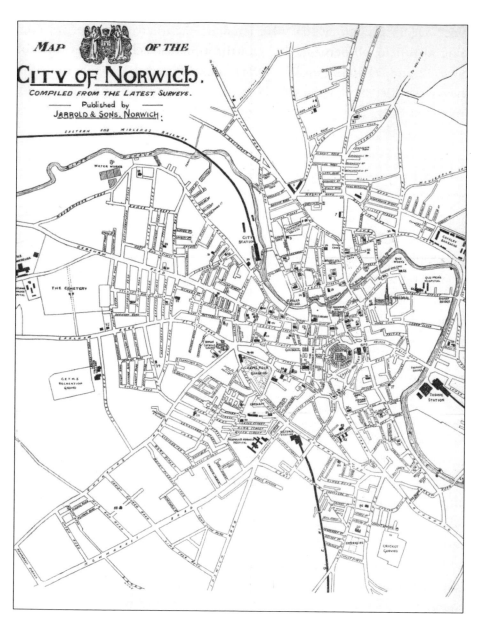

Norwich at the end of the 19th century

The Act put an end to all uncertainty as to the responsibility for repairs and improvements by constituting the entire city (all 40 parishes with their different rateable values and population numbers as well as the hamlets and liberties) into one parish. Thus the city's debt was spread over the whole city as well as all future costs in respect of improvements etc. It authorised the collection of the municipal sanitary and other rates by the Norwich Board of Guardians as it already collected the poor rate. The amount levied would be determined by the Corporation which would make an order on the Board for payment.

There was considerable opposition to the Bill and the reasons for this would be obscure, as neither the *Norwich Mercury* nor the *Norfolk Chronicle* gives much detail, were it not for the many reports by the radical newspaper, *Daylight* which wrote of the malversation of the city funds as a reason for opposing it:

'The report does not attempt to deny the facts, but simply states that, as the Corporation existed 200 years at least before the House of Commons, therefore it may bribe, booze and bamboozle the public generally, and its own constituents in particular, as much as it pleases, and the House of Commons has no right to call it to account.' [44]

While agreeing the Bill's main objective, which was to provide a much-needed new sewage system, *Daylight* campaigned against the Bill because of the additional clauses it contained. These clauses seem to have been the reason for the disorderly scenes at the meeting at St Andrew's Hall on 9th January which was adjourned as well as similar scenes at the later meeting on the 23rd.[45] As mentioned, newspaper reports about the reasons for the opposition did not go into details. The *Norwich Mercury* merely reported the disturbances, but *Daylight* made clear the causes for dissatisfaction. One clause was the proposal to prohibit more than two people congregating on a walking way. This was opposed because of the fear that meeting in a large open space, for instance the Market Place, could be declared illegal - a not unlikely suspicion in view of the parades and rallies that had taken place in the

Market Place in 1887.[46] *Daylight* cited other places in England where similar legislation was used to ban open-air meetings. A further reason for opposition was that the Board of Guardians would be charged with collecting and administering the rate for the Corporation. This was a hated institution and the niggardly provision of poor relief, although largely ignored by the press, was a constant theme in *Daylight* which also accused it of corrupt practices (including employing members of their own families). It was considered undemocratic: unlike the universal franchise of all ratepayers for elections to the Town Council and the School Board, the Guardians' franchise was very limited as only householders rated directly on assessments of £10 per annum and over could vote. Those whose property was assessed at £10 had one vote, those assessed at £20 had two votes, and so on, up to a maximum of six votes. Only ratepayers assessed at £25 per annum or over were entitled to be elected as Guardians.

There was a feeling that the Bill was being foisted on the City by stealth and opponents were warned that objections could lead to a delay or, even worse, a cancellation of the construction of much-needed sewers. The suspicion that the Bill was being hurried through was fuelled when the first public consultation was not properly advertised and was scheduled for a time when most people would be unable to attend.

Because of the opposition, it was agreed that the clause that it was feared might limit free association would be omitted from the Bill. However, the City was unwilling to take over administration of the rate on the grounds that it would be more economical for the Norwich Guardians, authorised by Parliament to administer the Poor Rate, to collect both rates. The City, while agreeing that the method by which the Guardians were appointed was unsatisfactory, thought that a committee comprising half town councillors and half Guardians could lead to difficulties. It did not think Parliament would agree to a system which would be unique for Norwich, especially as the Guardians administered the rates in every other part of the country. What would be acceptable would be for the Guardians to amend the franchise qualification for the election of Town Councillors.

And this was what happened. The *Norwich Mercury* reported in January 1893 that it had 'resolved to request the Local Government Board to repeal parts of the Norwich Poor Act of 1863 in order to make the general law as to franchise and election of Guardians applicable to Norwich',[47] and as a result the Bill was approved and passed through the Select Committee of the House of Common on June 18th 1889. The report of the Parliamentary Committee for the extension of the franchise for the election of the Guardians was awaited in November 1889.

Other reforms followed: the Common Lodging House Bye-law enacted in 1894 would bring lodging houses under the control of local government. The rules laid down ensured that overcrowding did not occur, that the sanitary arrangements were such as to prevent disease, and ensured suitable safeguards in the event of disease breaking out. The number of lodgers allowed in each lodging house was fixed and the degree of cleanliness to be observed in beds and bedding, the size and condition of rooms, the amount of fresh air and the sanitary arrangements to be provided was gone into in great detail and included the number of times the rooms, the privies and water-closets and the passages should be cleaned.

Yet there were still anomalies which remained and continued into the 20th century. The legislation, in its acceptance of privies rather than water-closets, was rather at odds with the Courts and Yards Committee's requirement that water-closets be installed in all tenements. Neither was any reference made to the provision of sanitary facilities apart from the positioning of privies, and inspection of drains, privies and cesspools in private houses and consequently approval continued to be given to building plans for houses which included a privy. This was the main weakness of the Act, which otherwise tried to legislate for every contingency. It seems likely that this was a failure in perception on the part of the councillors who did not really believe that the working classes needed (or even wanted) flush toilets.

The passing of the 1835 Municipal Corporation Act was the beginning of a slow process whereby Parliament brought local government under central control. Ancient towns, such as Norwich and Exeter, which mourned the loss of their ancient liberties were not only mourning the extension of the franchise and the increased regulation by councillors and aldermen, but also their freedom to decide their own destiny, to make improvements as and when they liked and not be subject to the *dictat* of central authority. This was not immediately apparent and, to begin with, local government continued as before: each local authority acting independently and Parliamentary approval being sought for every improvement made.

However, if the new legislation was to have a real effect and not just be elaborate window dressing, action would need to follow and legislation drawn up to address the problems caused by the growth of population and the industrial revolution; a system of government, rooted in past precedent, was unequal to the problems resulting from unfettered commerce. Although non-interference had been acceptable in a pre-industrial society with small-scale cottage-industry where most men, women and children were home-workers (as had pleased Daniel Defoe on his tour of England), the expansion of the factory system led to widespread exploitation, especially of children, and legislation to protect the vulnerable had become necessary.

Central government interference was also essential to tackle the problems caused by population movement which had led to uncontrolled building and the growth of slum properties, as well as the spread of previously unknown deadly diseases. This was a national problem and, like the regulation of industry, demanded a national solution.

Notes

1. Cited in the *Norfolk Chronicle* 12th February 1803
2. Peck's *Norwich Directory,* p. viii
3. *Norfolk Chronicle* 5th and 12th February 1803

4. Cozens-Hardy & Kent. *The Mayors of Norwich 1403-1835*, Hawes, T. (ed.) *An Index to Norwich City Officers* 1453-1835

5. Berry *A concise history and directory of the City of Norwich,* p. 45

6. *Norfolk Chronicle* 25th January 1812

7. A report of the meeting to oppose what was described as the Norwich New Paving Bill was held at the Duke's Palace Inn on the 1st March and its deliberations were reported in the *Norfolk Chronicle* on 5th March.

8. The lengthy correspondence was printed in the *Norfolk Chronicle* February-April 1825

9   NRO, N/TC 28/3 Paving Cleansing & Finance Committee No. 4

10 NRO, N/TC 28/3 Paving Cleansing & Finance Committee No. 4

11. Bayne, *A Comprehensive History of Norwich*, p. 406

12. Charles Suckling Gilman was a member of the old Paving Commission and for some time a member of the new Corporation.. In 1846 he was the leading promoter and secretary of the Norwich Mutual Marine Insurance Society, in 1843 he established the General Hailstorm Insurance Society and in 1849 he founded the Norfolk Farmers' Cattle Insurance Society. Mr Beckwith is probably Augustus Adolphus Hamilton Beckwith, solicitor and in the White's 1836 directory he is listed as 'Town Clerk'.

13. *Norfolk Chronicle* 6th April 1839

14. The controversy caused by the amendments to the 1825 Act was fully reported in both the *Norfolk Chronicle* and the *Norwich Mercury* between February 1839 and March 1840.

15. Councillor George Seppings, a merchant who lived in Lakenham Terrace in 1836, would have been very aware of the state of the hamlets. The most vocal opponent to Mr Gilman's Act was Councillor Thomas Osborn Springfield, a silk merchant, who had a house in St Mary's Alley in 1836.

16. NRO, N/TC/28/3 Lighting Committee meeting 30th March 1840

17. Browne, P. *A history of Norwich from the Earliest Records to the Present Time,* p. 125

18. [Stacy, John] *A topographical & historical account of the City of Norwich,* pp. 109/10

19. The Report of Robert Milne Esq. relative to the Water-Works and Mills in Norwich..... 10 March 1798. In addition N/EN/20/183 Norwich Corn Mills and waterworks with insert of Chapelfield [park] with details of

water supply system. R. Milne 1794. Milne drew a plan for the work to be done for supplying Norwich with water. On this plan it is drawn as considerably larger than the drawings of the reservoir in various maps, according to Milne's drawing, the reservoir was so large, there was very little left of the park.

20. [Hardy, C.] *Memories of Norwich and its inhabitants fifty years ago,* p. 5.

21. Lee, William   Report of an inquiry held before William Lee, Esq. of the Sanitary Condition of the City and County of Norwich, 1850, p. 25

22. Lee, p. 37

23. NRO, 18625/138 Spelman auction particulars 26th June 1850

24. NRO, 18625/173 Shuttle's Yard, Lower Heigham

25. Lee pp. 35-6. Mr W. Delf, a plumber and glazier, also admitted the drainage of Sussex Street was defective but said the water supply was satisfactory even though the water supply in this parish was said to consist of only two pumps, one of which was to water the street.

26. Lee, p. 57

27. Lee, p. 56

28. Reported in the *Norfolk Chronicle* 30th March 1850

29. Norwich Corporation meeting 1st January 1850 quoted in the *Norfolk Chronicle* 5th January

30. Lee, p. 5. The comments of the Editor of the *Norfolk Chronicle* are being quoted.

31. Quoted in the *Norfolk Chronicle* 8th June 1850.

32. Reported in the *Norwich Mercury* between 16th November 1839 and 4th March 1840

33. Reported in the *Norfolk Chronicle* 28th June 1851 and 12th July 1851

34. Reported in the Supplement to the *Norwich Mercury* February 18733. A full report is printed in *Norfolk Annals* Volume 2.

35. Norwich Drainage. 'The Memorial to the Board of Health and the Address of the Memorialists to the Sewerage and Irrigation Committee, with the Memorialists' replies to the Committee's Questions'. Printed by Jarrolds and dated 24th January 1868

36. NRO, TC336-7 1-4, 5-8 Bailey's Buildings, West Pottergate Street

37. NRO, TC337 68, 70, 72 Trinity Street

38. NRO, TC609 Cossey's Yard, Botolph Street included in auction of land in Sprowston

39. NRO, N/EN/1/12/3570 West End Street

40. NRO, N/EN/1/12/3772 Waddington Street and Armes Street

41. NRO, N/EN/29/2/4016 Mousehold Street

42. NRO, N/TC/D1/170 Sale particulars property auctioned by S. Mealing Mills and Thomas H. Keith

43. Elder-Duncan, J.H. *Country Cottages & Week-end Homes*, Cassell Co. Ltd., London [1906?]. This publication has plans and illustrations of cottages by well-known architects.

44. *Daylight* 25th February 1888

45 Reported in the *Norfolk Chronicle* 12th and 26th January 1889

46. Cherry, p. 22 refers to the problem of unemployment. A report in the *Eastern Daily Press* on 24th November 1888 refers to the clause which caused all the upset and E. Boardman is quoted as opposing it on the grounds that it will interfere with liberty of speech and action. Reported in *Norfolk Annals*, January 1893.

Chapter 10. Norwich in 1900

Norwich, it is feared, has seen its best days as a place of commerce; and would appear to be in that painful state of transition from a once flourishing manufacturing prosperity to its entire decline, and must, ere long, revert to its original condition of a capital of an extensive agricultural district.

When the Health of Towns Commission visited Norwich in 1845 its future prognosis was bleak. It is not surprising that it should make this pessimistic assessment: the textile industry was in decline and there seemed to be a lack of alternative employment, the shoe industry was in its infancy and was still small-scale despite the introduction of the sewing-machine which had been brought to Norwich in 1836.[1] If anything were to confirm the Commission in its belief, it was the fate of the Norwich Yarn Company.

This Joint Stock Company had been established in 1833 to give employment to the poor. Initially all went well and in April 1836 the *Norwich Mercury* reported the 'prosperous progress' of the Company and looked forward to the publication of the annual balance sheet. This was published on 11th June 1836. It was good news: the number employed had risen and a return to prosperity was envisaged. On the 18th of that month, at a special meeting, it was agreed to authorise an increase of capital because the company was unable to fulfil the demand for yarn. In December 1838 a new factory was completed near Whitefriars Bridge. However, the Company soon got into difficulties and in 1850, under the direction of the Master in Chancery under the Winding-Up Act, the factory was purchased with its machinery by the textile manufacturers, E. & R.W. Blake, finally closing down in May 1856.[2]

Bayne, writing in 1869, had optimistically listed all the textile manufacturers, but even he had to admit that the industry had been in decline for some time: the machinery used was out of date, the manufacturers could not keep up with changing fashion and, since 1840, large numbers of the workers had gone into the boot and shoe trade which offered them a better livelihood.[3] This had already been evident in 1838. White's 1845 Directory lists a total of textile manufacturers, the 1864 Directory thirty-one, whilst the 1883 and 1890 directories list thirteen and seven respectively.

Yet despite the loss of its main manufacturing base, the Commission's prognostication did not happen. In 1900 Norwich was no longer one of the most important cities in the country, but neither was it a solely agricultural district. There are a number of reasons why this pessimism was mistaken and this was bound up with its original position as the capital of a large agricultural county, the wealth that had accumulated over the centuries, and the strong and industrious work force (the descendants of those men, women and children of Daniel Defoe's encomium nearly a century before). This latter was very important if new industry were to prosper; there was not only a large number of hard-working men and women no longer employed in textiles, but also inherited wealth from the many centuries of textile manufacture which had resulted in the establishment of a number of banks and insurance companies in the late 18th and early 19th centuries.

Although the textile industry declined, a whole range of new industries were established and prospered. J. & J. Colman mustard manufacturers, which moved from Stoke Holy Cross early in the century in order to expand the business, was just one of a large number of businesses engaged in the food industry. The author of *Industries of Norfolk & Suffolk Business Review* published about 1885 and *A Descriptive Account of Norwich Illustrated,* published a little later, describe a number of businesses, many of which achieved international recognition. They vary from the engineering firm Boulton & Paul which, during the Boer War, was commissioned by the War Office to make bungalows to be sent to South Africa, to A. Caley & Son Ltd. who started making mineral water in 1863 and successfully enlarged the business to include cocoa, chocolate and cracker making. In addition the shoe industry, which probably employed the greatest number of men and women, commenced in the 1850s and exported boots and shoes throughout the world.

Burgess in *Men Who Have Made Norwich*[4] written in 1904 listed the number and variety of prosperous businesses. During the 19th century a great change had occurred and the authors, whilst acknowledging past prosperity, speak also of that age 'without railway, without penny postage, morning papers, matches or gas, to say nothing of electric light; without a thousand and one inventions that have given comforts to the masses such as monarchs themselves never dreamed of'.[5] This was undoubtedly true, but the 19th century had seen the city transformed in a more important, way: transformed from one which had changed very little since the Middle Ages, where a letter sent in 1842 addressed simply to 'Mr. Archer, butcher, opposite the Whip and Egg [*sic*], St. Mary's, Norwich'[6] could reach its destination, where each city and town in England had its own rules and regulations, and where in 1803 one hundred pairs of shoes were burnt in Norwich because they had been made contrary to Act of Parliament, to one where the whole country was governed by the same rules and regulations and where an outsider like Boots the Nottingham chemists was able to open a shop (there were three in Norwich by 1900).

Conclusion

Although Norwich entered the 20th century with a considerable amount of substandard housing and with much work to be done to improve sanitation, much of the necessary legislation had already been enacted. Attitudes were changing and by 1900 there was less opposition to improvements which in the past were considered either unnecessary or the interference in matters which were the concern of the individual only. Despite all the opposition to each and every move made to better conditions, the inhabitants of the City of Norwich entered the 20th century with a degree of regulation that was unheard of at the start of the century. Throughout the 19th century there had been a body of citizens which strove hard for improvements, their motives a mixture of altruism and hard business sense. Their success was limited, having to contend with a powerful opposition, whose motivation was not solely financial, but a sincerely held fear of a powerful executive.

Yet in spite of all the rhetoric, there was a certain inevitability which led to the passing of the various Acts. The changes brought about by the industrial revolution and the population explosion made central government's philosophy of *laissez-faire* untenable. The growth of industry and large factories, the building of thousands of small houses for the workers brought inevitable change. In the past, it didn't really matter that no parish would take responsibility for the repair of the roads. Their poor state inconvenienced only a few people. But the bad state of the roads was a serious disadvantage to commerce. Population growth also made change necessary. With a small population the overcrowding and squalor of the past may have been unpleasant but overcrowding affected no-one except those living in this condition but the combination of overcrowding and unsanitary housing led to the spread of disease which affected everyone, rich and poor alike.

Thorpe Railway Station, mid-nineteenth century, a symbol of change

Population growth and the industrial revolution changed the nature of life in a city and Norwich was no exception. The framework for life in the 20th century was established in the 19th century, and by 1900 the basic legislation for modern living forged. The progression was gradual but it was inevitable that the citizens of a modern city should lose some of their freedoms for the benefit of the many. The Corporation had finally accepted responsibility for the provision of services and assumed greater powers whilst at the same time the power of the individual necessarily decreased.

Notes

1. Mackie, Charles. *Norfolk Annals* Vol. 1, Norwich 1901. 29th August 1833
2. Mackie, Charles. *Norfolk Annals* Vol. 2, Norwich 1901, 31st May 1856
3. Bayne, A.D. *A Comprehensive History of Norwich*, Norwich 1860, p. 594.
4. Burgess, Edward & Wilfrid L. *Men Who Have Made Norwich*, Norwich 1904.
5. Burgess, p. 23.
6. This letter dated 8th February 1842 and pasted into a manuscript book was found among papers deposited at the Norfolk & Norwich Archaeological Society library by E.A. Kent.

Appendix 1

The population of Norwich according to the Census returns

Parishes	1801	1811	1821	1831	1841	1851
All Saints	701	657	741	692	676	688
St. Andrew	1858	1396	1518	1297	1295	1256
St. Augustine	1232	1394	1627	2022	2053	2111
St. Benedict	890	925	1125	1424	1319	1379
St. Clement	853	933	2364	2769	2836	3230
St. Edmund	446	492	677	762	727	890
St. Etheldred	252	261	273	627	308	395
St. George Colegate	1132	1379	1610	1513	1440	1581
St. George Tombland	750	739	797	709	778	794
St. Giles	1076	1043	1422	1595	1546	1611
St. Gregory	1057	1125	1244	1098	1107	1116
St. Helen	393	371	425	521	487	525
St. James	520	565	1268	1301	1311	1538
St. John Maddermarket	1698	827	957	814	738	708
St. John Sepulchre	1144	1233	1599	1832	1847	2014
St. John Timberhill	888	918	1101	1055	1108	1284
St. Julian	662	677	932	1069	1098	1296
St. Lawrence	899	992	1092	1008	974	1024
St. Margaret	662	797	938	868	865	840
St. Martin at Oak	1747	1857	2477	2524	2589	2678
St. Martin at Palace	936	978	1201	1217	1320	1317
St. Mary Coslany	1018	1097	1521	1361	1402	1565
St. Mary in the Marsh	616	-	583	611	498	518
St. Michael at Coslany	1031	947	1340	1202	1298	1347
St. Michael at Plea	446	501	389	357	395	423
St. Michael at Thorn	1198	1450	1750	2048	1860	2095
St. Paul	1395	1583	2160	2407	2783	2741
St. Peter Hungate	371	398	511	522	428	477
St. Peter Mancroft	2120	2137	2671	2901	2976	2992
St. Peter per Mountergate	1350	1291	1789	1975	2025	2297
St. Peter Southgate	378	389	530	627	465	493
St. Saviour	984	990	1266	1486	1419	1457
St. Simon & St. Jude	333	398	447	446	370	353
St. Stephen	2211	2198	2927	4110	4212	4361
St. Swithin	503	591	750	870	753	800

Hamlets & Close

Earlham	95	84	118	103	107	131
Eaton	278	294	419	529	621	785
Heigham	854	842	1503	5396	6050	7738
Hellesdon (Norwich part of)	81	117	248	382	324	371
Lakenham	428	441	1875	3810	4006	4776
Pockthorpe	979	1029	1313	1669	1878	2067
Thorpe (Norwich part of)	74	67	284	1211	1156	1811
Trowse, Carrow & Bracondale	353	345	505	607	788	724
Precinct of the Close	616	508	583	611	-	-
County Gaol & House of Correction	-	-	-	-	98	137
Total	**36,832**	**37, 313**	**50, 288**	**61, 364**	**62,344**	**68,706**

Note: St. Mary in the Marsh, or the Precincts of the Close, included in the Norwich Census 1831, in the 1841 Census was added to St. Faith's Union, and is enumerated therein, the number being 498.

The population of Norwich according to the Census returns

Parishes	1861	1871	1881	1891	1901
All Saints	667	591	368	706	1962*
St. Andrew	978	919	767	710	500
St. Augustine	1890	1730	1812	2419	2373
St. Benedict	1381	1659	1996	1982	1865
St. Clement	3961	4426	5199	407	836[1]
St. Edmund	753	734	726	593	*
St. Etheldred	614	587	632	745	1694*
St. George Colegate	1607	1463	1630	1486	1351
St. George Tombland	687	877	779	658	1068*
St. Giles	1586	1563	1438	1346	1211
St. Gregory	934	832	783	565	*
St. Helen	507	594	557	585	541
St. James	1353	1501	1557	1497	9113*
St. John Maddermarket	537	484	403	367	262
St. John Sepulchre	2219	2737	2909	2734	2732
St. John Timberhill	1302	1229	1208	1054	1015
St. Julian	1361	1588	1890	1742	*
St. Lawrence	877	656	613	485	963*
St. Margaret	664	657	699	570	1114*
St. Martin at Oak	2546	2450	2745	2426	2432
St. Martin at Palace	1085	892	755	692	586
St. Mary Coslany	1498	1277	1281	1131	1208
St. Mary in the Marsh	451	521	507	490	451

St. Michael Coslany	1365	1096	843	723	647
St. Michael at Plea	379	287	168	158	106
St. Michael at Thorn	2121	1719	1747	1595	1406
St. Paul	2907	2962	2690	4552	5434
St. Peter Hungate	399	360	387	303	258
St. Peter Mancroft	2575	2353	2246	1904	1557
St. Peter per Mountergate	2868	3061	2938	2767	2570
St. Peter Southgate	457	573	565	695	*
St. Saviour	1532	1492	1572	1364	1180
St. Simon & St. Jude	283	293	351	290	*
St. Stephen	4191	4178	4115	3584	3225
St. Swithin	699	826	774	692	*
Town Close Liberty	249	273	300	(Listed with Eaton)	299

Hamlets

Earlham	195	206	238	244	231
Eaton	930	1056	1237	1848	3152
Heigham	13,894	18,671	24,031	30,084	33,104[2]
Hellesdon (part of)	393	376	683	722	953[3]
Lakenham parish	4866	5265	6378	8653	
Lakenham St. Mark				5947	6196
New Catton Christchurch	(St. Clement Without)			6459	7985
Pockthorpe	2055	2173	1948	3365	*
Thorpe Hamlet	2388	2714	2864	5265	6450
Trowse, Carrow & Bracondale	687	485	503	290	
Trowse St. Andrew with Lakenham St. John and All Saints (part of)					3703
Total	**75,025**	**80,386**	**87,842**	**100,964**	**111,733**

* 1901: St. Julian with All Saints, St. Etheldred with St. Peter Southgate, St. George Tombland with St. Simon & St. Jude, St. James with Pockthorpe, St. Margaret with St. Swithin, St. Gregory with St. Lawrence
1. The parish of St. Clement Within and Without listed separately from 1891
2. In 1891 & 1901 divided into four parishes: Holy Trinity, St. Bartholomew, St. Philip and St. Thomas
3. In 1901 listed as Drayton St. Margaret with Hellesdon St. Mary (part of)

Appendix 2: Baths and Bathing

Where there were no proper sewers, there could not easily be baths. However, the provision of these, so essential in the 20th century, does not appear to have figured very highly on the list of must-haves, and even in the late 19th century, they were often not considered really necessary. It is difficult to judge what percentage of better-quality houses installed bathrooms once the sewage was up and running but the notion that artisan dwellings should have a bathroom does not seem ever to have been considered necessary. A catalogue published by the Norwich firm of Boulton & Paul in 1909 entitled *Bungalows and Cottage Residences. A small treatise on Country Houses and their Design and Equipment* gives designs of small country houses and in nearly every instance a bathroom is included. However, there is a design for a small lodge or gardener's cottage and this had no bathroom, and there was an earth closet which was approached from outside the house. The premises themselves were small but adequate. The building was a bungalow and it had a lobby, living-room with pantry off, kitchen with coal off, and two bedrooms. Perhaps more conclusively, in Elder-Duncan's book *Cottages and Week-end Homes* published in London about 1905 there is a plan for cottages built for outdoor servants in Bramley in Surrey. This, it is said, could be made suitable for a weekend or country home for middle-class people without servants as 'a bathroom could be arranged over the coal and woodshed'.

The author is fortunate enough to live in a house which had a bathroom included in the building plan. No. 31 Cambridge Street is a medium-sized terrace house built about 1880. The original owner/occupier was James Carver, a bank clerk, and two houses - Nos. 31 and 33 - were built at the same time. The Agreement between the vendor and the purchaser, stipulated that the houses should be completed 'in all things in a manner equal to the adjoining one' (No. 29) and in one house (No. 31), it should include 'in small room over hall a water closet and gas bath'. That a bathroom was a rarity in a house of this type at that time seems implicit in the separate instruction, as is the failure to have a bathroom fitted in the (slightly smaller) house beside it. According to the plan attached to the Indenture, No. 33 had a water-closet attached to the house but approached from the garden and No. 31 had an additional water-closet at the back also approached from the garden. And houses in Havelock Road which are slightly smaller than the ones in Cambridge Street were also built without a bathroom. Building Control Plans dated 28th July 1888[1] show only a water-closet entered from outside. As in Cambridge Street the houses had four rooms on the first floor, but the small room at the front of the house, which was to become a bathroom at Cambridge Street, is described as a 'dressing-room'.

Even higher status houses were without a bathroom, although by the late 1880s the number with them was increasing as were the number of applications for permission to install both an upstairs water-closet and a bathroom. There were exceptions, they were not always thought desirable in the same way as was an indoor water-closet. Plans for alterations and additions to Apsley House, West Parade, a large double-fronted house with six bedrooms which were approved in 1888[2] show a downstairs water-closet for servants entered from the yard and the installation of an upstairs water-closet. However, although one of the rooms was said to be a bed or bathroom, there is no evidence on the plan to show that running water would be installed in that room (unlike the upstairs water-closet). Another alteration, this time to build a new larder with bathroom over in Ipswich Road,[3] was approved in 1888 (it is unclear whether there was already a bathroom in this house). This was the home of E. Curl, esq. of Curl Bros. Draper Store. And newly built large houses seem by this time to have had a bathroom installed as a matter of course as happened when a house in Unthank Road was built in 1893.[4]

None of the plans of small terrace house which had been approved had a bathroom and this is not surprising considering that whether or not there was a water-closet, privy or earth-closet seems a matter of chance, and to have had little or nothing to do with location. Houses built in Denbigh Road in 1885, in Caernarvon Street In 1884, in Spencer Street in 1894, in Gloucester Street in 1893 had privies, in Bury Street in 1894 they had water-closets, in Silver Road and Wodehouse Street in 1894 they had earth-closets.[4] Except for the ones in Gloucester Street, none of these houses had a hall entrance. This is just a sample of houses built about that time, but there is no reason to suppose it is unrepresentative. Yet all the houses had a sink and Water Company water.

Appendix 3: House Rental Values

Building in the suburbs started about 1815 and the early houses tended to be very small with two rooms up and two down, often ranged around a courtyard with privy and bin and use of a well. In the absence of information about the actual quality and condition of the houses for rent and the lack of detailed information houses in a particular area, it is difficult to say how important was situation and why, all things being equal, a house in Waterloo Road for sale in 1845 (SPE524) had a rental value of £3.15s.0d.whilst in Union Place two houses were rented for a total of £9.15.0d. in 1846 (SPE555).

After about the 1830 small and large terrace houses predominated, all very similar, the size and number of rooms dependent on the width of the plot, the rent dependent on location: the nearer the main road, the higher the rent. Norwich had a significant number of houses that were owner-occupied but the majority were built or purchased to rent and in the 1850/60s an annual rent of £7 or £8 would get you a small house without a hall entrance, three rooms downstairs and three upstairs and a small garden in front, a larger one and/or yard at the back. In 1852 the rental value of a house in Norfolk Street (TC340) was £7 per annum. In Suffolk Street and Trinity Street houses sold in 1867 (TC152) and (TC149) had a rental value of £8 per annum. Rents for houses of this type increased during the century and similar houses (although by then with piped water and privy or water-closet) and in 1903 the covenants relating to a house on Bowthorpe Road, with a hall entrance, specified that the rental value should be not less than £12 p.a., the same as the rent for a house in Hill Street sold the same year.

The wider the frontage, the larger the terrace house and its situation made a difference. A quality house in Heigham Terrace, Dereham Road (TC526) with two sitting rooms, four bedrooms, one dressing-room, kitchen, scullery, store-room, yard and offices and a front and back garden had a rental value of £15 p.a. when it was built in 1847 and the rent for one on Richmond Hill built in 1849 was £15. But rents increased and in 1882 £16 p.a. could only get you a house in a street off the main road: in Cambridge Street a significantly smaller house with sitting and dining room, three bedrooms and bathroom, kitchen, scullery, basement and attic, garden front and back. In 1890 a similar house in College Road had a rental value or £18.

Except for the largest houses, the provision of water and sanitary facilities seems not to have been much considered during the century. Most houses (except the very smallest) had water laid on by 1900, but it was a matter of chance whether there were flush toilets. And even as late as 1912 one of four houses which was advertised in Trinity Street (TC 337) had to share a water-closet as there were two for the four houses. The records show that the provision of water closets was a matter of chance and that they often had to be shared between two or more houses. This was also the case with the provision of privies and it was common in the very smallest to have a row of privies at the back of the communal garden.

SOURCES

References

The documents in the Norfolk Record Office (NRO) include: (1) Spelman Sale Particulars prefixed SPE; (2) Town Clerk's deeds prefixed TC; Cozens-Hardy 21/3/1975 and (4) Building Control Plans prefixed N/EN which were submitted for approval for all properties built or altered after 1877.

The title deeds referring to Cambridge Street, the Eaton Glebe Estate and Havelock Road are copies in the author's possession.

Information about owners, lessees and tenants of property affected by the building of Prince of Wales Road is in the document 'Norwich New Street - book of reference' and an undated plan of the area of the Greyfriars is in the Library of the Norfolk & Norwich Archaeological Society.

Directories

Berry, *A concise history and directory of the city of Norwich*, 1811. Norwich, 1810

Blyth, G.K. *The Norwich Guide*, Norwich [1842]

Chase, W. & Co. (printer) *The Norwich Directory of Gentlemen and Tradesmen's Assistant*, Norwich 1783

Colman's *Directory of Norwich*, Norwich, 1877

Eyre Brothers, *Post Office Norwich District Directory*, London 1883/4

Harrod, J.G. & Co. *Royal County Directory of Norfolk*, Fourth Edition, Norwich 1877

Jarrold's Norwich directories, Norwich 1884-1905

Kelly, *Directory of Norfolk*, London 1879, 1900

Mathieson's *Norwich Directory*, Norwich 1867

Peck's *Norwich Directory*, Norwich 1802

Pigot and Co.'s *National Commercial Directory; Norfolk & Suffolk*, London 1830

Rogers' *Directory of Norwich and neighbourhood*, Norwich, [1859]

Simpson's *Norwich Directory and Court Guide*, 1864

White, Francis *History, gazeteer and directory of Norfolk and the City and County of the City of Norwich*. Sheffield, 1854

White, W. *History, gazeteer and directory of Norfolk, and the city and county of the city of Norwich*, Sheffield 1836, 1845, 1864, 1883, 1890

Maps

1783   *Plan of the city of Norwich* 1783 (included in W. Chase's Directory)
1789   *Plan of the City of Norwich* by Anthony Hochstetter
1802   *Plan of the City of Norwich* (included in Peck's Directory)
1810   *Plan of the City of Norwich* (included in Berry's Directory)
1830   *Plan of the City of Norwich* surveyed by W.S. Millard & Josh. Manning
[c.1834] *Plan of the City of Norwich* surveyed by Josh. Manning

1849 *Plan of the City of Norwich* 1849 (included in Muskett's *Visitors' Plan of Norwich)*

[1868] *Norwich* (included in Fullarton's publication *The Imperial Gazetteer of England & Wales)*

1873 *Map of the City of Norwich compiled from the latest surveys* by Morant, A.W.

1880-5 Ordnance Survey [City of Norwich].

[1897] *Map of the City of Norwich.* Published by Jarrold & Sons

1899 *Map of the City of Norwich* (Collins, Arthur E., City Architect Engineer & Surveyor)

Reports

Health of Towns Act. Report of an inquiry held before William Lee, Esq., Superintending Inspector of the Sanitary Condition of the City and County of Norwich, Norwich, 1850

Milne, Robt. The Report of Robert Milne, Esq. relative to the Water-Works and Mills in Norwich made 10th March 1798

Milne, Robt. Norwich Corn Mills and Waterworks (has insert of Chapelfield with details of water supply system) 1794. NRO N/EN/20/183

Report of the Commissioners 1845 - Second Report of the Commissioners for Inquiring into the State of Large Towns and Populous districts, - Appendix Norwich pages 280 to 286 (typescript version referred to)

Local Newspapers

Daylight
Eastern Daily Press
Norfolk Chronicle
Norwich Mercury

Norwich Council Committees (held by the Norfolk Record Office)

Artizans Dwellings Committee (NRO MS4382)
City Committee Book 1830-35
Courts & Yards Committee (NRO N/TC 9/7 and N/TC 28/19)
Executive & Sanitary Sub-Committee (NRO N/TC 9/7)
Housing Allotments Committee (NRO N/TC 29/3)
Housing of the Working Classes Committee (NRO N/TC 9/7)
Lighting Committee (NRO N/TC 28/3)
Lighting and Macadamising Committee (NRO N/TC 28/3)
Lighting and Watching Committee (NRO NM/TC 28/3)
Paving, Cleansing and Finance Committee (NRO N/TC28/3)
Paving, Cleansing and Finance Committee (NRO N/TC 28/3)
Paving, Cleansing, Sewerage and Lighting Committee (NRO N/TC 4/14)
Paving & Finance Committee (NRO N/TC 28/3)
Robinson's Yard, Oak Street (NRO N/TC 54/3)
Sanitary Purposes Committee (NRO N/TC 4/11-13)

Street Improvement Committee (NRO N/TC 9/7)
Town Council Meetings (NRO N/TC 1/3 and N/TC 1/34)

Bibliography

Astley, H.J. Dakenfield (ed.) *Memorials of Old Norfolk*, London 1908

Bayne, A.D. *A Comprehensive History of Norwich including a survey of the City*, Norwich 1869

Blake, Robert. *Esto Perpetua Norwich Union Life Insurance Society 1808-1958*, Norwich 1958

Blomefield, F. *An essay towards a topographical history of the county of Norfolk*, continued by C. Parkin. Second edition 11 volumes. London 1805/10

Blyth, G.K. *The Norwich Guide: being a Description, Historical, Topographical and Statistical of The City and its Hamlets; with an account of the public charities, and various local information*, Norwich [1842]

Bodington, P.R.. *Norwich High School 1765-1950*. Norwich n.d.[1950]

Booth, William. *In Darkest England and the Way Out*, London 1890

Boulton & Paul Ltd. *The Leaf and The Tree. The story of Boulton & Paul 1797-1947*, Norwich 1947

Briggs, Asa, *Victorian Cities*. London 1963

Britton, J. and Brayley, E.W. *A topographical and historical description of the county of Norfolk [1809]*. Separate Issue of *The Beauties of England Wales* Vol. 11.

Browne, P. *The History of Norwich from the Earliest Records to The Present Time*. Norwich 1814

Bull, J. (ed.), *1839-1981 The story of Keswick Hall Church of England College of Education*. Norwich, n.d.

Burnett, John, *A Social History of Housing 1815-1985*, London 1978

Cannadine, David, *Aspects of Aristocracy, Grandeur and Decline in Modern Britain*, London 1994

Chadwick, Edwin, *Report on the Sanitary Condition of the Labouring Population*. 1842

Cherry, Steven, *Doing Different? Politics and the Labour Movement in Norwich 1880-1914*. Norwich 1989

Chubb, T. and Stephen, G.A. *A descriptive list of the printed maps of Norfolk 1574-1916* and *A descriptive list of Norwich plans, 1541-1914*. Norwich 1928

Court, W.H.B. *A Concise Economic History of Britain from 1750 to Recent Times*, Cambridge 1965

Cozens-Hardy, B. and Kent, E.A. *The Mayors of Norwich 1403-1858*, Norwich 1938

Crescent History Group, *The Crescent, Norwich: listing of occupiers 1825-1978*, Norwich 1978.

Crouse, John (printer) *History of the city and county of Norwich from the earliest accounts to the present time*, Norwich, 1768

Darley, Gillian. *Villages of Vision*, London 1978

Defoe, Daniel, *Tour through the Eastern Counties.* First published 1724; Ipswich 1969

Delves, E. *A Brief Historical Description of the Hamlet of Heigham,* Norwich 1879

Digby, A. 'The Relief of Poverty in Victorian York: Attitudes and Policies' in Feinstein, C.H. (Ed.). *York 1831-1981. 150 Years of Scientific Endeavour and Social Change,* York 1981

Eade, Sir Peter, *Some Account of the Parish of St. Giles, Norwich,* Norwich, 1886

Eade, Sir Peter. *The Norfolk and Norwich Hospital 1770-1900,* London 1900

Excursions in the County of Norfolk: comprising a brief historical description of every town and village, Two volumes. Vol. 1 - 1818, Vol. 2 - 1819. Supplement c. 1825

Frostick, Raymond, *The Printed Plans of Norwich 1558-1840. A Carto-Bibliography,* Norwich 2002

Goodwin, E.A. *Selections from Norwich Newspapers 1760-1790.* Ipswich n.d. [1972]

Gourvish, T. *Norfolk beers from English barley: a history of Steward and Patteson, 1793-1963* Norwich 1987

Great Gothic Fane. The Catholic church of St. John the Baptist, Norwich. With historical retrospect of Catholicity in Norwich, London 1913

Gregg, Pauline, *A Social and Economic History of Britain 1760-1965,* 5th Ed. revised, London 1965

Griffiths, Elizabeth & Smith, Hassell, *Buxom to the Mayor'. A History of the Norwich Freemen,* Norwich 1987

[Hardy, C.], *Memories of Norwich and its inhabitants fifty years ago by a nonagenarian,* Norwich, 1888

Harrod, Henry. *Gleanings amoung the Castles & Convents of Norfolk.* Norwich 1857

Hawes, T. (ed.) *An Index to Norwich City Officers 1453-1835,* Norwich 1989

Hawkins, C.B. *Norwich: A Social Study,* London 1910

Hibgame, F.T. *Recollections of Norwich Fifty Years Ago,* Norwich, 1919 (Reprinted from *The Norfolk Chronicle* published in 1913)

House of Jarrolds 1823-1923. A Brief History of One Hundred Years, Norwich 1924

Jewson, C.B. *The Baptists in Norfolk,* London, 1957

Kent, E. A., 'The Houses of the Duke of Norfolk' *Norfolk Archaeology,* Vol. 24, 1932

Longmate, Norman, *The Workhouse. A Social History,* London 1974

Mackie, Charles, *Norfolk Annals. A chronological record of remarkable events in the nineteenth century* (compiled from the files of the *Norfolk Chronicle*). Vol. I 1801-1850; Vol. II 1851-1900

Mantle, Jonathan. *Norwich Union. The First 200 Years,* London, 1997

Matchett & Stevenson (Printers) *A Norfolk & Norwich Remembrancer and Vade-Mecum,* Norwich, 1822

Mayhew, Henry, *The Life and Labour of the People of London*, London 1861-62

Middelbrook, S. *Newcastle upon Tyne Its Growth and Achievement.* Newcastle 1950

Muthesius, S. 'Nineteenth Century Housing' in *Norwich in the 19th Century*, edited J. C. Barringer. Norwich, 1984

Newton, Robert. *Victorian Exeter 1837-1914*, Leicester 1968

Norwich High School 1875-1950, Norwich n.d. [1950]

Norwich Union Insurance Societies 1797-194. Souvenir of the One Hundred and Fiftieth Anniversary of the Societies' Foundation, Norwich 1947

Nottingham University and W.E.A. Group Study. Foreword Asa Briggs. *Nottingham in the eighteen eighties. a study in social change*, Nottingham 1971

Patterson, A. Temple. *Southampton a Biography*, London 1970

Poore, George Vivian. *The Dwellinghouse.* London 1898.

Pound, John 'Poverty & Public Health 1800-1880' in *Norwich in the 19th century*, edited J. C. Barringer, Norwich 1984

Rawcliffe, Carole & Wilson, Richard (eds.) *Norwich since 1550*, London 2004

Rowntree, B. Seebohm. *Poverty. A Study of Town Life*, London c.1901

Rye W. *Norfolk Families*, Norwich 1911-13

Sandred, K.I. and Lindström, B. *The Place-names of Norfolk.* Part I *The place-names of the City of Norwich*, English Place-name Society, 1989

Sparks, W.L. *The story of Shoemaking in Norwich*, Norwich 1949

[Stacy, John] *A topographical & historical account of the City & County of Norwich*, Norwich 1832

Violet, Sister, *All Hallows: Ditchingham. The story of an East Anglian Community*, Oxford 1983

Wearing, Stanley J. *Georgian Norwich. Its Builders.* Norwich n.d. [1926]

Wicks, Walter. *Inns and Taverns of Old Norwich*, Norwich 1925

Young, J.R. *The Inns and Taverns of Old Norwich*, Norwich, 1975

Catalogues

Boulton & Paul Ltd. *Catalogue Bungalows and Cottage Residences. A small treatise on Country Houses their Design and Equipment*, Norwich 1909

Elder-Duncan, J.H. *Country Cottages & Week-end Homes*, London c.1907

Industries of Norfolk & Suffolk Business Review. A Guide to leading commercial enterprises, Birmingham n.d. [c.1890]

Articles and Publicity Material

Browne, W.J. Utten, *A few observations respecting Municipal Reform, suggested by passing events*, Norwich, n.d. [1837]

Builder, The (Publisher: George Godwin, London)

Earth Closets, to the Ratepayers of Norwich [from] An Anxious Ratepayer. Poster 7th January 1868

Jewson & Sons Ltd.(pub.) *Number 18 and Number 19 Colegate*, n.d. [?1950]

245

Norwich Drainage, *The Memorial to the Board of Health, and The Address of the Memorialists to the Sewerage and Irrigation Committee, with the Memorialists' Replies to the Committee's Questions,* Norwich 1867

Register of deaths 1839-70, 1870-78, 1878-1914 (found in the Norfolk & Norwich Archaeological Society Library)

Rye, W. 'Some Ancient Parts of Norwich. Mr. Walter Rye on Pockthorpe and District', *Eastern Daily Press* 1902

Picture Credits

The illustrations in this book have been drawn from many sources, most of them out of print and out of copyright. The author is grateful to the Norfolk and Norwich Archaeological Society for the use of the pictures on pages 32, 45 & 65. Those on pages, 113, 177 and the back cover are from postcards. The picture on p.33 is from *Norwich Guildhall* by Ernest A. Kent. The picture on p.38 is taken from Sir Peter Eade's book, *Some Account of the Parish of St Giles.* The photo on p.42 is taken from *The Norwich Union Fire Insurance Society 1797-1897* by Ernest Felce. Pictures on pages 51, 53 & 56 are from *Illustrated Norwich.* The picture on p.83 is taken from John Howard's *Doors and Doorways of Old Norwich* 1890. The drawings on page 48 and 85 are by Henry Ninham. The picture on p.84 is taken for the *Norwich Planning Handbook* of 1972; we have been unable to trace authors or publishers. The modern photographs were taken by James O'Donoghue who also did the redrawn maps.

INDEX